# Thinking in Pictures

JOHN SAYLES

# THINKING IN PICTURES

## THE MAKING OF THE MOVIE
## Matewan

BOSTON
HOUGHTON MIFFLIN COMPANY

*Library of Congress Cataloging-in-Publication Data*
Sayles, John
Thinking in pictures.

1. Matewan.    2. Moving-pictures—
Production and direction.    I. Title.
PN1997.M3943S29    1987        791.43'72        87-11881
ISBN 0-395-45388-7
ISBN 0-395-45399-2 (pbk.)

Printed in the United States of America

P 10 9 8 7 6 5 4 3

Photographs on page 55 by Nora Chavooshian; all other
photographs by Bob Marshak, copyright © Red Dog Films, Inc.

# Contents

# Exhibits

# About the Book

THIS BOOK is about the thought processes that go into making a movie. Movie-making can be analyzed in terms of choices, most of them conscious. (There are nonrational elements in movie-making too, choices you can explain only by saying, "It *felt* right," but I won't deal with those much here.) I'll be talking about the choices that get made at each stage of production, using the making of the movie *Matewan* (on which I was screenwriter and director and controlled the editing) as the main example. The book is set up in the order the movie was made, starting with the writing of the screenplay and moving on to the shooting and editing. Throughout there are exhibits — documents or pictures from the phase being discussed. Most of these are examples of the kind of detailed planning that goes into every aspect of movie production.

The most important exhibit is the screenplay itself, found in the back of the book. This is the shooting script, the version we went into production with, rather than a transcript of the finished movie. Those who have seen the movie will notice scenes not existing in the screen version, scenes altered and moved around. I'll be discussing how and why this happened. Whether you've seen the movie or not, it might be a good idea to read or at least breeze through the screenplay before you get into the rest of the book.

One of the main ways that storytelling on film differs from writing fiction is that the choices you make are extremely practical as well as aesthetic and intuitive. I've never had to change a line of fiction because the sun was or wasn't out, because heavy machinery was operating in the neighborhood or union meal penalty started in five minutes, yet movie-making, especially on a low budget, is full of these compromises.

The making of *Matewan* offers a good example of the effect these practical considerations have on what gets shot and how, as well as the effect of collaboration, the bringing together of many viewpoints, talents and technologies.

I'd like to think of this book as a kind of reporting from the front, a reporting of internal as well as external events in a situation I witnessed firsthand, from the beginning. It's a book I would have liked to have when I first started working for the movies, and I hope it will be useful evidence to anyone interested in the process of storytelling on film.

# THINKING

# Thinking in Pictures

A STEAM ENGINE thunders toward us, belching black smoke.

Men with guns walk down an empty street, spreading out as they come, faces grim.

People cluster around a new-dug grave on the side of a steep hill, a cold wind moaning through the ragged trees that surround them.

A coal-blackened man crawls through a narrow seam under tons of slate, the top dripping, the ribs sweating cold water, puddles at his knees. The headlamp clipped to his hat gives only a candle's worth of light as he grits his teeth and chops into the coal face in front of him, tunneling deeper into darkness like a man digging his own grave.

Reading these pictures in a sentence gives you one kind of feeling, depending on your experience and imagination. Seeing them on a movie screen, animated by flickering light and existing in sequential time, can give you a very different feeling, can tell you different things. Understanding the differences between the two experiences is the basis of telling stories on film.

Narrative film, what we ordinarily think of as "the movies," is a combination of literary, theatrical and purely cinematic elements. The story itself and the dialogue — the literary elements — can be written down, though except in books like this they are rarely published and never considered "literature" on their own. The acting has its roots in theater, though the style may be altered quite a bit from what would go down on a stage. The picture may have some aspects of painting when it is still, but the minute it cuts, moves or somebody moves within it, we are brought into purely cinematic areas.

When you are making a narrative movie you hope all three elements

work together to tell the story. If one of the elements drags on the others, or contradicts them or is distractingly awkward, it can take the viewer out of the flow of the story. Crummy dialogue and inappropriate acting take me out of a story faster than anything else. I start to see the typing on the screenplay page, start to hear the voices at the story conferences, and see only actors instead of characters. Some people are more sensitive to the look of a movie and can handle or don't even notice lapses in the dialogue and acting. I think all of us are more lenient with these elements in a movie in a language and from a culture we don't understand. We have gotten used to a certain reductive stiffness in subtitles (which have to be condensed and simplified just to fit on the screen) and may accept an over-the-top performance from a Japanese actor that a Japanese audience would be rolling its eyes over.

If one element is strong enough it can sometimes carry the other two. A knockout performance can grab us in an otherwise crummy movie, and there are horror movies in which the dialogue is dopey and the acting wooden but the story and its cinematic telling are so together it's still worth the ride. In the first couple movies I directed, *Return of the Secaucus Seven* and *Lianna*, we didn't have the time, money or experience to do much visual storytelling and so we concentrated on the other elements, trying to keep the technical end simple and competent. Both movies were written and planned with this approach in mind, and both are mostly involved with interpersonal dynamics in enclosed spaces. In *Secaucus Seven* we substituted the movement of cutting from character to character within a large ensemble cast for the camera movement we were avoiding. In *Lianna* we worked on establishing a kind of cumulative mood and identification with the characters through a series of episodic, dramatic scenes, once again using music and cutting to fill in for camera movement. Only in later movies I've directed, *Baby, It's You*, *The Brother from Another Planet* and *Matewan*, did we have the time and money (or the experience to make up for the lack of them) to tell much of the story in pictures.

I "started" as a fiction writer, publishing some short stories and a novel called *Pride of the Bimbos* in 1975. The novel was originally a movie in my head. I started with a couple scenes that I saw dramatically, saw the setting, imagined a certain graininess to the image, heard a country-Western soundtrack compressed through a tinny juke box speaker. But in 1975 I was working in hospitals and factories or was on unemployment, had no track record as a writer or movie-maker, had no connections whatsoever in the movie business. I hadn't even gone to film school. A practical look at the situation told me any screenplay I wrote was going to sit on the shelf for a long time, especially one about a white-trash kid, a midget shortstop and a six-foot-six black hustler with violent

revenge on his mind. I began to rethink the story as fiction, mentally adapting it into a long, episodic short story that eventually became a novel. But the pictures and sounds were there first, and in the writing I did my best to give the reader the idea and the feeling of what I had first "seen."

The transition I was able to make from writing fiction to making movies was a case not of graduating from one to the other, of moving up or down, but of eventually having the practical means to do another kind of storytelling I'd always been interested in. Ideas for stories usually come to me in their own form — short story, play, novel, movie. The form seems like the best way to tell the story. Now and then I'll be able to adapt a story from the form it presented itself in to another, and with some of my early fiction this was a kind of sublimation — if I couldn't make the movie maybe I could write a story about it and make the movie later.

I eventually got to make movies through writing. I had to get a literary agent to sell my second novel, and his literary agency had a connection with a Hollywood talent agency that handled books as potential film "properties." I contacted that agency, wrote a screenplay to show them what I could do, and they agreed to represent me if I'd move to the West Coast for a while. I got my first assignment, rewriting a movie called *Piranha* for Roger Corman, at least partly because Roger's story editor, Frances Doel, read fiction for pleasure (a rarity in Hollywood) and had actually read some of *mine*. I got to direct *Return of the Secaucus Seven* because I made enough money writing screenplays for other people to finance the movie myself. The budget was so low ($60,000 out of pocket to get to a first print) that I had to back up a bit and stop thinking in pictures, as I had been able to do in writing for others, and start thinking in budget.

My experience as a screenwriter up to that point had been primarily visual. Movies I had written such as *Piranha* or *Alligator*, at their most basic, were about tension and motion, teasing the audience with the possibility of the creature in question leaping out from who knows where and eating the second lead. In writing the screenplays for these I first imagined the stories as if they were silent movies without title cards. Since the piranha were water-bound (until the sequel, in which they had bred with flying fish) the most important image became the river in which they lived. The next image that came was a dam, a manmade attempt to control nature and a chance to keep the little buggers from getting out to the ocean. Since Roger Corman had asked for a *Jaws*-like attack on a crowded beach, that beach appeared as the end of the race and the structure of the movie was then graphically laid out like a board game — river, dam, beach. The original idea I'd inherited had a logical

weakness — if you know there are piranha in the water, why not stay out of the river? The contrivances that this led me to work up also led me to the central image — people on a jerrybuilt raft, surrounded by piranha-infested water, poling down a wilderness river to warn the people gathering for a resort opening on the beach.

Not much dialogue is needed to keep this kind of story afloat and I didn't write much. In fact, I deliberately tried to keep the lead role "actor proof" by keeping his dialogue down to single sentences. When Bradford Dillman, a good, experienced actor, was cast, I was able to flesh out the rest of his lines knowing the movie wouldn't stop dead while he said them. No director had been chosen while I was writing the drafts of the script, and so I wrote it as if *I* were going to have to direct it the next day, a full shooting script with each cutaway detailed and nothing left for a director to fill in. Joe Dante eventually directed it and managed to make a pretty good movie despite a minuscule budget and heavy logistical problems. He, of course, did more than fill in the action described in the screenplay, taking it as suggestions he was free to use or not use as he saw fit. And though this is almost always the case with screenwriters-for-hire, if you're doing your job you are often writing in pictures.

Visiting the set of *Piranha* and talking to the people involved in making it helped me learn one of the basic rules of film production, which is that talk is cheap and action is expensive. When good actors are going at some well-written piece of drama, you don't generally need or want to move the camera around a lot or keep cutting all over the place, for fear of breaking the immediacy, the "lock" of tension or emotion between one character and another. Unless the actors need to redo them dozens and dozens of times to get them right, dialogue scenes are easier and cheaper to shoot than action scenes that need precision camera work, the hitting of exact marks and lots of different angles to build the sequence. So when it came to writing *Secaucus Seven*, I concentrated on telling the story through the words of the characters (as self-contradictory as they sometimes were), and the images were more about establishing a certain cultural setting and grouping certain people together than about telling the story in pictures. There are a few mostly visual sequences, most notably the basketball game in which two of the characters vent their sexual jealousy on the court, but this was something we could shoot in a semidocumentary style in a very short time.

*Secaucus Seven* was, in fact, a story that couldn't be told only in visual terms, no matter how much time, money or experience we had. It is a story about the complex relationships of human beings, and since human beings do most of their communicating verbally (even when they lie), to make these characters mute would be to reduce them to stereotypes. This goes against most concepts of "pure cinema," but pure cinema is at

its weakest when trying to deal with human beings in a narrative form. Stories become limited to fairly broad strokes, like cartoons and even the best of the silent comedies and dramas, or the visual metaphors become so complex in themselves that you have to do an incredible amount of mental translating into highly literary language to understand what is going on. The dead sheep on the radiator may indeed represent man's descent from communal to popular culture, but you probably have to go back to something you read in a book to figure it out. Probably the most vital examples of purely visual storytelling we have today are TV commercials and rock videos. Although some of these are real knockouts viscerally and can be lots of fun, the stories they tell are pretty simple, usually variations on "Buy this stuff, it'll help you get your shit together," or "Be a rock star, look at how many models dressed in underwear you'll meet."

Many of the movies we've made independently could never have been made through the studio system. There is a homily in the movie business that movies are good only at telling stories with strong, simple lines, that complexity is beyond them because you can't "get into people's heads" as in fiction and drama. This idea exists probably because it's hard in *any* medium to really get into somebody's head, and if simpler movies are making money why mess with the formula? On the other hand, one of the problems you run into in writing screenplays for film studios is that when it is appropriate to tell part of the story in pictures and you write it down that way, most of the powers that be don't get it, or don't think that the *audience* will get it. Some of the problem is that the pictures don't yet exist in their final form and some of it is that people are used to being *told* everything. Long stretches without dialogue make most studio executives and independent money people as nervous as huge, unbroken speeches do, and you end up having to add dialogue that is simplistic and redundant and hope the eventual director will have the sense and the power to cut it out or not shoot it in the first place. We see Indians on the plain, mounted and armed to hunt. We see buffalo thundering across the plain toward them. We cut to a closer shot of the Indians, watching, bodies tense, gripping their lances. We cut back to the buffalo, thundering. We cut back to the Indians, and at this point nine times out of ten somebody in power will pop up at a story conference and say, "Couldn't one of the Indians say 'Here come the buffalo'?" Good observation, Yellow Deer, you're really on your toes today.

The point is not that studio guys are dense, because most of them aren't, but there is a tradition, much reinforced by TV, of having a running commentary while you're doing anything visual so nobody gets lost. The reluctance to buck this tradition is understandable. There's a lot of talk about how visually literate kids today are, but a lot of that literacy

is the equivalent of being able to read *Spider-man*, without the captions, real fast. When you throw any kind of complexity in, visual or verbal, things haven't changed much. The main use I make of preview screenings is to see if people "get it" or not. If enough people are confused about a plot point we still have time to lay in a line or two to help clear things up. So maybe you do shoot the equivalent of the guy saying "Here come the buffalo," but only use it if you have to.

When thinking in pictures it's important to consider whether a certain image will have the same meaning to someone else as it does to you. No matter what your experience of the Vietnam War, *Platoon* is a rugged movie to enter into, a meaningful assault on the senses. But the images in it are bound to have a different resonance for people who have been in combat than for people who haven't. The trick is not to ignore one group and concentrate on the other, to become either a caterer to the elite or a panderer to the masses, but to pick and build your images so that *anybody* can get into the story on some level, so that maybe people are drawn in deeper than they thought they could or would want to go. And you have to do all this without lying to them.

Much is made of the differences between fiction and movies, yet in some ways they have more in common than movies and theater. It is possible in fiction to "move the eye" around a setting, very much the way a tracking shot in movies does, by selecting and ordering details. This is something that is very difficult in theater, because our eyes tend to follow anything that moves and to travel around the whole set when nothing is moving. Attempts to move the eye by spotlighting tend to make us as aware of the spotlight as of the object being lit, whereas in fiction and movies there is nothing *but* the object being described or seen on screen. Generally in theater the eye is moved by the actors, whereas in both movies and fiction the eye can be led to wander away from characters to other important parts of the story.

But finally, fiction is words describing images, where in movies you have the images themselves. Fiction relies more on the imagination of the reader, while movies often seem to be imagination made solid. This potential for solidity in movies, their ability to make you feel the tangible weight of objects, the immediate consequences of actions, has something to do with why some stories present themselves as movies and some don't. We do some of our understanding straight from the gut, and if we can be made to feel the damp and cold of the mine shaft, feel the weight of the pick, breathe the dust-thick air, we're going to have more of a handle on a coal miner and his feelings than we could get just from reading and thinking. Thinking in pictures is a way to inhabit the bodies of characters as well as their minds. Trying to bring those pictures, those feelings, to other people is a lot of what movie-making is about.

# Why <u>Matewan</u>?

THERE'S NO PLACE in America like the hills of West Virginia and eastern Kentucky. There'll be a river, usually fast running and not too wide, and on the flatland along its banks a railroad track and maybe a little town, only two or three streets deep before the land starts rising up steep all around you. You've got to look straight up to see the sky and often there's a soft mist shrouding the holler. The hills hug around you — stay inside of them for a while and a flat horizon seems cold and unwelcoming. It's always been a hard life there, with not enough bottomland to farm and no easy way to get manufactured goods in or out of the area. The cash crops had to be torn out from the ground, first timber and then coal. It's a land that doesn't yield anything easily.

In the late sixties I hitchhiked through the area several times and most of the people who gave me rides were coal miners or people with mining in their families. They spoke with a mixture of pride and resignation about the mining — resignation about how dark and dirty and cold and wet and dangerous it was and pride that they were the people to do it, to do it well. The United Mine Workers were going through heavy times then. Their president, Tony Boyle, was accused of having his election opponent, Jock Yablonski, murdered. The coal companies and most of the political machinery that fed on them and even the UMW hierarchy denied even the existence of black lung disease and refused any compensation for it. All this was added to the usual mine accidents and disasters and wild fluctuations in coal prices. But every miner I talked to would shake his head and say, "Buddy, this aint nothin compared to what *used* to go on. I could tell you some *stories*." The stories would be about their grandfathers and uncles and fathers and mothers, and the older men

would tell their own stories from when they were young. The stories had a lot of the Old West to them, only set in those embracing hills and coffinlike seams of three-foot coal. It was a whole hunk of our history I'd never heard of, that a lot of people had never heard of.

In 1977 I wrote a novel called *Union Dues* that begins in West Virginia coal country and moves to Boston. Before I wrote it I did a lot of reading in labor history, especially about the coal fields, and that was when I came across the story of the Matewan Massacre. In a book about the Hatfield and McCoy feud in Mingo County, there was a mention of a distant cousin of the Hatfields named Sid, chief of police of the town of Matewan, who was involved in a bloody shoot-out in 1920, during the mine wars of the era. It got me interested, but accounts of the incident were few and highly prejudiced. The rhetoric of both the company-controlled newspapers of the day and their counterparts on the political left was rich in lurid metaphor but short on eyewitness testimony. But a few characters stuck in my head — Sid Hatfield; the mayor, Cabell Testerman, who wouldn't be bought at a time when the coal companies routinely paid the salaries of public officials and expected their strikebreakers to be deputized and aided in busting the union; a man known only as Few Clothes, a giant black miner who joined the strikers and was rumored to have fought in the Spanish-American War; and C.E. Lively, a company spy so skilled he was once elected president of a UMW local. Aspects and details of other union showdowns in the area also began to accumulate — the transportations of blacks from Alabama and European immigrants just off the boat to scab against the strikers; the life of the coal camp and company store; the feudal system of mine guards and "Baldwin thugs" that enforced the near slavery the miners and their families lived in. All the elements and principles involved seemed basic to the idea of what America has become and what it should be. Individualism versus collectivism, the personal and political legacy of racism, the immigrant dream and the reality that greeted it, monopoly capitalism at its most extreme versus American populism at its most violent, plus a lawman with two guns strapped on walking to the center of town to face a bunch of armed enforcers — what more could you ask for in a story? And yet it was a story unknown to most Americans, untold on film but for a silent short financed by the UMW in the aftermath of the massacre. The movie was called *Smilin' Sid* and the only known print was stolen by coal company agents and never seen again.

Though there were familiar Western elements to the story, it had a unique character because of its setting. The hills of West Virginia, the people and the music have a mood and rhythm to them that need to be seen and heard to be felt completely. There is a cyclical sense of time there, a feeling of inescapable fate that in the story resists the optimism

and progressive collectivism of the 1920s workers' movement. Politics are always at the mercy of human nature and custom, and the coal wars of the twenties were so personal that they make ideology accessible in a story, make it immediate and emotional. It was this emotional immediacy that made me think of making a movie about the events in Matewan.

If storytelling has a positive function it's to put us in touch with other people's lives, to help us connect and draw strength or knowledge from people we'll never meet, to help us see beyond our own experience. The people I read about in the history books and the people I met in the hills of Kentucky and West Virginia had important stories to tell and I wanted to find a way to pass them on.

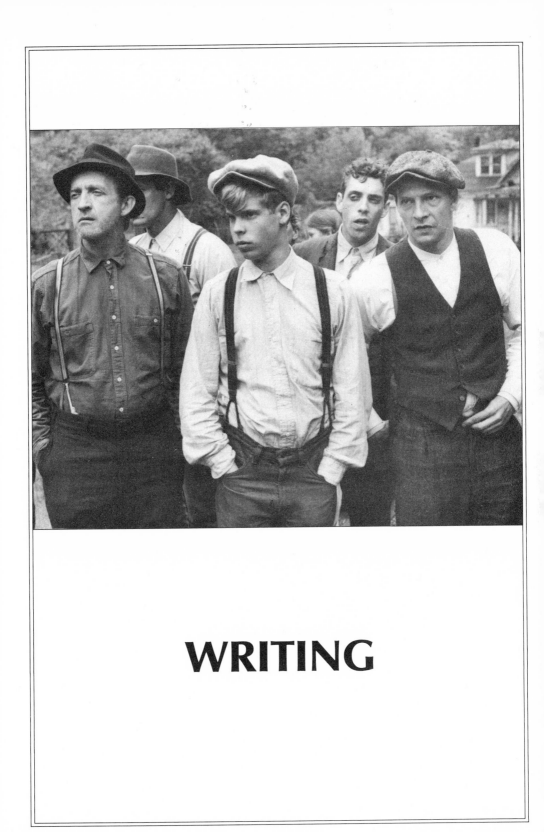

# WRITING

# Writing the Screenplay

## The Story

In 1920 the minefields in eastern Kentucky and southwestern West Virginia are totally nonunion, to the point where the coal operators in that area can undersell their competitors throughout the country. The United Mine Workers union, still a young and volatile organization, targets several counties to be organized. The mine owners, hoping to stop and reverse the spread of what they see as a malignant cancer, hold Mingo and Logan counties in West Virginia in a military grip — controlling political officials and police, posting armed guards at the mines and coal camps, sending spies into the midst of the miners and creating a "judicious mixture" of native miners, blacks and recent immigrants who they believe can never rise above their basic prejudices to resist collectively.

A strike begins near the town of Matewan, on the Tug Fork River just across from Kentucky, in the land where the Hatfields and McCoys ambushed each other in the decades after the Civil War. The mayor and chief of police of the town, Cabell Testerman and Sid Hatfield, refuse a bribe offered by agents from the Baldwin-Felts Detective Agency, which functions as the enforcing arm of the state's coal operators. Hatfield forbids the agents to evict striking miners from company housing within his jurisdiction. The Baldwins threaten to arrest him and try him in a neighboring county. Evictions take place and the Baldwin agents walk to the train station to leave town. They are met in the street by Hatfield and Testerman. Shots are fired, possibly started by the men in the street, possibly by miners inside a nearby building. The shooting explodes into

a massacre. Most of the Baldwin agents, the mayor and a few miners are killed.

These are the bare bones of the history I started with.

## Beyond Genre

American movies present an endless series of lean strangers riding into town from who-knows-where. The celebration of the individual is the backbone of our mythologies, the promise inherent in most of our laws and attitudes. Much of our political energy is spent in finding ways to get people to live with each other on some peaceful and equitable level without confining or appearing to confine that individualism. This may be why dramas of collective life have always had a stronger hold on European and Asian audiences than on Americans. The lone man against the mob, whether he's mounted on a horse or on a motorcycle, is a typical American movie protagonist, and whether he chooses it or has it forced upon him, he is usually the bringer of violent justice.

American labor history is a violent one, the violence being condoned or condemned depending on which side of the picket line you stand on. The first major decision I made in writing *Matewan* was to not just pick a side and then root for that side to be left standing when the smoke cleared, but to question the violence itself, to question it politically, strategically, morally. Accounts from both sides of the Matewan Massacre mention the horror of the killings, the grim hatred of the people involved in town toward the dead Baldwins. To bring the questioning of this violence to the foreground I made the fictional protagonist of the story, the union organizer Joe Kenehan, a pacifist. Not a reformed gunslinger who pulls his holster and guns off the wall in the last reel to wipe out the bad guys and thrill the audience, but a real pacifist, a guy who does not kill people no matter what. A guy trying to preach turning the other cheek in the land of an eye for an eye. And in having Joe question violence, pacifism is also questioned.

So right away I had to be aware that I was messing with genre expectations. The plot and structure of the Matewan story resemble the classic American Western so closely that the movie is going to automatically evoke a whole lifetime of movies that play by certain rules, that maintain certain codes.

In Westerns such as *Shane, High Noon, Gunfight at the OK Corral, The Tin Star* and countless others, there is a relentless build to a final confrontation, in which the hero either finds the courage to stand up for the first time or returns to the violence he hoped to have left behind, in order to blow away the bad guys. Honor and courage are codified here,

and wearing a badge is usually a sign of goodness and responsibility. The deprecations of the bad guys build up throughout the movie, till there is no choice but to meet on Main Street with your irons strapped on. The story of *Matewan* has this same stark shoot-out at the end. But the goodness of wearing a badge is much more relative in this situation, where the oppressors are the ones who generally hand the badges out, and the primary hero has set himself outside the code of the gunman. So if Joe Kenehan doesn't pull that gun off the wall, if you go against the genre expectations of the audience, you'd better know how and why you're doing it or you're just going to lose them.

The first step in making Joe's pacifism acceptable, maybe even attractive, was to make him seem a familiar rather than exotic character. So I made him a Wobbly. The Industrial Workers of the World (IWW) was a very home-grown, American, populist, working-stiff kind of organization. It had little of the rarefied ideological bent and European influence of the Socialist and Communist parties of the time. Lumberjacks, longshoremen, railroad men, farmworkers — the salt of the earth joined in a kind of global idealism. They struck hard and often, lived constantly on the front lines, advocated noncompliance and sabotage of the World War I effort and were broken as a major force in only a few years by the federal government and their own lack of political infighting skills. But the Wobbly spirit remained alive in fact and fiction, in the Tom Joads and Woody Guthries of the Depression, in the rhetoric of Huey Long and the selling copy of the New Deal. Joe Kenehan is not a slogan-spouting Marxist with a book education, not a little Indian guy in white robes preaching a kind of mystic Eastern acceptance, not a stranger at all but just about the most regular fella you'd want to meet, a railroad worker who's had it up to here with the bosses and their bullshit and has started to do something about it. My hope for Joe Kenehan was that the audience would be halfway down the road with him, identifying with him, rooting for him, before they could stop and realize this sucker doesn't carry a *gun.* What gives?

Once Joe is established as the protagonist, the backbone of the movie then becomes "Can he get justice for the miners without a gun?" There may be scenes about other things and other characters, there are, you hope, many other questions to be asked in the story, but that is the spine you have to keep coming back to, the central question that drives the plot. Movies that make the audience ask questions almost invariably have to push beyond genre, beyond the satisfying ritual of the expected. You can reasonably say of a standard thriller or horror movie or Western that it is not so important who does what to whom and why, but how the story is told, how the audience's emotions are manipulated. In the movies I've worked on that attempt to push beyond genre, it's *always*

important who does what and why, and the manner of the storytelling is important only in its effectiveness in bringing the audience to its basic questions.

To pull that off, though, and to keep the audience emotionally involved with the story, the movie has to make them willing not only to think beyond the boundaries of genre but also to reevaluate what they know or think about the world ("Without a gun? Fat fucking chance."). The main way I try to do this is to get them to enter into the point of view of the characters, especially the characters who think Joe Kenehan *might* succeed.

## Point of View

Point of view is a tricky thing, especially in movies. In fiction, in the relaxed time environment of a novel, it is possible to deal with multiple points of view fairly easily, assuming the voice and world view of a new character with each successive chapter if you want. In movies this gets real confusing real fast. Unless you make a formal point that what you are seeing is a certain person telling his or her side of things, as in Kurosawa's *Rashomon*, point of view follows some pretty basic, visceral rules. The camera, used solely as a recording eye, provides a kind of omniscient point of view. When camera movement and editing montage are added, the point of view can become either a self-consciously authorial one (the camera tricks and jokes in Buster Keaton or Alfred Hitchcock movies are examples of this) or be assigned to a certain character. The simplest form of this assigned point of view is to have a character on the screen look at something, then pan or cut to what he's looking at. The character may not be the protagonist, may be about to get rubbed out in the next shot, but for that moment we are in his physical point of view.

A method of assignment of point of view borrowed from literature is to use a narrator, or multiple narrators (sometimes used in conjunction with flashback, as in *Citizen Kane*). The narration is used as an introductory device — once the action starts the story can become very immediate and even drift into someone else's point of view. If the narrator is a nonparticipant in the story, a neutral voice (as in some of Truffaut's adaptations of literary works, such as *Jules and Jim* and *Two English Girls*), it can have a distancing effect, sending us back out to the omniscient or authorial point of view for a little emotional rest before we jump into the heat of the story again. In *Badlands* and *Days of Heaven*, Terrence Malick used narrators who, though characters in the story, were so emotionally affectless that they created a kind of Zen-like remove

from the turmoil on screen, the vocal equivalent of an extremely high crane shot.

The most difficult form of point of view to pull off is the psychological point of view. In this you don't only see what a character literally sees, but you see *how* he perceives it, how he sees the world. Probably the most successful recent example of this is Martin Scorsese's *Raging Bull*, where we get inside Jake LaMotta's head, inside his physical rhythm, for long periods during the film. Psychological point of view, when obvious, is usually associated with tilted camera angles and characters on drugs, but when done effectively there is nothing quite like it to bring the audience inside somebody else's skin, to really connect.

In *Matewan* I tried using several different types of point of view for different purposes. To personalize the backbone of the film, Joe's struggle for justice without violence, I created Danny Radnor. Danny is an adolescent boy, a coal miner, preacher, and union man who has both the Old Testament values of righteousness and retribution and the New Testament dreams for peace and justice within him. Joe's fight becomes a struggle for Danny's soul, a fight to help him see beyond the cycle of blood feuds and meaningless revenge the company fosters among the miners. What is positive to me in *Matewan* is the sense of mission passed on from Joe to Danny, and so I try to concentrate on their points of view throughout the story.

The entire movie is framed by a narration spoken by Danny as an old man, called Pappy in the screenplay (Pappy is heard but never seen). The narration is a reflection on things past. The movie opens with immediate action — men work in a coal mine while Danny, as a boy, spreads word of an impending strike. We are literally and figuratively in the dark as we watch — Who are these people? What's going on? As soon as we start to figure out what's up, we are catapulted out of the mine and the narrator's voice begins. "Hit were 1920 in the southwest field," he tells us, and these were the conditions and this was the situation. This voice, this storyteller, is somebody who was there in the pictures we're seeing, but we aren't sure who he is yet.

Next we see a mysterious stranger on a train. The men behind him are talking about strikes and union agitators, but he doesn't let on where he stands. The train stops. He steps out to see why, and through his eyes we see a transportation of blacks from Alabama attacked by the local striking white miners. The man, Joe Kenehan, watches but doesn't take part.

At this point we've been invited into two characters' points of view without being introduced to them in any detail. One of the things I was aiming for in this movie was a kind of trust and empathy for the characters based on experience rather than generic expectation. In a pure genre

Western, the hero rides into town and he's Gary Cooper or Gregory Peck or whoever and we know we like him before he does anything because he's the *hero* — that's the kind of movie it is. That kind of instant identification is good and useful but it has its limitations. When the hero doesn't act like a hero the audience knows he is just playing possum, he will turn around in the end and fulfill the genre's code. In *Matewan* I wanted Joe and Danny to go beyond that. When they mess up there has to be a real fear in the audience that this is it, this is who the character is going to remain, we've put our hopes on a loser or a coward or a pacifist and how come we're still feeling friendly toward him? By giving both of the characters an oblique entrance into the movie, I hoped to let the audience find them on their own time, to discover and make friends with them rather than having the relationship thrust on them as a given. You stack the deck of course, and bring out what you think is likable or sympathetic in the characters, but finally you make the audience do some of the work. People generally value what they work for more than what is handed to them without asking.

Throughout the movie I alternate between the two characters' points of view. Danny as an old man returns three times as narrator and many scenes are seen through his eyes as a young boy. This gives me both an insider and an outsider as guides for the audience. Joe, the sympathetic outsider, can ask many of the questions the audience would like to ask about this place and situation. Danny, the insider who because of his youth and disposition is less suspicious than the other miners, can answer many of those questions. The audience can choose either or both as a way into the movie.

## Fictional History and Historical Fiction

In the screenplay there are both fictional characters based on composites of people I've read about and known and characters based on actual historical figures who were involved in the Matewan Massacre. Mixing the historical and the fictional is something that has been done numerous times, but it's something you always have to do carefully. Well-known historical figures become a kind of public property and over the years lots of writers take a crack at them — think of the wildly different movie interpretations of Custer or Jesse James or Napoleon. You feel that if one interpretation does them an injustice they'll get another day in court, the record will be gone back to. Since the historical figures I was dealing with were not widely known, I felt a responsibility to stick pretty close to the verifiable accounts of their actions and shied away from their personal lives. The burden of personalizing the story then fell on the

fictional characters. I didn't want the audience to be able to feel this was a story of long ago and far away, about people they could never be or know. In some sorts of movies you want the exact opposite, you want a kind of generic simplicity that can become mythic if you do it well enough. In Sergio Leone's Westerns he stripped away the specifics of place, personal history and even name, until he could make a movie appropriately titled *The Good, the Bad, and the Ugly*. But while the mythic is stirring, it can make you think "this really doesn't have anything to do with *me*, those are allegorical figures up there on the screen." So I tried to particularize, to humanize, to provide historical and domestic detail. The nature of the detail is often not so important as the *fact* of it — the dollars-and-cents amounts miners had to pay for heat and housing in 1920 may be hard to translate into modern prices but we recognize the reality of being concerned with a raise in the rent and a drop in the paycheck — we've been there counting pennies.

The characters have an archetypal outer appearance — Joe is the stranger in town, Sid the representative of brooding violence, Few Clothes the John Henry of coal, Turley the company man — but they also have to work on a merely human level, to seem to have a life outside of the story, other fish to fry. One thing I've tried to do in all the movies I've written for myself to direct is have the world populated by more than one or two people, to present a community. The norm in star-vehicle screenwriting is to have a couple of leads and the rest of the characters there only to provide background and plot advancement. "A love story set against the turbulent backdrop of the Hundred Years War" and so on. I'm more interested in how individual or political acts affect communities of people — parents, friends, children, co-workers. To pull this off, to have all these characters seem three-dimensional, they need not only more screen time than is usually provided but also more depth of character.

## Character

In pure generic films, character is often a matter of physical appearance or physical business, done in fairly broad strokes. The character wears a certain uniform or a black hat or a Mohawk haircut or has squeaky shoes, chews gum, giggles before shooting people and uses a nasal inhaler. There was a time when a "character actor" was someone expected only to deliver a certain type — Edward Everett Horton didn't play a longshoreman one week and an Apache warrior the next, he played Edward Everett Horton and he did it very well. Character depth entails a complexity that is unnecessary and even unwanted in most genre films. Part of the appeal

of a generic character is that the audience knows exactly what he or she will do in a certain situation — that's the payoff. Once a character is established with some complexity, though, the audience has to wonder, and the character acts on a more human level.

Often I'll try to achieve this complexity by subverting stereotype. Early in the movie *Lianna* we meet a football coach, the husband of one of the main characters. He looks and acts, on first meeting, like a generic big lunk of a football coach. But later when he has a conversation with his wife's best friend who has just come out of the closet as a lesbian, his reaction isn't what we expect from the stereotype. It is a believable reaction, so the effect isn't only comic or anachronistic, and because it is unexpected it prepares us for the unpredictable nature of the rest of the community's reaction to Lianna's coming out.

In *Matewan* I try to give even the most negative of characters something else to play besides evil. At one point we learn that Hickey, one of the Baldwin agents sent to town to stir up trouble, is a war hero with a traumatic past in the trenches. This information is meant not as an excuse or a Freudian explanation for his actions but to give him some room to breathe, to remind us that the man's life is not contained by this one incident in it, as well as to establish him as a guy familiar with killing.

Similarly, Bass, James and Doolin, three of the Baldwins brought to town for the final confrontation, are introduced as a trio of working stiffs horsing around rather than as poker-faced grim reapers bent on murder. I didn't want the bad guys shot down at the end to be totally faceless, to be easily written off as human beings.

The language of the movie is also very particular, both to its time and its place. West Virginia mountain dialect can vary from county to county, even from holler to holler. I was aiming not for scientific accuracy but for something evocative and consistent, a rhythm and color to the dialogue that would place it geographically as well as make use of the simple beauty of expression you find there. For this you listen and you read, you pick up syntax and vocabulary and try to keep some difference between the speakers. Part of the character of a people is their voice, and part of the attraction of storytelling for me is carrying that voice to other people.

## Structure and Pace

The rule of thumb in screenwriting is that a page of dialogue and description will turn into roughly one minute of running time on screen. There are of course exceptions — when I worked for Ivan Tors, who had pro-

duced *Sea Hunt*, he told me that when writing for underwater scenes you had to allow one and a half to two minutes per page. When you say "Mike swims over to the hull and searches for the eel," it takes less than an eighth of a page to describe but it takes a good thirty seconds for Mike to swim to the hull. Action sequences where you detail all the little shots and cutaways may actually boil down to less than a minute per page. But in general, if you've got 110 to 120 pages of script you're talking about a two-hour movie.

In terms of audience rhythm and patience, I subscribe to certain broad rules. By the end of the first half hour they better know what the game is and who the players are. The proposition of the movie, the backbone question that will be decided, must be stated. New characters can be brought in after this point, new subpropositions raised, but all the basic stuff should be established.

The structure of *Matewan* is basically four peaks, each with its own build-up, each peak representing either a defeat or victory for Joe in his attempt to bring in the union without killing. After the introductory section, where the narrator sets the stage for us, the first quarter begins with the fight between the native miners and the blacks from Alabama and peaks with the scene at the driftmouth, when both the black and Italian scabs walk out and join the natives in the strike. So the first structural quarter of the film is about whether Joe can get the three groups to overcome their prejudices and oppose the company together, and it results in a temporary victory for Joe.

The next section begins with the united miners building a tent camp and the antagonists, Hickey and Griggs, raising the stakes in their battle against the union. They shoot up the tent camp at night, then the miners go against Joe's wishes and plan retaliation, but they're betrayed and end up being ambushed themselves. This quarter peaks with the ambush and its aftermath. Joe's attempts to lead the miners away from the violent revenge cycle the company wants to lure them into ends in a defeat for both Joe and the miners.

The third quarter begins with finding the body of Hadley, an ambushed miner, and the beginning of the plot by C.E. Lively, who the audience now knows is a spy, to discredit Joe with the miners. The plot continues, seems to be working, and is derailed only at the last minute by Danny. The question of whether the miners will be tricked into turning on Joe ends with a temporary victory.

The last quarter begins on a high note with a montage of the strikers organizing, then crashes with the murder of Hillard Elkins and the arrival of the back-up Baldwin agents in town. The section peaks at the end with the shoot-out, the Matewan Massacre.

Within each quarter there is a setup and a build-up leading to a climac-

```
                        MATEWAN BREAKDOWN

1-3        Int. coal mine - word spreads

3-5          Miners walking montage, Pappy VO

5-7          Joe in train - black miners attacked

7-8           Joe and Bridey - Joe sees town

9-11           Joe and Elma - Danny and Hillard return

11-13        Turley and blacks in shed

13-14        Elma's table - Sephus comes for Joe

14-16         Sephus and Joe to C.E.'s, grill Joe

16-23          Miners bitch, Joe speech x-cut with Hardshell rap

23-28          Danny sermon x-cut w/Joe at Italians

28-29         Sid and Joe on steps

29-31          Bridey w/Hickey and Griggs

31-33          Joe and Elma in back - Hickey and Griggs get Joe's room

33-34         Few and Fausto in mine

34-36         Joe, Sephus and C.E. talk strategy, Bridey interrupts

36-38          Black miners confer, Italian miners confer
```

## Breakdown Sheet

I used breakdown sheets during the production for a quick graphic form to orient myself as to where we stood in the flow of the story. In the rush of shooting it isn't hard to paint yourself into a corner, setting a tone or style in one sequence that will be impossible to match with what has to come next. Lighting, cutting, music, emotional intensity — all have a flow that must be kept track of. If you end one sequence with an extreme close-up the next one might benefit from a wide shot. When shots or entire sequences are altered or dropped completely due to time pressures (or new ideas), you have to consider the structure of the story as a whole rather than just the immediate impact. The breakdown sheets provide an overview that can help you avoid throwing things out of whack. During the writing and rewriting stages they can give you a sense of overall story rhythm. What has happened by page 30? By page 60? What do we know? Who have we met? What should we think or hope will happen next?

| | |
|---|---|
| 38 | Bridey and Joe on path, Hillard calls |
| 38-42 | Eviction confrontation, Sid saves Joe |
| 42-43 | Miners vote to bop scabs |
| 43-44 | Hickey and Griggs ride Danny at dinner - Danny exits, sees hills |
| 45-50 | Mine shaft confrontation - scabs walk out |
| 50-51 | Tent-camp-building montage, Pappy VO |
| 51-52 | Joe w/Danny and Elma at tent camp |
| 52-53 | Sid and Cabell meet Hickey and Griggs in apothecary |
| 53-56 | Night, tent camp shot up |
| 56-59 | Morning, tent camp recovers - Elma and Bridey tend wounded |
| 59-60 | Miners meet without Joe |
| 60-63 | Tent-camp confrontation - hill people save Joe |
| 64 | Joe looks for men - C.E. give Danny a bomb |
| 64-66 | Hickey _ _ _ _ dinner - Joe comforts her on porc_ |
| 66-69 | BOOM1 |
| 69-71 | Woun_ Miss_ |

| | |
|---|---|
| 72-73 | Miners search for stiffs on slope - C.E. gets letter |
| 73 | Danny darkness speech to Joe |
| 74-78 | C.E. plays Bridey x-cut w/Joe working on miners - Bridey lies and miners vote to kill Joe |
| 79-80 | Hickey catches Danny in his room, warns |
| 80-89 | Few and Joe x-cut w/Danny sermon |
| 89-90 | C.E.'s burned, he escapes |
| 90-92 | Organizing montage, Pappy VO |
| 92-94 | Rosaria and Mrs. Elkins make friends |
| 94-95 | Joe and Danny pitch and catch |
| 95-100 | Danny and Hillard get caught - C.E. and Turley - Hillard killed |
| 100-102 | Baldwins arrive |
| 102-104 | Hillard funeral |
| 104-105 | Camp, lull before the storm - Danny rejects Joe |
| 105-106 | Night int. Elma's - Sid walks the street |
| 106-110 | Lead-up and shoot-out |
| 110-111 | Danny in mine, Pappy VO |

tic peak, as well as the through-line keeping everything connected to the backbone proposition. Danny's relationship with Joe changes and deepens within each of the sections, the character of violence in each section escalates. The existence of sections rather than one long build to a single climax helps give the movie some scope, some of the psychological feeling of interrelated events happening over time.

One of the main aspects of movies that distinguishes them from other forms of storytelling is their very special relationship with time. Only recently has the phenomenon of home video rental allowed viewers to "put down" a movie the way they might put down a book. But the images still have a tangible duration in time, rather than just taking up so much space on paper. The structure of a movie is, in many ways, its realization in time — both actual elapsed screen time and perceived time. By perceived time I mean both the very subjective perception of whether a movie or scene seems long or short, and the perception of how much "story time" has passed from scene to scene within the movie.

Generic films and their offshoots, television dramas, tend to have the most codified structures and time schemes. You can set your watch by a formula drama like *The Fugitive* with its rigid structure: the introduction of Richard Kimble in his new guise, possible conflict or danger appearing, possible friendship or love relationship appearing, Kimble forced to reveal his true identity, new acquaintances forced to either hide or reveal his identity, near capture and narrow escape, and the afterward with Lieutenant Girard glumly sniffing the cooling trail — each element in a fixed time niche relative to the commercial breaks. *Hill Street Blues* seemed a revelation when it first hit TV not only for the high level of the writing and performance but for its successful grafting of the soap-opera structure — repeating characters in parallel stories — onto the cops and criminals genre. The actual time of such a show is fixed by network format, and on *Hill Street* there is the added structure of the "day in the life," starting with the precinct shift briefing at the beginning of every episode. Sequences not falling within that single day are usually placed after the natural transitional break of a commercial. In a feature film you have no commercials and running time has less absolute boundaries.

The monster movie (think of *Mothra, Them, Gorgo, Alligator*) is a good example of strict generic structure and time scheme in a feature. There is a mysterious first manifestation of the creature, often off screen, hinting at its destructive capabilities. There is the meeting of the adventurer-hero with the scientist (and usually his beautiful daughter) who will explain things. The first major confrontation, in which the creature fully reveals itself, finds the local authorities' puny efforts to destroy it inadequate. There is a realization of the ultimate threat of the beast (multiplying its own kind, making a beeline for downtown Tokyo, etc.), and the

heroine is put in peril and barely saved. A final, major military confrontation often fails, leading to a rampage by the creature, followed by its destruction or banishment through some flash of insight by the hero. It is an efficient structure, with room built in for reversals of fortune and rest periods between confrontations in which the hero and the scientist's daughter can get together. The time scheme is a basic straight line toward a D-Day of some sort — the creature's arrival in the big city or the hatching of its beastlings. A race against time is built in and usually physical movement of the creature toward the final confrontation. It is a streamlined machine of a movie that can withstand clunky dialogue, terrible special effects and wooden, badly dubbed acting.

In *Matewan* I was able to use some of the structure provided by genre but also to stray from it. Like many a Western it ends with a shoot-out on Main Street, but the path it takes to get there is not a straight one. I wanted a cyclical structure to be contained within the dovetailing actions leading to the shoot-out. If all the movie is about is who got shot and who didn't, the history ends there — it doesn't inform anything we do today. But people still go underground to mine coal, people with power still pit races and ethnic groups against each other to keep them from taking control of their own lives, religion is still used for oppression as often as for liberation. The last shot in the movie is not the dead Baldwins on the street but Danny walking back into the mine, his voice as an old man telling us how he went on to work for the things Joe Kenehan stood for. The final confrontation is preceded by others like it, the narration tells of Sid's murder by C.E. Lively at a later date — we have seen only a piece of an ongoing battle, a cycle of violence and revenge with no definite end.

Cyclical life, a sense of continuity, good and bad, is the opposite of the favored Hollywood ending of ultimate triumph (Rocky at center ring, victorious, wrapped in the American flag). The counterculture movies of the sixties had endings that were much more downbeat but just as finite — Cool Hand Luke or Butch and Sundance or the hippies in *Easy Rider* all blasted dead by the forces of oppression. The finite ending sends the audience out with a definite jolt, a sense that justice (or injustice) has been done. A more ambiguous ending is a trickier thing to pull off and demands more preparation. You can't ask people to think about things that are difficult unless you can make them care about and identify with the characters in the story on a deeper level than genre movies are usually willing or able to evoke. A *Jaws* where the shark remains undefeated is a great genre picture with an inappropriate ending. But when Moby Dick rolls back into the depths in Melville's novel it works fine, because the story is about a lot more than catching a whale.

## DUAL PURPOSE SCENES

In *Matewan* I try to build this identification between audience and character by getting the audience involved in the lives of the people of the community without dampening the "page-turning" aspects of the plot. This means doing more than one thing at a time, having scenes of action also be scenes of character and exposition whenever possible. The norm in the monster movie is to separate the two — the raging beast amok followed by the explaining scientist with charts and graphs. In *Matewan* I try to pack as much into every scene as I can.

The movie starts with Sephus underground, performing the cramped, back-breaking everyday actions of prepping and shooting a coal face, cross-cut with Danny running through the mine spreading word of the company's last offer on the tonnage rate — the mundane and the dramatic brought together. The first shot of Joe, the mysterious stranger on the train, is backed with overheard throwaway lines from two coal brokers about the situation brewing in the county. The nonverbal actions of the various principals during the attack on the black miners tell us about the character of each — Joe a noncombatant, Hillard rushing in headlong and getting nailed, Few Clothes fighting defensively and trying to sort out what's going on, Danny more involved in helping Hillard out of the rumble than in fighting himself. The scene in the supply room between Turley and the black miners, seemingly a litany of details from coal camp life, is also a microcosm of company/worker relations. The moment Few raises an objection he is asked for his name — isolated and marked as a troublemaker to be gotten rid of. Whenever Elma Radnor appears, she is usually working as well as talking or listening. Chopping, hauling, cleaning, cooking — when she finally breaks down and says to Joe she's "just tired is all" we have a good idea from *what*.

The problem with packing a lot into each scene is that if you choose to cut it for whatever reason, you're cutting more than one thing. I try to have plot and character information stated and reinforced more than once in the course of the movie, so when it comes to editing we're not married to a whole scene for the sake of a single line or detail. Even with such precautions, people do get lost. When the Baldwins discover C.E. Lively hiding after they've ambushed the miners, I had written for Griggs to shout "Hold it boys, it's C.E.!" We considered cutting this during the editing, figuring even Griggs wouldn't be dumb enough to yell out the name of their best spy when miners might still be around. But after we showed the rough cut a few times, a number of people expressed confusion over just who it was standing under that lantern, a distressing problem considering C.E. is about to swing into action in his plot against Joe. We left the line in.

## CONTEXT

The pace of a movie can often be quickened by bringing the audience into a scene as late as possible, skipping the knock on the door, the introductions and build-up, and getting right to the meat of the action. This asks the audience to understand what's going on in the scene partly by the context it's in. In a horror film you see a familiar building, there are cop cars and ambulances flashing in the street, the woman-in-peril's best friend's cat is running loose — uh-oh, they got her. If you break from genre and don't have those seventy years of movie history to provide the context, then you have to be more careful in building it within the story. You have to set the pins up before you can knock them down. That Griggs is the one to actually murder Hillard is foreshadowed by his willingness to shoot Danny over a matter of passing the peas in an earlier scene. Sure, he's the one who'd do it, no questions asked. The scene where Danny rejects Joe's pacifism in the tent the night before the shoot-out sets us up for Danny's showdown with Doolin by the river — will he shoot him or not? Each confrontation between Elma and Hickey informs their eventual armed meeting in the backyard.

The one time I use a cavalry-to-the-rescue kind of appearance, the arrival of the hill people to bail Joe out at the tent camp, I lean on their mythic, generic stereotype as violent, sharpshooting individualists. Once the audience has their initial "Let's see the Baldwins fuck with *these* guys" reaction, I try to push beyond the stereotype, to show some of the formal manners and sense of basic justice they also possess. The patriarch of the group invites the tent people to share the game in the area, and politely asks them not to shoot any of his hogs.

Throughout the script Sid Hatfield and Hickey prepare us for the face-off on Main Street, each a representative of doom, a fuse burning closer to explosion. The context of Joe's travels his first night out — secret knocks, codes and questions at the back door, armed guards everywhere — gives us as much a sense of the company's oppression as any of the miners' accounts in the first meeting or Pappy's narration. The main subplot, the relationship between Mrs. Elkins and Rosaria, works in a more subtle way. A hard generic stand could be taken that we don't need this stuff, it slows down the action. But in an important way the coming together of these two people *is* the action of *Matewan*, the concept of "union" that goes beyond the forming of a trade organization, and to subtract it from the context of the story would leave you with just another horse opera.

# Working with Time

## STORY DAYS

In both the writing and editing of a movie you manipulate time in various ways. One basic method is to use the natural rhythm of a "story day" — events that happen from sun up through the night of one day — grouped in a defined section of the picture. Silent movies relied heavily on their "Night Falls . . . " and "Came the Dawn . . . " title cards to separate sections of a story. Time of day can become a plot device — "They never attack at night" or "They always attack at night." Night is the enemy in many a horror movie, and daylight the hero.

In *Matewan* I used the transition from night to day at times for a sense of renewed energy, as in the tent-building and organizing montages that follow long, tense, nighttime confrontations.* Other times I use the morning to reveal the damage done the night before, as in the recovery scene after the Baldwins shoot up the tent camp or the discovery of Hadley's body after the ambush. And sometimes, connected with the arrival of the morning train, the new day brings more danger to Joe and the miners. Direct confrontations happen by day, while surreptitious ones, plots and ambushes, happen by night. The people in the movie are still strongly connected to nature and its rhythms and I wanted that sense of natural day-to-night transition in the story. Sections of the movie are often ended with the restful quiet of a slow fade to black.

## MONTAGE TIME

Another form of time manipulation is the use of compressed-time montages. Sometimes you want to convey the feeling that many days have passed or are passing without spending a proportionate amount of screen time to get the feeling across. Shorthand such as titles, seasonal changes, changes in the look or age of the characters, long dissolves and fades can be used, and each has its own rhythm. A way to make the time pass without losing forward energy is to jam lots of moments from the transition into a montage sequence. In the sequence in *Matewan* where the strikers organize after Joe is saved by Danny's sermon, dissolves, straight-cut pieces of scenes, narration and music are all combined to show us a month or more passing and the union beginning to spread.† Montage

---

  * A montage is a kind of movie shorthand, collapsing many events over a period of story time into a short sequence, ordinarily with the use of fast cutting or dissolves.

  † A dissolve is when one shot fades into the next, both images sharing the screen for a moment. In a straight cut there is no overlap.

sequences of this kind are a strain on a low-budget picture, especially a low-budget period picture. A sequence lasting two minutes in final form that calls for many different locations and extras, that entails many travel hours and hours of prep by the art department, is extremely inefficient in terms of shooting cost per minute. So my efforts in writing the sequence focus on telling the transition story with as few shots as possible. It is hard to gauge at what exact point the audience's time meter will register satisfaction that months have passed, that it's time to get back to the regular story again. On a bigger budget you can overwrite and overshoot and then carve something out of all that footage. Not having this luxury in the movies I've directed has been both an instructive kind of discipline and, at times, an exercise in frustration. I've used out-takes, camera mistakes, flash frames and actors mugging out of character in editing montages, just to have enough shots to build some rhythm with.* Music helps a lot, as does camera movement when you can afford it. A pan or a track or even a zoom that would seem self-conscious and obvious in the rest of the movie can be just what you need in a montage sequence. Dissolves and jump cuts take on a completely different character.† The closest cousin to a transition montage is the rock video, with its compressed time scheme, reliance on effects and musicality.

This kind of sequence doesn't have to rely on a lot of cuts, though. Sometimes something slow and stately — a long master shot or a series of slow dissolves — can accomplish the same thing. The Japanese are masters of these, and till recently their movies had a markedly more seasonal pace than the American shorthand. The rhythm of the writing and cutting does affect the energy of the time transition and the sense of just how much time has elapsed. The biggest structural risk I took in *Matewan* was to have so little actual story between Joe's salvation (on page 144 of the screenplay) and the beginning of the final shoot-out (on page 173). The danger is that the upbeat climax of Joe being saved is so close to the end that it might make the massacre anticlimactic. So in the organizing montage I tried to do two things — to show the union gaining strength and its people gaining solidarity, forcing the company to up the stakes in its oppression; and to make the audience *sense* that a lot of time has passed, that the incident with Joe is long gone and we're on to new developments now.

---

* "Out-takes" are takes of a scene not used in the editing. Often this is because of blown lines or technical problems. "Flash frames" occur when the camera operator takes his eye away from the eyepiece while still shooting, allowing ambient light to flood onto the film, overexposing the shot. The explosion of the bounty hunters in *The Brother from Another Planet* was done with flash frames.

† A "pan" is when the camera swivels from side to side while staying in the same spot, much like when you turn your head. A "track" or "tracking shot" is when the camera is moved forward, backward or sideways either on a dolly on wheels, on a crane

The story could have moved straight from the aftermath of Hillard's murder, from Sid's line "Baldwins coming in the morning, Kenehan," to the final shoot-out. But for the audience to question the violence I felt they needed some time to think about it. The long night before the showdown is a kind of slow montage, a suspension of time in which Joe can have his last try to save Danny and both the characters and audience can reflect on what is about to happen. The shots themselves expand in screen time far beyond what the page length would indicate and help establish the sense of doom, of tragic fate so prevalent in the history and music of the hill people.

## EMOTIONAL TIME

Time can also be manipulated for emotional or psychological purposes. Picture a man on a crowded subway platform suddenly lunging in front of a speeding train, then picture a slow, endlessly formal execution by firing squad. Both may leave a man dead, but they have vastly different emotional effects. One is a complete shock, the other gives us time to consider the event, to hope it won't happen.

In planning this sort of time manipulation I tend to do much more detailing and breaking down of individual shots in the screenplay than usual. On page 66 in the eviction scene, Sid gives the Baldwins an ultimatum. Next we see —

JOE

Watching, tense —

DANNY

Watching —

CABELL

Sweat breaking out on his forehead —

In the final cut we didn't happen to use those exact cutaways, but we did shoot them and shots like them, and the inclusion of those shots in the screenplay informed how the scene was blocked, shot, acted and edited.

---

arm or hand-held by the operator. A "zoom" is when the focal length of the lens is changed during the shot, making the subject larger or smaller in the frame. It is possible to pan, track and zoom at the same time. "Jump cuts" are straight cuts that derive their impact from rapid juxtaposition of images unlike in composition, size or angle. See the shower scene in Hitchcock's *Psycho.*

I wanted time to stop a bit for the characters and for the audience, to give them a moment to wonder if the shooting was going to start so soon. There is a lot of white space around those simple cutaways on the script page, white space without dialogue, white space that graphically looks like tension to an experienced screenplay reader. The flow of the eye over text is stopped, the sentences become shorter, you hold your breath . . .

Watching —

Tense —

Sweat —

Then Hickey gives in and a cheer goes through the crowd and the tension is released. The placement of the words on the page is essentially a literary technique that has to be transferred to film during the movie-making. The exact tempo of this exchange will be worked out in the editing, but the editing depends on what and how much is shot and this in turn is based on the control of emotional time in the script itself.

## RUNNING TIME

Because movies are expensive to make there is also a kind of economic time to consider. A reel of film ready to project is roughly twenty minutes in length. Each time you go past another twenty minutes of running time it means another reel that has to be shipped. The distributor has to pay for that shipping. Theatrical prints are charged for by the foot — the longer the movie, the more expensive each print is. Different theaters have different turnaround times for getting the old audience out and the new one seated, and there are a limited number of "prime-time" movie-going hours each week. If you go much past 110 minutes in running time, you can forget about having a 6:00, 8:00, 10:00 and midnight show — go much longer than 2 hours and there's really only room for two rather than three prime-time shows a night. Exhibitors start to get nervous. No matter how good or popular your movie, three shows at 65 percent capacity in a five-hundred-seat theater will outgross two full houses.

These are the economics of theatrical distribution, and they've fucked up lots of movies that should have been longer and been ignored in lots of movies that could have been shorter. Even if you are free of distributor pressure, or the bulk of your money is expected from videocassette, where length is not much of an extra expense or liability, there has to be a sense of balance informing the running time of the movie. Is your epic-length movie about an epic subject? What are you delivering with that extra reel? In the case of a conscious "blockbuster," the sense of size and production value may be important to the image of the movie as an "event," of something not available on TV or not sufficiently visceral if

seen on the small screen. A thriller, horror movie or comedy might run out of gas at 100 minutes but be perfectly satisfying at 90.

What I think is more important than assigning minute lengths is how the movie *feels* — are you immersed in the story till the final scene or looking at your watch waiting for it to end? I've been to 2½-hour movies I didn't want to end and 88-minute action pictures that seemed like the Bataan Death March. The balance comes in assessing what you have and what the market will bear. If your movie is going to depend on good word of mouth and a sense of audience satisfaction to succeed, it's probably better to lose a few shows a week rather than cut for length and leave plot or emotional gaps in the story. If you've got a star who at the moment turns everything he or she touches into gold, the distributors will make more if it's short enough for more shows and the exhibitors may not care one way or the other if they can sell more popcorn during the slow parts. If you have a mediocre to bad movie in a known genre or with hot actors to advertise, you chop it short, get as many shows in before the word spreads and dump it to videocassette and cable in a few months.

In the screenplay stage of *Matewan* my awareness of economic time mostly affected the scope of the story. The massacre kicked off all kinds of historical events that would have been nice to include, but to do them justice would have sent us into David Lean territory, three hours with an intermission. Aware of the "difficult" nature of the subject matter, I felt this kind of length would have put economic pressures on the movie that would, in terms of casting and story compromises, bend it badly out of shape. So I aimed for a jam-packed two hours and hoped the story didn't expand too much in the shooting.

# Writing for Low Budget

WRITING FOR low-budget production is a kind of formal exercise, something like writing in iambic pentameter or for *The Days of Our Lives*. You have certain parameters and you try to tell the story as well as you can within those parameters. The first requirement is some knowledge of what costs money in making a movie and what doesn't.

Anything set in a historical period costs more for costumes, props and sets than the same story in a contemporary setting would (unless you're doing Adam and Eve in Griffith Park). Shooting on location brings with it the expenses of lodging, per diems, travel days, long-distance phone calls and shipping of film materials. Each speaking part you add means another day or more of Screen Actors Guild (SAG) minimum wage, even for a few lines. Music you don't own the publishing or performance rights to can cost a fortune. Precision camera movement calls for a crew that can pull it off — the best people in those categories are expensive to hire. Star actors cost a lot more than SAG minimum and can run you into lots more maintaining them in the style to which they've become accustomed. Special effects and stunts are expensive and increase your insurance bills. Action scenes are more expensive to shoot in terms of shots and man-hours per screen minute than dialogue scenes are. Special equipment — cranes, Steadicams, helicopter mounts — all cost a lot. Each additional day you shoot has a price tag on it. A high shooting ratio — number of feet exposed in relation to length of finished movie — is a great strain on a low budget. Expensive location rentals and the insurance that sometimes goes with them mount up. The various guilds and unions charge more for night than for day shooting. Shots that depend on a certain kind of weather will almost always run you into delays and down time (time on the set when you can't shoot).

"Low budget" is a somewhat relative term. As of this writing, anything under $5 million is considered low budget by the major Hollywood studios, and their average production cost $11 million. We had well under $4 million to make *Matewan,* and as we first sent the script around to studios, most commented that it just couldn't be made on that amount of money. We were signatories to both the SAG (Screen Actors Guild) and NABET (the union representing most of the crew members) minimum agreements, and had to spend a good deal of money in legal and completion bond (a form of insurance for the investors) fees in order to raise the production money. Though $4 million would have been an extravagant budget on *Secaucus Seven* (made for $60,000) or *Lianna* (made for $300,000), it was an extremely low figure on which to attempt something on the scale of *Matewan.* (As a comparison, *Silverado,* a recent Western with a cast of near stars, reportedly cost $26 million.)

The ideal low-budget movie is set in the present, with few sets, lots of interiors, only a couple speaking actors (none of them known), no major optical effects, no horses to feed. It's no wonder so many beginning movie-makers set a bunch of not-yet-in-the-Guild teenagers loose in an old house and have some guy in a hockey mask go around and skewer them. *Matewan,* of course, has a period setting, a cast of dozens, numerous exteriors, lots of night scenes and a climactic shoot-out. Rather than eliminate all these elements, I tried to minimize and control them.

Several scenes of the steam train coming in and out of Matewan were condensed into an important few. We had use of the train for only a day and a half and shot the shit out of it, moving and stationary, day and night. I cut down on scenes with motorcars. I cut a prologue scene in which Joe leaves from a city train station, and constantly rewrote the interior mine scenes as we got cost reports on various props and operations. Two old ladies staying at Elma's became one Mrs. Knightes, and Elma lost three or four little children who would have caused continuity reshoots and work-hour problems no matter how well behaved they might have been.* The fire at C.E.'s restaurant was written in a minimalist style, and I tried to set a lot of action at the tent camp, where we could easily move the tents around to provide different "looks" for different scenes. The conversation between Bass and Doolin and James was moved from inside a moving train to Main Street, and a scene in the black section of town disappeared. Once the production schedule began to gel I traded some lines among the smaller characters to cut down on people paid a week's salary for saying two lines on the wrong day.

After all this was done we were still faced with the task of shooting a semi-epic period piece in seven weeks for under $4 million. We began to plan like crazy and lean on the talent of our collaborators.

* Kids are great at being kids, but usually not so good at picking the fork up with the same hand at the same moment take after take and not looking at the camera.

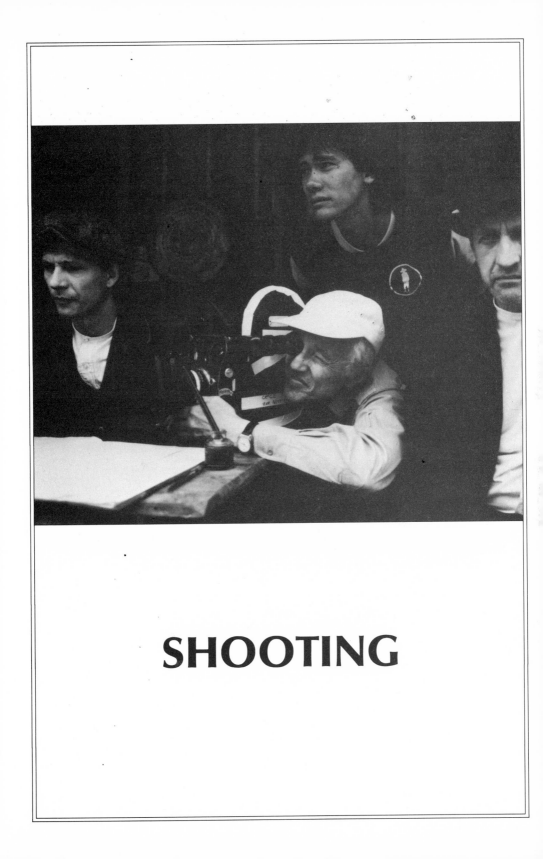

# SHOOTING

# Preproduction

## A Note on Fund-raising

If you have any great ideas on how to raise money to make movies, send them to me in care of the publisher, because I don't. Of the five movies I've directed, two were totally financed by me from writing screenplays for other people, one was funded through a public offering, one was financed by a major studio and *Matewan* was pieced together from a combination of my money, distributor's money, outside investors' money and home-video presale money. Only on *Baby, It's You*, the studio picture, did I not have complete cutting control and that turned into a major fight. That experience combined with other misadventures in fund-raising has led me and the people I work with to believe that there is such a thing as the right money and the wrong money.

Anyone who has tried to get financing for an independent feature may think this idea is insane, that the only way to survive is to grab it and spend it quick the minute anyone really puts some cash on the line. I see the choice as do you want your troubles now or do you want them later. I know people whose movies will never be finished or released because their investors are doing battle with each other in court, I know people whose movies are released chopped up or unfinished or with inserts they had nothing to do with stuck in — all because they didn't have control of the production or lost it along the way. There are directors who work for major studios who claim they've never been fucked over and investors who say they've never been burned, and I hope for them their luck continues. But making a movie is an expensive and difficult process, and any agreement between movie-makers and financiers should be approached cautiously on both sides.

Co-producers Peggy Rajski and Maggie Renzi confer on the set.

It is most important that both parties have a very clear idea just what they're going to get out of the experience, that they agree on that idea, and that it is written into a legal contract. Movie-makers have to be honest with themselves, then have to pass that honesty on to potential investors. If you've got something that really could be the next *Rocky*, great for you. But if you've got a movie with a no-name cast and "difficult" subject matter, that with solid reviews, intelligent marketing and good word of mouth will probably gross $2 million tops theatrically on the art circuit, you'd better know it and you'd better let the investors know it. A certain amount of hype can help draw money to a project, but it's best if the hype is only an extension of your own true enthusiasm for the movie, of the energy you hope to put into it. If you promise people *Star Wars* they're going to be disappointed with *My Dinner with André*.

It's important to remember that investors often get involved in movies for reasons beyond the chance to make big profits. Some want to be patrons of certain directors or actors, some are interested in a particular subject matter, or bringing movie production to their home state, or learning about a new business, or meeting actresses or whatever. Some want to have a say in the production, usually during the casting and editing periods. Some want a screen credit. It doesn't matter especially what it is as long as it's understood and agreed on by both parties from the start and, whenever possible, spelled out in great detail in a contract.

It took *Matewan*'s co-producers, Peggy Rajski and Maggie Renzi, some

three years, from 1983 to 1986, to put the money together for *Matewan*, and a couple times the money was nearly there and fell apart at the last minute. Sometimes it fell apart because both parties realized that what the investors wanted in terms of control was not what we were offering. Other times this was apparent early enough to save a lot of phone calls and meetings. Though it was discouraging to tread water for so long, not knowing if we'd ever get to make the movie, it's good those deals didn't come through. Once any investor's money has been spent on a production it becomes much harder to walk away and start from scratch, and you can end up talking to lots of lawyers trying to get your own story back.

When you have the issue of creative control clearly defined it opens you up to listening to advice without having to play strategic games. Executive producers, investors, and studio heads all have good ideas sometimes.* So do grips, gaffers, production assistants, sound editors, friends, relatives and strangers who wander into your screenings.† If you've held out for the right kind of investor you can listen or not listen to his ideas based on their merit as ideas, not based on the rank of the person telling them to you.

With *Matewan*, Peggy and Maggie were trying to sell a movie with several strikes against it as a mass-audience "property." The story was political, the hero an early socialist, the ending not upbeat and there was no room in it for a rock soundtrack. Though we were considering approaching a few actors with alleged box-office appeal, we were careful to say we weren't likely to land any of them and weren't going to make offers to stars who weren't appropriate for the characters as written. What we *were* able to offer was a completed screenplay, a detailed production budget and our track record of staying on schedule, on budget and out of court and paying all our deferments. The rap was, "We think this is going to be a good movie, we think at this budget it can be successful commercially, would you like to get involved in it?"

---

* An "executive producer" is usually associated with the money on a project, rather than the nuts and bolts of the actual movie-making (the way a producer or "line producer" is). An executive producer may never come on the set or meet any of the people involved in the shooting.

† A "grip" is a crew member who deals with the mechanics of moving and placing the camera, as well as any work involving special rigging. Grips build platforms and tracks for the camera, move it on a dolly for tracking shots and secure it (and the camera operator) on special mounts, such as in helicopter or moving-car shots. They help put up and take down reflectors and scrims to control sunlight.

A "gaffer" is basically an electrician, in charge of working with the director of photography to hang and focus lights, and to tie into or establish power sources.

"Production assistants" are usually the lowest paid and most overworked members of the crew, used for crowd and traffic control, fetching and carrying, guarding equipment, guiding extras on and off the set and anything else that needs doing that nobody else has time or inclination to do.

## Private Offering for a Limited Partnership

This is a page from the offering we sent to potential investors in *Matewan*. Most of the language is dictated by law, the offering monitored by the Securities and Exchange Commission. It basically tells you you're a sap for even considering sinking your money in a movie. It's sort of like telling somebody looking in your refrigerator, "Oh, I think the milk is sour, but help yourself." It's all true, of course. But every once in a while somebody does invest in an independent feature and they make a killing, and/or get to see a movie they feel proud to have helped make happen.

Eventually Peggy and Maggie teamed with Cinecom, the distributor of our *Brother from Another Planet,* to raise the money. Cinecom has had great success on a level of the distribution ecosystem somewhere between art-circuit specialty films and big studio releases, most notably with *The Brother, El Norte, Stop Making Sense,* and *Room with a View.* At the time we made the deal with them they were ready to take the step from merely acquiring and distributing movies to putting some of their money into the production before shooting started. Though this eliminates competition for the final product, it greatly increases the financial risk. As a movie-maker what you want a distributor to do is maximize your movie's potential, getting as many people to see it as you can on the best financial terms possible. Cinecom has a good history of doing this without spending too much money in the process.

In 1984, after one of the times the money fell apart, we quickly made *The Brother from Another Planet* with money I'd made from screenwriting. Cinecom won the right to distribute it after lots of competition, and our relationship with them began. At that time, however, they weren't yet ready to take the leap into production financing, and we were back out on the open market trying anything possible — big studios, small studios, known film investors, rich people allegedly hot to invest in movies, you name it.

Since script, casting and cutting control were pointedly to remain in our hands, a lot less time was wasted in discussions about how the money would materialize if we'd only change this, cut that, or cast whoever. A lot of people weren't even vaguely interested and Maggie and Peggy kept digging, kept following every lead no matter how unlikely it might seem. In the three years basic costs rose sharply — raw stock, guild and union minimums, food and housing costs and insurance rates went crazy — so the price of shooting the movie went from $1.8 million to $3.6 million as we sat around not shooting it. But there was never a temptation to take easier money with the wrong strings attached to it — to risk destroying the movie just in order to finally make it.

## Collaboration

Now that the screenplay section is past, you'll be hearing a lot less "I" and a lot more "we." This is not the royal we or the corporate we or the patriotic we, but the collaborative we. No matter how centralized control is on a movie, it is always a collaboration. Each performance is a collaboration between actor, screenwriter, director, cinematographer, editor, costumer, and so on. The way Ingrid Bergman was dressed, made up, lit, shot and supported by background music in *Casablanca* were all integral

Members of the costume department spray coal schmutz on a miner.

Blocking the tent camp actors and extras, Rosaria and Fausto in foreground

to her performance. Nobody else could have delivered that performance quite like her, but it was the result of a collaboration.

When Peggy, Maggie and I look for crew people to work with, we look not only for the best technicians we can afford but for people who are interested in and have a feeling for the story. A dolly grip with a sense of the rhythm and tension of a scene is going to give you a better tracking move than somebody just staring at marks on the floor. When I talk to production designer Nora Chavooshian about a set I rely on her not only to look at old pictures and do something appropriate for the period but to consider the mood of the scene, its function in the flow of things, the psychology of the characters — to help me tell the story. We look for actors who not only say the lines and play the character but who can take the part somewhere extra, who can expand the story in the right direction. Just as I feel that my job as a writer is to channel and focus other people's stories, other people's words, I feel a director is there to channel and focus the various talents of crew and cast. The producers not only raise the money and run the production but maintain a certain philosophy of operation throughout, a balance that serves both the story and the people working to tell it. When I talk about us having final control on a movie, it means controlling the overall collaboration.

A low budget and tight schedule are constant frustrations, and often you have to tell people that their ideas are great but not affordable, or not top priority at the moment. But when people sign on we let them know that the challenge is to find ways of doing great stuff that don't cost a lot or take up too much time. Some very talented people reach a point where this is just a pain in the ass — why try to make pictures with crayons when there are a dozen other productions offering you oil paints? But we've been lucky in attracting people who are able to do good work under ridiculous conditions, and are willing to take the ride with us.

## Casting

Cast a movie well and half your troubles are over. An audience will forgive or ignore all kinds of shortcomings in direction, production value * and editing continuity if there are strong, believable characters to get involved with, and this means getting the right people in front of the camera.

* "Production value" is generally meant as the "richness" of the overall look of a movie. This is not the same as quality, though it can help a picture a good deal. Something minimalist like Jim Jarmusch's *Stranger than Paradise,* though well shot and appropriately designed, is said to be low on production value. David Lean's *A Passage to India* is loaded with production value.

Casting for movies is a tricky business, a combination of timing, practical, tactical and economic factors, taste and pure luck. Movie acting demands different things than commercials or soap operas or theater work, and the skills for these are not necessarily transferable. People look different on screen than they do in real life or on the stage. Pure acting ability and range may be secondary to looks or vocal quality or "type." Budget factors affect who you can cast — on a lower budget movie you can afford fewer of the amenities and perks that stars and more established actors may be used to, much less six- or seven-digit salaries. Some actors care more (or have agents who advise them to care more) about these things than others. Since there is usually no money to pay for pre-shooting rehearsal on a low-budget feature, the actor's "process" has to be taken into consideration — how much time and trouble will it take for that actor to give you the necessary performance? Actors don't take every part they're offered. Sometimes an actor can't afford to work for scale, or turn down a better part, or get out of a series or soap opera contract or leave a family behind for seven weeks. Chemistry between actors is important, as is relative age and difference in size. Relative fame can be a factor, too. If you put together an ensemble piece with one major superstar and a group of unknowns, the audience may expect the star to have the most important part and feel cheated if he or she doesn't.

The decision to use well-known actors requires some thought. If the actor is known mostly for one thing, an important role in a long-running TV series maybe, you'd better be casting that actor for the same basic role or plan to give the character lots of time and attention early on in the movie to help the audience forget all those *M*\**A*\**S*\**H* episodes. Many actors settle into one or two distinct personas at some point in their career, and you cast them precisely for that standard performance. The minute they come on the screen they carry a host of associations, a movie history, with them. A woman alone at night who answers the doorbell to find Peter Lorre on the front steps is in for a different evening than one who finds David Niven. That sense of movie history can be useful in genre movies and parodies (*Airplane* benefited from a number of such performances) but can get in the way if the story you're telling has more to do with the real world than the world of movies.

The ideal is to find an actor with the talent and magnetism that may make him a hot property someday but who hasn't yet been pegged by the audience. Or, with luck, you can land one of the few actors whose fame is based on their range and acting ability itself, actors flexible enough to quickly make you forget the other dozen times you've seen them.

For *Matewan* we had a short list of actors of this kind who we thought would be good for certain of the larger parts. Some never responded (or their agents didn't), some weren't interested, some may have been inter-

The Baldwins walk to meet Sid and Cabell.

ested but were busy shooting something else. Since the funding of the movie wasn't based on our casting any well-known actors, it wasn't a disaster when we struck out, and we felt we had done our best to give our investors an edge in making their money back. The brief star search over, we settled down with our casting director, Barbara Shapiro, and started seeing actors.

In fact, we started seeing actors three times. There were two false alarms when the funding was all but in the bank, we started casting the movie, and then the money fell apart. Three years passed. Actors grew older, lost their hair, became hot properties, quit the business, had their voices change and grew several inches. We offered parts to a few actors I had worked with before, they accepted, then had to wait around hoping the movie would happen someday. A wonderful actress named Susan Kingsley whom we wanted to work with was killed in a car crash. Some kids we'd thought of to play Danny grew too old and we started to consider them for Hillard. Our main effort narrowed down to the search for Joe, Elma, Danny and Few Clothes.

We saw hundreds of actors to play Joe Kenehan. We were after someone in his late twenties or early thirties, someone who seemed very American in a Midwestern, Henry Fonda–Gary Cooper kind of way, somebody who could be smart and down to earth at the same time, someone the

audience and the characters would take seriously but who had some sense of humor. Not so easy to find. We saw a lot of really good actors, but the dream of having the character just walk in the door one day and say "I'm it" and you can't imagine him any other way, didn't happen.

Barbara Shapiro and I and usually Maggie Renzi and Peggy Rajski would greet the actors and ask what they had been doing and explain the story and the character and then have them read for us. We had them read the scene where Joe first organizes the men in C.E.'s restaurant, which is a pretty long speech, as well as the scenes where he first meets Elma and where he plays catch with Danny. We asked them to stand when they read the speech. This rap to the miners proved harder to handle than we expected. Readings ranged from bombastic rhetoric to a lack of power and conviction, and I kept seeing the typing on the page when people read it. Granted, I had *done* the typing and knew the speech inside out, but I was convinced it could work in the movie and not seem theatrical. I didn't give the actors much direction at first, but if they were in the ballpark physically but blew the reading I'd make a few suggestions and have them do the speech again.

Chris Cooper came in the first or second day of our original round of casting and read really well and we wrote down something like "Good reading, definitely see again." The thing that stood out about his reading was that I forgot which line came next and just listened to a guy making up a pretty good argument from his own feelings and whatever other organizing speeches he'd heard in his life. When he walked out we were relieved but not finished in our search — it was actually to his disadvantage that we saw him so early in the process, since you tend to force yourself to keep an open mind for the other people you haven't seen yet and hope they'll be even better. But we did have a standard to compare the other actors to: were they as good or as right for the part as Chris Cooper?

Barbara Shapiro continued to bring people in. She had cast *Lianna* with us and the second time the money for *Matewan* fell apart she did a great one-week job of casting *The Brother from Another Planet*. She knew us well enough to be able to interpret our sometimes vague feelings and comments and we knew and trusted each other's taste in acting. Her job in this case was both to look for the type of actor we specified and, as time passed and parts remained unfilled, to expand our horizons. As the beginning of shooting approached and important roles were still not cast, her job was to say "Does he have to be white?" or "What if she's a little older?" or "Shouldn't we take a look at so-and-so again?" The casting director sends the script around to the various agencies and receives "submissions," lists of clients the agency thinks might be suitable for the parts available. Since agents routinely sacrifice a bit of their credibil-

ity in favor of enthusiasm for the allegedly enormous acting range of their clients, Barbara would edit these lists down to the ones who were at all plausible and arrange for them to come in to audition. Some actors reach the point (or their agents convince them they've reached the point) where they don't audition anymore, or only audition for people with a lot more clout than we have. This is fine if their body of work is really substantial enough that you can see them on tape in many different roles, and maybe a brief meeting is all you need to have. But we ran into a few actors who wouldn't audition even though they'd done only one or two movies and plays. They may have been right about the policy in terms of their careers, but we didn't have enough evidence to consider them and looked elsewhere. On the other hand, there were actors who were established enough that they could have reasonably said they didn't need to audition who came in anyway and gave good readings, and that willingness weighed in their favor when we were making decisions.

The audition process was as much a performance by us as by the actors, and we had to do it many times a day with no letup. Even when an actor came through the door and was obviously physically wrong for the part, we did our whole rap and had him read. Actors put out for you by coming in and going through the bizarre experience of performing for a job, and you have to give them the courtesy of paying attention. Often we'll file away the names of actors who aren't right for anything in the present project but impress us enough to think of them for something else.

You can get a slight idea from an audition as to how actors deal with direction, how they move and talk. For a better look you have to call them back and, when you're close to final casting, put them on videotape. The taping is not so much to see what they look like on camera but to eliminate both your own late-in-the-day burnout factor and to avoid having to call them in again and again.

The hardest part of casting for me is the depressing number of good actors and nice people you see who you're not going to be able to hire. Auditioning is an exercise in exposure, acting a part you haven't had enough time to work on in front of strangers who will most likely reject you. Some of our fatigue at the end of a casting day was from sympathetic anxiety, some from the discipline of pretending to be involved in a full five-minute reading when the first two lines told you all you needed to know.

By the time we were ready to cast *Matewan* for the third and final time, we had filled all but the most central roles. We were taping various actresses auditioning for Elma and we had Chris Cooper come in to read with them. Somewhere during this process it became clear that this was the guy. When we thought of Joe Kenehan's voice it was Chris Cooper's voice we heard and it became hard to imagine another. Once he was set

in our minds it was easier to place Elma in age and type. The first time we saw Mary McDonnell in 1983 I wrote "Really good actress, a bit young." By the final casting three years later Mary didn't look much different but seemed older in terms of experience — whatever she had lived was available and apparent in her acting. It was clear she could convey Elma's hard past and knowledge of a hard future without "playing" it. Sensing this is an intangible, gut-feeling kind of thing, like much of casting. Technical skills can take you only so far in movie acting, and Elma had to be somebody the audience wanted good things to happen to. Watching Mary read I got that same feeling.

The search for Danny made us all nervous. Danny had to still be boy enough to make his preaching and organizing seem precocious, had to be down to earth enough to make him believable as a coal miner, country enough to place him in West Virginia in the twenties and a good enough actor to pull off long sermons, speeches and emotional scenes. Casting out of New York we saw some good kid actors, but all were pretty urban and had trouble with the accent and feel of a coal-country kid. There were lots of kids making good money doing commercials who couldn't act much and a few real little monsters. We were close to shooting and about to eat the expense of a trip south to do some digging when Barbara got word from the Actors' Theater of Louisville that they had a kid who'd started acting with them on and off who was pretty good and nice to work with. We crossed our fingers and eventually were able to arrange for Will Oldham to come up and read for us. When you've struck out so many times you tend to put a lot of hopes on your longest shots and even start to rethink the role — "Well, if he's *any* good maybe we can cut down on the sermons a bit, just get him to talk loud and we'll cut away to the other characters' faces a lot" — that kind of thing. Will came in and he was the right age and had a bit of Kentucky in his voice, which broke now and then like Jimmy Stewart's, and he read the first sermon and it wasn't bad at all. I asked him to read it again and make it a little less text-bound and a little more just like a guy telling us a story, and *bang*, there it was in the reading. He was smart and seemed like he'd be easy to work with and as a bonus his parents were what you always hope for, people who care about their kids but don't lay a lot of pressure to perform on them. Writing a large, difficult part for anyone under twenty is a self-destructive act and I consider myself lucky to have escaped so successfully this time around.

The casting of Few Clothes seems to have been our reward for surviving all the ones who got away, all the actors who got cold feet or last-minute conflicts on our previous movies and sent us back into casting only days before we started shooting. Few Clothes is mentioned in the history books as a giant of a black miner who was rumored to be a good

shot from his days in the army during the Spanish-American War, kind of the John Henry of the coal fields. We needed somebody not only big but with the kind of power that could keep him walking head up and alive through the treacherous racial minefield of the rural South in 1920. We saw lots of good actors, but the combination of size and the kind of power that comes across even when held in restraint was hard to find. Now and then we'd consider making an offer to James Earl Jones, but after three-and-a-half-movies' worth of dealing with name actors and their agents it seemed so unlikely, he seemed so clearly out of our league, that we never took any action on it.

We were already in West Virginia, doing preproduction work, when we decided what the hell and contacted Jones's agent. We sent a script and a litany of warnings about the low budget and modest nature of our production, and in a few days we got a simple yes. James Earl turned out to be one of the best prepared, most helpful actors I've ever gotten to work with. He understood the mixture of strength and savvy Few Clothes needed to help his men survive in a deadly confrontation far from home, and brought even the moments where he just sits and listens to life.

Sometimes you just get lucky.

Each part we cast has its own history, its own set of factors that influenced the decision. Jace Alexander was dragged in at least three times to read for Hillard, though his first audition years earlier was excellent. We just needed to be sure he hadn't grown past the age we wanted Hillard to seem. Kevin Tighe, who plays Hickey, flew from California to New York to make a tape for us in August of 1986, when we were already in West Virginia, and we didn't meet till the night before he started shooting. Three different actors fell through for the small part of Bass because they had better offers that conflicted, and we ended up casting the part locally.

We left several of the smaller speaking parts to be cast in West Virginia. The idea was to both save some transportation expense and get some of the feeling and sound of the local people into the movie. Avy Kaufman was in charge of our extras and small-part casting and set up shop in the Econolodge in West Virginia shortly after we started preproduction. She advertised in local papers, contacted schools and nursing homes, went through the piles of letters and pictures that we'd been sent since the project was first announced in the Charleston newspapers three years earlier. She had an open-call audition in a local theater, then began to have people read who might be right for any of the parts, taping them with home-video equipment. Every night when I'd come back from location scouting she'd have another tape full of interviews and auditions for me.

The interviews, especially those with active and retired coal miners

Descriptions - Local Speaking Parts

PAPPY - A man with an old-sounding voice and a hill accent. Doesn't appear on screen but should be able to read narration naturally and nontheatrically.

LUNGER - An old white retired miner, 55 to 70, with a real case of black lung. He is a boarding house resident who tries not to cough at table but fails. (Probably no lines)

MRS. KNIGHTES - A older white woman, 55 to 80, who can seem tough and a bit out of it at the same time. We'll probably play her as hard-of-hearing so she should have a good strong voice. A coal foreman's widow with a bit of dough socked away, very proud.

TOLBERT - White miner, 30 to 45, a strong-looking muleskinner.

STENNIS - White miner, 40 to 50, a tough, older coal loader.

OLD MINER - White miner, late 50s, could have a mustache. A good storyteller.

REDNECK MINER - Angry white miner in his 30s or late 20s. Should look like he's got a temper.

REV. JUSTICE - Tall white male, 40 to 50, stern and distinguished-looking. (Probably no lines)

SHEB - A white mountain man in his early 40s, a bit scary-looking. Need a good pokerfaced yup-and-nope type of guy.

ISAAC - A mountain patriarch, late 40s to 60. Tall, strong-looking, could have a beard. Piercing eyes -- needs to be a pretty good actor.

AL AND LEE FELTS - White men in their late 30s, early 40s, well fed but not fat, with an air of authority. Bosses. They get shot on the spot so don't need to be in great shape for the shoot-out.

## Extras Casting

This is a page from the list of descriptions I gave to Avy Kaufman before she began to look for local extras and actors. Though we were willing and occasionally did cast away from type, these descriptions gave her a basic look, age and personality profile to start from.

and with their wives and widows, were often more useful than the readings. People not used to auditioning tend to literally read dialogue off a page, and many of the older people's failing eyesight was a real obstacle. But when Avy got them telling stories, their natural qualities would come out and you'd be able to see who was there to work with. Beyond the practical consideration of filling the parts, we heard interesting, moving stories, stories that fed back into the movie and the importance of making it. Some of our actors not from the area were able to use the storytelling tapes to work on their accents, while others benefited from hearing the firsthand experience of people who had lived through the coal wars.

The connection with our local actors and extras became one of the nicest parts of working on the movie. There were miners and preachers, musicians, union organizers, white-water rafting guides, retirees from nursing homes, workers from our Econolodge, a couple extended families with beautiful kids, black people, white people, people with Italian ancestors and looks and some pretty good natural actors. We relied on them to show up again and again at ridiculous hours and work long hours for good food and low pay, hoping it would be interesting enough or enough fun to keep them coming back. They were enormously supportive and resourceful, and their blood connection to the land and history we were telling about, the character that shone through on and off screen, fed us all.

## Production Design

I define a "period" movie as anything set in the past rather than the present or the future. If it is a recent period being re-created, people will have their own memories of the time. If the period is a little older, they'll have movies, photographs, and paintings to inform them, and if even further back there's whatever they know of history and, significantly, whatever movies they've seen set in that period. How a movie-maker handles period has an enormous bearing on the story being told. In old-fashioned Hollywood costume dramas, period was often used to spice up an insipid or routine story line, or used for its value as spectacle, or because the leading lady would look great in the clothes. More recently, period has been used by some movie-makers to present a simpler, more clearly defined moral world than the one we live in now, a world that may not have existed but that lives in people's private mythologies. Others go back to revise, muckrake or find allegories for our lives today. And many still use period because the leading lady will look great in the clothes.

The style of these productions can be very different, from the bright and clean shorthand where everybody is clearly wearing costumes and nobody is wearing real clothes, to the kind of historical obsessiveness that insists on headless nails holding together a colonial-era barn even if there are no shots close enough to see those nails. Whether the style of the period design is appropriate depends a lot on the theatricality of the story and acting style. A series for children about Robin Hood might work better with broader strokes in its design than an adult-oriented feature about the battle of Culloden. The more detailed or "realistic" design is not automatically better or more serious. The Monty Python period movies have designs that rival most straight dramatic epics, and somehow this is part of their effectiveness as comedy.

What is most important is not the objective accuracy of the design but what it evokes subjectively in the audience. The design is telling its own story to the viewer, in its own voice. The voice may be hard-boiled and grim or gentle and nostalgic about the same time and place. Do you want to emphasize what is different about that time and place or what is surprisingly like our lives today? Is it, in fact, mostly a great chance to see some popular actors dress like cowboys and ride horses, or do you want to say something new or different about the West? Practical considerations come in here. Yes, Western streets were often a mire of mud and horseshit, but that stuff is a major pain to shoot in. Does it really add to the story or couldn't we just say it hasn't rained in a month and the horses are being careful?

The time and place of *Matewan* is important to the story in many ways. The isolation of the West Virginia hills and hollers, the unfarmable slopes and thick woods that surround you everywhere, all helped shape the raw strength of the natives and the coal companies' ability to divide and conquer, to maintain a feudal system of coal camps and mine guards. The time, 1920, had its mass strikes, unemployed veterans on the march and the beginning of the anti-Red, anti-foreigner Palmer raids. We wanted to capture the hard beauty of the hills, the functional weight of everything manmade, the inescapable domination of the company. We wanted the images to reflect the muscle and effort that it took to build anything up in the wilderness of those hills, to feel like even the newest things were used and worn.

The cornerstone of our production design was finding a town to serve as our main set for the town of Matewan. We scouted the actual Matewan, but it had grown and modernized so much we could never have afforded to transform it. Instead, we used the town of Thurmond, West Virginia. Once a wild river town with big hotels, gambling and prostitution, Thurmond is now a quiet handful of buildings along the New River in one of the state's best white-water rafting areas. The main street is

Driftmouth before and after set construction

Thurmond buildings before and after set construction

not really a street but a series of railroad tracks, with a beautiful old train station and wheelhouse still standing and a huge cement coal dock straddling the track at the other end of town. The population is down to around sixty or seventy people. Hills rise up steeply just behind the single row of buildings on the main street and from the banks of the other side of the river, just as in the real Matewan. The buildings are almost all brick, most built before the First World War. The telephone lines strung along the tracks are the same green copper wire stretched on low poles that existed in 1920. Water tanks and work towers still stand from the days when the railroad yard handled as much freight as Cincinnati. It has the blend of natural beauty and industrial function we were looking for, far from the drone of airplanes and highway traffic. There was still an enormous amount for our production designer, Nora Chavooshian, to do, but there was an important number of things we *wouldn't* need to do — bury power lines, cover or dig up sidewalks, remove hundreds of TV antennas, reroute highway traffic, etc. The basic buildings were there, the hills and the river were there and the remnants of the mammoth coal and railroad works were still standing.

Nora kept the ideas of "functional" and "worn" prominent throughout the production design. The facings she designed for buildings, the loading docks and wooden sidewalks, even the interiors in Elma Radnor's boarding house all look like they've been through hard times. Things may be clean but it's not because they're new. Nora and the director of photography, Haskell Wexler, worked together on controlling the texture and color of what went in front of the camera, establishing a period look with design rather than with filters or by treating the film stock. Period movies such as *McCabe and Mrs. Miller* and *The Godfather* broke new ground with the use of diffusion and film-fogging techniques that have now come to be a kind of shorthand, capitalizing on our psychological resistance to seeing old times rendered in sharp detail and bright colors. Just as costume designers will wash pure white clothing in tea to age it, recent period films often look like the light has been strained through tea, making a kind of diffuse golden cream. We felt this gauziness would rob the images in *Matewan* of their solidity, would lose the hardness and weight of those trains and coal docks, the tangible heft of the guns, the impact of a pick against a coal face. So instead the bright, contemporary edge was taken off by using a limited palette — blacks, grays, browns, grayish blues and greens — almost no pure reds or whites or yellows. Cynthia Flynt and her costume department distressed the miners' clothing to reflect a lifetime spent crawling in coal, a thousand washings in harsh lye soap. People do what they can with what they've got for clothes, but it's all been through some hard winters.

Another feature of our design plan was to keep much of the period

Overview of Matewan main street set, Thurmond, West Virginia

detail incidental, to keep it in the background. The purpose of the story is not nostalgia. We wanted places to look lived in and details to be accurate, but not stylized to the point where people in the audience would be buzzing about the props. Nora's scenic artists painted some beautiful signs, then schmutzed them down till they were nearly unreadable.

There were disappointments. We never found a large enough grouping of coal camp houses still standing (unadorned by aluminum siding or brickette) to establish a large company coal camp. Nora had only a row of six in Eunice, West Virginia, to work with, and even that taxed her budget with the repair and dressing of their exteriors. The camp appears in daylight only once, in the sequence where the men first come out of the mine, in a single long tracking shot. We spent the time and money on that set in hopes that that one shot and the few night exteriors of the camp would lock it in the minds of the audience, just as one or two wide exterior shots of a ship at sea may be enough to establish it psychologically so that the rest of the picture can be shot on an interior set.

The number of tents and extras we could afford was pretty limited, and we had to keep moving both around into new configurations to suggest a larger tent camp stretching off in many directions. This was the one case

where we wanted the audience to be a bit disoriented geographically, to be lost in the jumble of the tents and not notice they were the same ones, slightly redressed, used over and over. The coal tipple and chute mentioned in the script as standing on the hill over the town never materialized and we couldn't afford to build one. Our limited time and resources in the mine meant we never got a shot of a mule hauling a coal car, and the shot we tried of miners riding a man-trip out into the light from the inside didn't work. But somehow Nora and her crew managed to piece things together, to beg, borrow and rent props and come up with a place that's three-dimensional and solid, a place that seems to have a life beyond the frame lines.

The sense that you can pick up any of those tools and use it, that the people go home in those clothes they're wearing, all helps to tell the story. When the Baldwins make their final walk to face Sid and Cabell, the coal dock looms behind them, the size and power of the company backing them up. The Italians in their coal camp house have religious statues and pictures from the old country on the mantel, but their walls are papered with the *Charleston Gazette,* the words incomprehensible to them. The tent camp, in a clearing hacked out of thick woods, is a hodge-podge of tents, cookfires and clotheslines separated by muck, where the various racial and ethnic groups have no hard walls to raise between each other. There are so few automobiles that just the sound of one is a sure sign of danger. Each setting not only has to carry on the through-line of the design philosophy, of the period detail, but has to make a storytelling point.

My conversations with Nora about the design of *Matewan* were about historical, psychological and practical issues. We'd look at pictures, talk about structures, signs and materials specific to coal country in the twenties, talk about the function the buildings and props would have played in the lives of the characters. Nora drew a plan for the main street of Matewan based on the existing structures in Thurmond, and we talked about which doors had to open and close, which windows we could keep the shades down on and which had to be prepared for squibbing in the shoot-out scene.* We talked about the mood we wanted associated with each set and location, about the mood of the scenes to be played there. Elma's dining room was designed to provide a note of warmth and civilization in contrast to the starker, plainer interiors in the movie. Though not elegant, it has patterned wallpaper, tablecloths, softer light. With cinematographer Haskell Wexler, Nora worked on the location and type of lighting in the room so the warm and comfortable rosy glow of Joe's

---

* "Squibs" are small explosive charges the special effects department places on objects or bodies. Set off manually or by radio, they appear to be the impact of a bullet (when they work).

first dinner could realistically become close and hellish when Hickey and Griggs are at their worst. The effect is not so stylized as to *tell* you what to feel, but it affects your feelings.

Time and again an actor would walk onto one of Nora's sets and say "Okay, *now* I get it." The mood of the place would help feed their acting, help them inhabit the character. And in the natural settings — in the woods at night, inside the coal mine — there were moments of eerie identification. The cold mist really was cold mist, mud and cutting wind supplied free of charge, and the dark and the damp of the mine left us all cramped and shivering after a few hours underground. We could only push on and hope that we could just catch it all on film, that somehow the experience could be passed through the movie to the audience.

## Production Scheduling

Nowhere in movie-making is the balance between practical concerns and creative process more in evidence than in production scheduling. Even large-budget movies have to make compromises here. Movies are rarely shot in sequence, though that would seem best for the actors. Instead, an actor may do his death scene in the first week of production, get married in the fourth and meet his future wife in the eighth. On low-budget features this is usually done without the benefit of rehearsal before shooting starts (since the Screen Actors Guild requires that actors be paid for rehearsal time).

Peggy Rajski, who was our production manager as well as a co-producer, had an enormous number of factors to consider in each scheduling decision. Actors were one of our major expenses and the total cost depended on how their time was juggled. Guild minimum at the time was $1439 for a weekly player (a week defined as 48 hours, with no day lasting more than 10 hours without going into overtime) and $379 a day for a daily player (a day defined as 8 hours). Sometimes it was cheaper to consider an actor as a weekly player than to pay him for each day separately. Once an actor started working, 10 days had to pass before he could be brought in again without paying him for all the days in between. Travel days to and from location had to be paid for, and night shooting, defined as any work day starting after 11:59 A.M., was paid at a higher rate. Actors had to be fed a hot meal within 6 hours of their first call or a penalty was levied on the production for each actor affected. So Peggy had a kind of handicapping job on her hands, trying to minimize the amount of time we were paying people (and paying for their living expenses) when they weren't working.

This alone would be hard, but other factors complicate the equation.

Neither the actors nor the crew go off the clock while you're traveling to and from a location, so you try to group as many shots in a single location on the same day or days as possible. The scene of the miners first walking out of the driftmouth and the scene of their nighttime confrontation there are far apart in the story, but we shot them on the same two nights. It made no sense to bring everybody up that mountain more than once, and the difficulty of getting there overruled the desire to clump all of some actors' working days together, so we ended up eating some actor down time.

Since we had so many exterior scenes, susceptible to weather problems, Peggy had to plan for "cover sets," interiors we could move to and still get some shooting done till the weather improved. A cover set needs to be fully prepped by the art department, and the actors in the scenes there have to be ones who are going to be around that day. We were pretty lucky with weather and it was late in the shoot when we had to scramble into our one remaining cover set, the interior coal mine, where the rain never falls and the sun never shines. You almost always lose time in the confusion of switching from plan A to plan B and this cut down on our effectiveness in the mine shooting, but we couldn't have afforded to sit around watching the sky for those two days.

Time of day and time of year also had to be considered in scheduling. We shot in September and October and had to worry about the color change of the trees in the mountains that surrounded almost every exterior shot. You don't want to go from early fall to early winter too many times in the movie, or to have the hills flash from green to red in reverse angles of the same scene. The walking-out montage was shot on many different days in many different locations and all Peggy could do was try to plan them for early or late in the day and trust in Haskell's mastery of filters to even out their look.

Two-thirds of the way through the picture C.E. Lively's restaurant is burned down. Nora had a façade built on the main street of Thurmond (the interiors were shot in a church basement up the hill) that was visible in wide shots of town. The burning of this façade was a watershed in scheduling exteriors in town, and those scenes were classified as pre- or postfire and kept on one side or the other of our shooting of the event.

A good deal of guesswork went into predicting how long each scene would take to shoot. I had some idea of the coverage — the number and type of shots — I wanted on each scene, and we made a whirlwind tour of the locations with our director of photography, assistant director, key grip, gaffer and production designer. We'd time how long the travel took, estimate what the setup time would be, check out how the sun moved if the shot was an exterior, and we came back with a dozen variables that couldn't be foreseen.

All the known variables had to be synthesized and priorities set. What was important enough to make something else suffer? The budget didn't always win, but neither did the easiest way of shooting things. The one restrictive cage around the process was, unfortunately, the available shooting days. We knew we could afford to rent equipment, hire actors, staff and crew and put them up and feed them on location only for some forty shooting days, and Peggy had to cram everything into that too-small container.

The production schedule is worked out on a strip board, a folding contraption that holds long strips of cardboard in place next to each other. At the top of the strip is written the number of the scene, its location, the page number it is found in the script and the number of story pages it takes up. Each strip is lined and numbered and if an actor is scheduled to work in that scene his code number appears on its numbered line on the strip. Strips are blue for night exteriors, yellow for day exteriors, pink for day interiors and white for night interior scenes. Various stickers or symbols can be added at the bottom to indicate if special effects or equipment will be needed or things like whether the scene is before or after the restaurant burns. The strips are detachable so scenes can be shuffled easily from day to day (days are separated by plain black strips) or week to week (weeks are separated by two black strips in a row). The days are grouped in sequence, reading from left to right. So if a high priority is getting a certain actor's scenes all shot in a one-week period, you can start by finding all the strips with his or her number on it and grouping them together. Similar groupings can be made of strips bearing a certain location, or of night-exterior strips, or of day-exteriors on which a steam train will be needed. An easy pattern rarely emerges, but you get a useful graphic representation of what the various possibilities are.

Once we started shooting, the strip board was in constant flux. We might go over schedule on one scene and have to bump another to a later day, or might discover in the editing room or at dailies that we needed to reshoot something, or a major variable like the availability of the train might suddenly change.* Most lunch hours Peggy and I and the assistant director, Matia Karrell, had to meet and make decisions about whether we'd go into overtime that night or move something to another day or rethink the coverage. Moving the strip is easy, but alerting fifty extras of a major change the night before and dumping the burden of getting them

---

* "Dailies" or "rushes" are screenings at the end or beginning of the day of previously shot scenes. They may not, in fact, occur daily, but whenever there's enough footage back from the lab. On *Matewan* the entire cast and crew were invited to dailies, though on some pictures attendance is restricted to producers, director and camera department.

all dressed for a certain scene a week earlier than planned on the costume department can be a bitch. Turnaround times, budget scenarios, weather predictions and other variables had to be considered, sometimes projecting several weeks into the future.

The struggle was day to day, sometimes shot to shot. We made some bad guesses, but were always able to shoot *something* and averaged a reasonable number of setups per day. Though the production scheduling could never overcome the fact that the movie was overambitious for

## Call Sheet ▶

This is an example of the call sheet, given to each crew and cast member the day before shooting. All cast and crew members should be able to find out what they'll need to prepare for by reading it. The top quarter includes the general crew pickup call (individual members and departments may have to leave earlier, and this information is specified on the back of the sheet), the location or locations of the shoot and a weather prediction and times for sunrise and sunset.

The next section refers both to the script and the strip board. The set and scene descriptions are listed, and opposite them information on their numbers in the script, the "story day" they take place on (for continuity purposes), the code numbers of the cast members involved, time of day the scene takes place, number of pages the scene takes up and its location. On the line immediately below is the cover set, in this case INT. COAL MINE.

The next section is about the actors. The actors' names are listed opposite their character names and numbers, their pickup, make-up and set call times posted, and information as to where they will be leaving from.

After this comes Atmosphere and Stand-ins and Special Instructions. Stand-ins and extras are listed with their pickup times, and any special wardrobe information is listed. Transportation here refers to a condor lift, originally planned for a high-angle shot, but the machine was so smooth we were able to use it as an inexpensive crane. Props information is both general and specific, and any special effects equipment or preparation necessary is listed.

The final part of the front page is information about the next couple days, allowing people to prepare ahead if they have time.

On the back of the sheet, in addition to the individual pickup times for each crew member, there are often special notes. The ones for this day were "The location is very dirty and muddy. Please dress accordingly," and "Dailies will be at 3:00 p.m."

With this sheet the costume department can see who they'll have to dress for the scenes, as well as have clothes on hold for the cover-set actors. The various drivers know when they have to have their vehicles waiting and where, and the cover-set actors know to hang by the motel till they get word they definitely won't be needed. Our extras coordinator, Avy Kaufman, sees who she has to call if the schedule has been changed and everyone can go over the scenes in the script and prepare themselves mentally.

| | | | DAY: | Saturday, September 20,1986 |
|---|---|---|---|---|

PRODUCER: Peggy Rajski
    Maggie Renzi
DIRECTOR: John Sayles
PROD.MANAGER P. Rajski
1st AD: Matia Karrell
2nd AD: Benita Allen
(304)877-6455  Ext.237
PROD. OFFICE: (304) 877-6433
Econolodge
1000 Highway 16, Mt.Hope 25880

**SET CREW CALL**

4:30P

**LV HOTEL**

4:30P

DAY: Saturday, September 20,1986
    16    DAY OUT OF   42
SHOOTING CALL: 5:30P
WEATHER: Partly sunny,high near
80/ Sat night partly cloudy
60 - 65
LOCATION: Summerlee Tipple
Rte 38 Lochgelly Rd, Summerlee

SUNRISE: 6:10A    SUNSET: 6:25P

| SET # SET | SCENES | DAY | CAST | D/N | PAGES | LOCATION |
|---|---|---|---|---|---|---|
| EXT. COAL TIPPLE: Sun sets behind Tipple | 128 | 17 | - | sunset | 1/8 | LOC 1 |
| EXT. RAILROAD YARD: Mine guard sees miners crossing the R.R. Yard | 11 | 1 | E(16) | DSK | 1/8 | LOC 1 |
| EXT. HILLSIDE: Danny & Hillard start to climb down to coal car | 120 | 16 | 2,3 | N | 2/8 | LOC 1 |
| EXT. COAL YARD: Hillard is caught & murdered,Danny hides | 122 | 16 | 2,3,5,7,8,E(4) | N | 3 5/8 | LOC 1 |
| EXT. COAL YARD: Coal car on tracks | 119 | 16 | - | N | 1/8 | LOC 1 |
| EXT. COAL YARD: Deserted Coal Yard in Moonlight | 118 | 16 | - | N | 1/8 | LOC 1 |
| INT. COAL MINE | 1,2,5,43,44, | | 4,2,10,15,21, 42 | | | BECKLEY MINE |

| CAST & DAY PLAYERS | PART OF | P/U | M/U | SET CALL | REMARKS |
|---|---|---|---|---|---|
| Will Oldham | 2. Danny | 6P | 6:30P | 7P | P/U @ Econolodge |
| Jace ALexander | 3. Hillard | 6P | 6:30P | 7P | P/U @ Econolodge |
| Ken Jenkins | 4. Sephus | COVER SET | | | |
| Bob Gunton | 5. C.E. | 6P | 6:30P | 7P | P/U @ Econolodge |
| Kevin Tighe | 7. Hickey | 6P | 6:30P | 7P | P/U @ Econolodge |
| Gordon Clapp | 8. Griggs | 6P | 6:30P | 7P | P/U @ Econolodge |
| James Earl Jones | 10. Few | COVER SET | | | |
| Joe Grifasi | 15. Fausto | COVER SET | | | |
| Tom Wright | 21. Tom | COVER SET | | | |
| TBA | 42.Black Miner | COVER SET | | | |

**ATMOSPHERE AND STAND-INS** REPORT TO LOCATION

STAND IN: Danny @ 4:30P

EXTRAS:
Sc 11: Mine Guard (1) @ 4P
       Native IC (4) @ 4P
       Native New (11)
Sc 122: Mine Guards (2) @ 4P
        (RPT frm above add 1)
        Mine Guards H.G (2)  @ 4P

WARDROBE: Doubles on Hillards  Jackets

**SPECIAL INSTRUCTIONS**

PROPS: Coal Cars,coal Lunch Pails(sc1`
       Gun Rifles,Jacknife,coal,sack
       Razor(sc 122)
       Coal Car, Tarp, Coal (sc114)

MECH SPFX: Shotgun blast, throat slit
           A&B Blood, compressor
           (sc 122)
M/U SPFX   BLOOD (sc 122)

TRANSPORTATION: Condor lift (sc 122,123,119,118)

**ADVANCE SHOOTING NOTES**

| SHOOTING DATE | SET # | SET NAME | CAST # | LOCATION | SCENE # |
|---|---|---|---|---|---|
| MONDAY & TUESDAY Sept 22&23 1986 DAY 17&18 | | EXT. DRIFTMOUTH - D, DUSK Night | 2,4,6 1,2,3,4,5,6, 10,12,15,20 21,23 | | 112,6,7,53 |

## Crew Call Sheet


| STAFF/ITEM | TIM |
|---|---|
| DIRECTOR:J.Sayles | 4:30P |
| 1st AD:M.Karrell | 4:30P |
| 2nd AD:B.Allen | 3:00P |
| SCRPT SUP:J.Tintori | 4:30P |
| UNIT MGR:D.Pokorny | 2:30P |
| PA: B. Wenk RTO | 4:00P |
| PA: E.Gelchis | per dept / 4:00P |
| PA: L.Heyward RTO | 10:30A |
| PA: R.Penzi RTO | 3:30P |
| PA: B.Brewer RTO | 4:00P |
| PA: K.xxxT.Collins | 2:30lv |
| PA: G.Jacobs | 4:00P |
| PA: L.Gorchov RTO | 2:30lv |
| PA: S.Cox | 10:30 lv |
| PA: M.Brewer | |
| Dir Photo: H. Wexler | 4:30P |
| Cam Op: T. Sigal | |
| Cam Op: M. Dubin | 4:30P |
| 1st AC: S.Sakamoto | 4:30P |
| 2nd AC:D. Sarjeant | 4:30P |
| ADDT'L CAM ASST: | |
| 2nd UNIT: | |
| VIDEO ASST:S.Apicella | 4:30P |
| STILLS:B.Marshak | 4:30P |
| CAMERAS: | |
| ADD'L CAM: | |
| STEADICAM: | |
| PA's: Mark Brewer | 10:30lv |
| Mark S. RTO | 4:00P |
| T. Collins RTO | 4:00P |
| Jesse RTO | 4:00P |
| Rachel | 2:30 lv /4:30P |
| KEY GRIP:S.Czapsky | 4:30P |
| 2nd GRIP:R.Feldman | 4:30P |
| 3rd GRIP:A.Blum | |
| ASST GRIP:S.Garrett | 4:30P |
| ASST GRIP:M.Latino | 4:30P |
| GAFFER:M.Flam | 4:30P |
| BEST BOY:L.Breschel | 4:30P |
| Co.ELEC:R.Bruce | 4:30P |
| ELEC ASST:C.Lashley | 4:30P |
| ADD'L ELEC: | |
| 2nd UNIT: | |
| PUBLICIST:M.Renzi | |
| CRAFT SER:S.Cox | 2:30P |
| 2nd UNIT CRAFT SER: | |
| M'U(KEY):J.Sarzotti | 4:30P |
| M'U ASST:D.Halsey | N/A |
| HAIR: | |
| EFX M/U | |
| STUNT COORD:E.MOURINO | |
| STUNT PERSON: | |


| STAFF/ITEM | TIME |
|---|---|
| COST DES: C.Flynt | 3:00P |
| COST SUP:H.Shulman | 4:00P |
| ASST COST DES:S.Lyall | 3:00P |
| ADDT'L COST: | |
| XTRA CSTNG:A.Kaufman | |
| APM:S.Green | O.C. |
| POC:C.Turner | O.C. |
| APOC:P.McCarthy | O.C. |
| OFFICE PA:B.Bernstein | O.C. |
| OFFICE PA:L.Bika | O.C. |
| TEACHER:M.Preston | 6:00P |
| EFX(KEY):P.Kunz | O.C. |
| EFX ASST: | O.C. |
| ANIMAL TRAINER | |
| POLICE: | |
| FLAGMEN: | |
| Paramedic | 8:00P |
| FIREMAN: | |
| SECURITY | |
| PERMITS | |
| 1st AID: | |
| SOUND MXR:J.Sutton | 4:30P |
| BOOM:L.Schnall | 4:30P |
| WALKIES: | |
| PLYBK (AUD) | |
| PLYBK (VID) | |
| CATERING: | |
| BREAKFAST: | |
| LUNCH: | 95 @ 10:30P |
| DINNER: | |
| COFFEE: | |
| LOC MGR:P.Marcus | 10:30 lv for Driftmouth/ 3P @ Summerlee |
| LOC ASST: | |


| STAFF/ITEM | TIME |
|---|---|
| PROD DES:N.Chavooshian | O.C. |
| ART DIR:D.Bishop | O.C. |
| SET DEC:L.Pope | O.C. |
| SET DEC:A.Michenivich | O.C. |
| SET DRSSR:L.Kyle | O.C. |
| SET DRSSR:N.Gilmore | O.C. |
| ART ASST:D.Boxer | O.C. |
| ART PA:L.Johnson | O.C. |
| ART PA:J.Butcher | |
| PROP MSTR:A.Edgeworth | per dept |
| ASST PROPS:J.Cohen | per dept |
| PROP PA:C.Gibbon | per dept |
| TRANS COORD:D.Pokorny | |
| DRIVER CPTN: Sonny | PER COORD |
| TRANS EQUIP: | PER COORD |
| CAM TRUCK: B. Brewer | 2:30lv/4:30 on set |
| PROP TRUCK:C.Gibbons | per dept. |
| WARDROBE:L.Scott | per dept. |
| WINNIE:C.Lashley | 4:00lv/4:30 on set |
| SFX TRK: | |
| GRIP TRK: | 4:00lv/4:30 on set |
| ELEC TRK:S.Adkins | 4:00lv/4:30 on set |
| ELEC/GRP SHTL: | 4:00lv/4:30 on set |
| GENNY P/U: | 4:00lv/4:30 on set |
| 15 PASS:Terry C. | 4:15/4:30 lv |
| 7 PASS: Louisa | 4:15/4:30 lv |
| 7 PASS:Mark S. | 4:15/4:30 lv |
| DIR SEDAN: Brian | 4:15/4:30 lv |
| CRAFT SER: R.Bower | |
| PICTURE CARS: | |
| 15 pass: Jesse | 4:15/4:30 lv |

### NOTES

Ralph Renzi & Mark Brewer
RTO @ 10:30 AM for Unit
Pre-Rig at Driftmouth.

The location is very dirty &
muddy. Please dress accordingly.

Dailies will be at 3:00 PM.

the time and money we had, it did provide a solid base from which we could choose most of our compromises, rather than having them forced upon us.

## Location Scouting

One of the most important steps in our preproduction was location scouting. A good location for a scene not only serves the action but serves the production in a practical way and has its own story to tell. Paul Marcus, our location scout, began to look for the places we would shoot as soon as we got to West Virginia. We talked about each location mentioned in the script, looked at old photos and drawings with Nora Chavooshian, and Paul would go off with county maps, a home-video camera and the suggestions of people we'd met in the area.

We had decided on the town of Thurmond as the location for Matewan's main street over a year earlier, when the head of the West Virginia Department of Tourism, Carolyn Ketchum, brought us there. Since this was our central location, we set up production offices nearby in Mount Hope, just north of the city of Beckley and a half mile from the interstate highway up to Charleston. Since travel time is expensive and cuts down on shooting time, one of Paul's priorities was to find locations as close as possible to our base. In most cases the scenes we'd planned called for synch sound recording, so what a location sounded like was as important as what it looked like.* We were not near busy airplane routes, and in a movie about 1920s rural life we had to keep the soundtrack free of car sounds as well. Locations had to be accessible to our cars and trucks but far enough off the beaten track to avoid constant delays because of buzzing traffic. Paul came back each day with a videotaped record of his findings for us to review, and then we'd decide which places I'd want to see in person.

I had some idea of the kind of coverage planned for each scene. For one we might need 360 degrees of shooting space with no inappropriate buildings or roads in any direction, while for another scene only one narrow angle might be enough. The eviction scene was shot in a tiny hollow called Laurel Creek, and though we needed to move the camera a lot to cover all the characters and action, there was a large, nonperiod building

---

* "Synch" or synchronous sound recording means you are recording the sound at the same time you are taking the picture, as opposed to "dubbing" or "looping" the sound by adding it in a sound studio later. Americans have gotten used to synch sound, while audiences in many European countries are more tolerant of looping. Federico Fellini still loops much of the dialogue in his movies, especially ones with multinational casts like *Satyricon*.

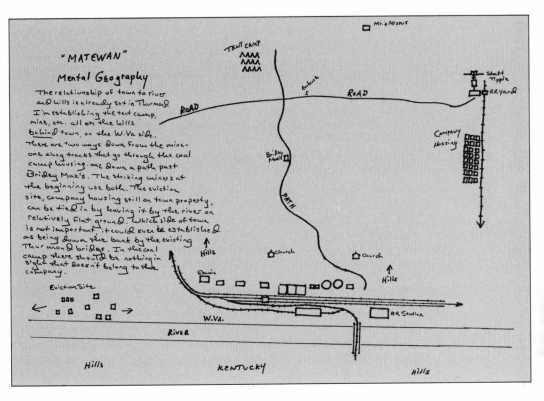

The handwritten text within the map reads:

"MATEWAN"

Mental Geography

The relationship of town to river and hills is already set in Thurmond. I'm establishing the tent camp, mine, etc. all on the hills behind town, on the W.Va. side. There are two ways down from the mine- one along tracks that go through the coal camp housing. one down a path past Bridey Mae's. The striking miners at the beginning use both. The eviction site, company housing still on town property, can be tied in by having it by the river on relatively flat ground. Which side of town is not important—it could even be established as being down the bank by the existing Thurmond bridge. In the coal camp there should be nothing in sight that doesn't belong to the company.

Map labels: Mr. & Misrus · TENT CAMP · Ambush X · ROAD · ROAD · Shaft Tipple · RR Yard · Company Housing · Bridey Mae's · PATH · Hills · Church · Church · Hills · Eviction Site · Stores · W.VA. · RR Station · RIVER · Hills · KENTUCKY · Hills

## Mental Geography

This map combines the building locations in Thurmond with my mental geography of where the scenes in the story take place. Though the relation of the town to the river and to the Hardshell church are the only ones that exist in fact, it was important to have a sense of where we wanted the actors and audience to feel they were, trying to be consistent in screen direction, especially in regards to uphill and downhill.

directly across the tracks from the house we wanted to shoot in front of. This meant we had no true reverse angle to shots angled directly toward the house, and the few times we needed one we had to move the actors down the tracks a ways to have neutral trees in the background. The location was limited by the building, but so right in every other way that we lived with it. In the case of the scene at the back door of C.E.'s restaurant at night, we wanted a close, restricted feeling and were able to use the side door of the church we shot the Hardshell preacher scene in. Nothing around it was appropriate for the scene, but since it was night and we had only a few narrow-angle close shots to cover it, this didn't matter.

Another factor in choosing locations was the ability to set up support

services. Bathrooms, dressing rooms, a place to eat, a place to get out of the rain — if these don't exist near your location you have to bring your own, which is expensive and time-consuming. One of the most difficult locations to find turned out to be the exterior of the coal mine, where we see the miners first walk out and later have the driftmouth confrontation.* Through a combination of following rumors and guesswork Paul found an abandoned mine that had not had its opening cemented over. It was high on the side of a mountain slope, down a rarely used dirt road that needed repairs before our trucks could get down it. We shot there for two long nights and the logistics of getting people and equipment there, feeding them and making sure nobody fell off a cliff in the dark were as complicated as the shooting itself. We set up tents for dressing and eating, pulled up our generator and other support trucks and put a couple portable toilets as near to the set as we could get them. The sequence is a very important one to the movie and we couldn't have afforded to do this kind of support effort for less vital scenes.

Once we had chosen a particular location, the location manager part of Paul's job began. In Thurmond, where we were staging a third of the movie with both interior and exterior scenes, we stayed in constant contact with the people who lived in the town and owned the property we were shooting on. Film crews can seem like wild marauders even when they're being as careful as possible, so it's important for the location manager to keep people informed of what's happening in their front yards and when, to get legal permissions, to try to foresee inconveniences that will be caused and find ways to help the residents around them. The residents of Thurmond let us shoot in and around their buildings, paint and put façades on some buildings, cover their satellite dishes now and then, move their cars and themselves out of shooting range over and over for several weeks — and it was Paul's job to keep them willing to cooperate.

We had a location budget and tried to keep a sense of fairness and proportion in paying people for the use of their property. Insurance costs were a major drain on this budget, especially for the scenes involving the use of railroad property and equipment (the railroad people were extremely helpful but had no control over the insurance companies). Some locations proved to be too expensive and we had to look elsewhere.

Locations are a big part of visual storytelling. A good location has its own character, and that character adds to the mood of the scene. Shooting in West Virginia gave us the sense of isolation and containment so particular to those hills and hollers. Help doesn't come galloping across

---

* The "driftmouth" is the portal where the miners enter and exit the mine. The driftmouth confrontation is the scene in which the scabs throw down their tools and join the striking miners.

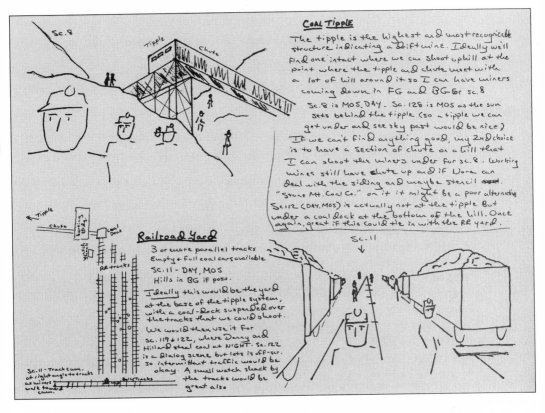

## Location Drawings

These are a few of the drawings I made for Paul Marcus to take on his scouting missions. We never did find a head house and chute standing that wasn't far too modern and we couldn't afford to build one. We did find a railroad yard with tracks running under the enormous building where coal was graded and then dumped into the coal cars below. It had been out of operation for many years, however, and it was a chore dragging abandoned coal cars out of the woods and into the shot. Since we couldn't afford to fill hundred-ton cars with coal, we built a crib across the top of a few of them and piled a few tons of coal on top of that for the illusion.

the plains here, it comes puffing up or down a steep mountainside. The height that someone lives on the slope becomes a kind of social ranking, with the townspeople by the river at one end and the high hill people on the other. The river becomes a symbol of escape, even if it's only to the wilds of eastern Kentucky. The town of Thurmond, with its railroad track for a main street, its little outcropping of buildings huddled together under the dominating shadow of coal docks and water towers, gave us a town under the thumb of an industry, a perfect setting for a

showdown. Bridey Mae's cabin, beautiful, isolated (and actually on a back acre in the suburbs of Beckley), gives us a clue to her character, her hunger to be accepted by the townspeople. The narrow, low-ceilinged dimness of C.E.'s restaurant seems to fit his suspicious character. The outside of Elma's boarding house, weathered but solid, tells us something about the woman who runs it. Though we pieced together the locations from a fifty-mile radius, I started with a mental geography of the town and environs and we tried to stay true to that in our choice of location and screen direction, especially uphill and downhill. Though I wouldn't expect a viewer to be able to draw me a map after seeing the movie, I do think this sense of relative distance helped us stay oriented and fed into the storytelling somehow.

At their best, locations have such a strong personality that they help the actors and crew internally as well as practically. The cramp and damp and absolute darkness of the coal mine made a big impression on the actors who went underground before we started shooting. The two little country churches we shot in had a sound and feel to them that made singing and sermonizing seem natural, and those West Virginia hills have a real power to them, a power that can't help but tell its own story to the audience.

# Production

## Cinematography

Cinematography is a good model for the entire process of making a movie. It's a constant barrage of choices to make, each choice creating and defining the next. Cinematography is the art of balancing elements — light and shadow, contrast, focal length, f-stop, depth-of-field, composition, focus and camera movement, color, diffusion — all of which affect each other and affect the story the image tells. Add to these the pressures of time and money and nature and you've got a juggler with dozens of variables flying through the air all at the same time. Put a filter on a lens and you eat up some light — an adjustment has to be made elsewhere. Go for deep focus in a dark and difficult location and you increase the time it will take to light. Move the camera and the subject apart several times in the same shot and the extra burden shifts to the focus-puller.* Establish a look for an exterior scene and prepare yourself for having to match it a day or a week or a month later in reshoots when the sky is in a different mood.

We were lucky enough to get Haskell Wexler to be our director of photography on *Matewan*. Haskell has loads of experience, including work on period pieces like *Bound for Glory* and *Days of Heaven*, and has a long-standing knowledge of and involvement in the kind of politics *Matewan* is about. We were asking him to handle the most difficult thing for a D.P. — to shoot indoors and out, above and under ground, day and

---

* The "focus-puller" is the assistant camera operator (A.C.), who moves the focus ring on the camera lens as the distance between the camera and the object that must remain in focus changes. The A.C. is also in charge of changing lenses and filters, keeping the camera loaded and clean and keeping camera logs as to lens, focal length, f-stop and filter on each shot.

night, and to give the whole picture a consistent, unified period look, all without much time and even less money. The question was never just "How good can it look?" but "How good can it look if we've only got an hour to light it and shoot it?"

The first thing we had to do was establish a philosophy of lighting. There are various conventions in movie lighting that are totally unnatural but are generally accepted — think of the light that floods up from the dashboard in most interior car shots at night. These conventions represent a deal between the movie-makers and the audience, a deal that changes terms from time to time. The old high-key style of lighting that developed on enormous studio sets and back lots gave way in the sixties and seventies to a more "naturalistic" style, influenced by European cinematographers using more mobile equipment and by the availability of more light-sensitive film stocks. What looked "realistic" to audiences began to change, though elements of the old style still remain and can be used effectively. A sense of unreality (as in some comedies, horror movies) or hyper-reality (as in film noir) might be appropriate in some situations, but a more natural look can give a weight and tangibility to objects and people that more stylized or theatrical lighting designs can't. That tangible quality is something we felt was very important to *Matewan*, and our philosophy became to attempt a kind of "psychological realism."

Natural light, that provided by the sun or by practical sources such as house lamps and candles, is not often adequate to give a natural look on screen. Our eyes react differently to natural light than they do to light on a movie screen. If we walk into a dark room our eyes adjust gradually till we see more, but if we see a picture of a dark room, we'll never see more unless the exposure of the photograph changes. This change of exposure is not physically realistic, but if done well it can give viewers the psychological *feeling* that their eyes are adjusting.

Getting this kind of feeling on film was most difficult in the coal mine scenes. In the mines in the twenties there were sometimes electric lights strung sparsely overhead along the top of the main shaft, but usually the only light in the "rooms" that branched off from the shaft was the single flame of the miner's headlamp, providing only a few foot-candles' worth of illumination. Though we were equipped with "fast" film stock and lenses, the carbide headlamps didn't throw enough light to register on film with anything near the brightness the eye would see under those conditions.* If we had made the decision to go with battery-powered

---

* The "speed" or ASA rating of a film stock refers to its sensitivity to light. A "fast" film will give you a clear, fine-grained image at relatively low light levels. In the past few years the speed of movie film stock has more than doubled, allowing cinematographers to shoot at night without enormous arc lights and to use more "natural" lighting sources indoors.

Haskell Wexler takes a light reading in the company supply room set.

electric headlamps, which were just starting to be used in that era, Haskell's job would have been easier. A much more powerful bulb and bat-
tery could have been used and the source light from the headlamp would
then be adequate to light the scene. But we both felt the open flame of
the carbide lamps was more dramatic, more evocative of the period and
the primitive conditions the Mingo County miners labored under. So we
went with the open flames and had to add supplemental light to get an
exposure.

In a certain kind of movie you might accept the old convention that a
candle can throw its own shadow on a wall, but this would have been a
joke in the context of *Matewan*. The position and character of the supplemental light became very tricky — if the actor got between it and the
surface it was illuminating a shadow would be thrown and it would be
clear that the light wasn't coming from his headlamp. Haskell used a
diffuse kind of spotlight that had to be aimed past the miner without
focusing on a spot on the miner's body, and be moved in synch with the
miner's head, trying to throw the same light on the wall the headlamp
would throw if it were strong enough. Getting this right took time. The
other major problem was that the open flame of the carbide lamp was a
visible constant in its light level, and everything else in the shot had to

be balanced according to its (extremely low) intensity. A common way of dealing with low-light scenes is to light them brightly, thus increasing your depth-of-field (the distance from the camera within which the image is in focus) and later bringing it down to darkness by underexposing in the printing process. An open flame, however, would then no longer be the brightest thing in the room and would go dull in the printing down. In order to preserve the illusion that the flame was the only light source we were forced to work in truly low light levels, with a depth-of-field of inches or less. With this little depth even slow movement, like a miner crawling toward the camera, becomes an extremely critical focus problem. This slowed us down even more in the two days we had allotted to finish the mine scenes, and there were shots we never got to or had to simplify a great deal. But the few period mine scenes I could recall from movies seemed overlit and stagey, and we were determined to capture the claustrophobia and discomfort of working in "low coal," crawling through muck puddles on your hands and knees with the top only three feet above you.

The main concession we made to brightness was to throw more bounce light on Sephus's face in his scenes alone at the coal face, hoping that the audience would identify with him quicker if they could see human features. In the later scene between Fausto and Few Clothes, after the audience has had time to meet them, we could forget about their faces and let their back-lit silhouettes and their voices identify who they were. In other scenes we often let characters go in and out of light. Once you've seen who a character is, your mind tends to help you picture him even after he moves into the dark, and you feel less lost if you hear lines without seeing features.

The coal mine, with all its problems, was at least consistently dark. For this reason it became our cover set, the location we held in readiness till rain drove us in from a planned exterior shoot. Close to 70 percent of *Matewan* takes place outside, at the mercy of sun and sky. On a tight schedule this makes it hard to keep the image consistent. If a scene is supposed to happen within a few minutes of sequential time outdoors, but because of actor availability or the amount of coverage necessary it has to be shot in one long day or over a period of days, the light conditions are going to change constantly. The sun is in or out of the clouds, the shadows lengthen and shorten, they move across the street and up the walls in the background, the color temperature of the sunlight changes throughout the day. At the bottom of the New River Gorge in Thurmond the sun took longer to clear the mountains to the east and dipped below the ones to the west around 4:30, cutting our available daylight by as much as an hour and a half.

In the case of the climactic shoot-out we had three days scheduled to

film all the action. Shadows covered the main street in Thurmond from one direction in the morning and from another in late afternoon, and there were often clouds and sometimes a morning mist. We calculated that there were more hours of natural shade than of direct sunlight in town and therefore decided to establish the shoot-out with a diffused-light, early-morning look. We planned to shoot whenever the sunlight was not open and direct, and when it was, to do our shots that were very tight with a building close in the background. In this kind of shot you can block the sun off the confined area on screen by erecting a big tent of scrim in the light's path. There are, however, large differences in exposure level and light temperature (which affects the color tint of the picture) throughout even an evenly overcast day. Haskell smoothed these out using his light meter and filters, often calling out a meter reading, f-stop and filter number the instant before the camera rolled.

By the second day of the shoot-out we had finished all our tight shots against buildings and were left with wide shots or shots that had open street in the background. When the sun came out strong we either sat and waited or trekked up to the Radnors' boarding house set at the other end of town to do a few pickup shots. Even a quarter mile is a big move when you have trucks full of equipment that have to wind up and down narrow hill roads to get there. We got a couple stretches of cloud cover, though, and made our shots roughly in order of importance, so at the end of three days we had enough to make a sequence, if not everything we had planned. The footage came back from the lab printed to Haskell's instructions and was amazingly consistent, looking like all the action could believably have taken place in the five minutes of screen time it would eventually fill.

The montage of men walking out of the mine and down into town posed another light-planning problem. Each shot was in a different location, often many miles apart, and yet once again the action had to take place in a short span of sequential time. Though the sky can change rapidly in real life, it is psychologically jarring on screen to start with a character in bright sunlight, cut away to the object he's looking at and then cut back to him in deep shade. Whether we articulate what's wrong consciously or not it still tends to pull us out of the flow of the story. The solution we tried with the walking-out shots was to spread them throughout the schedule but to try to shoot them always at the very beginning or very end of the day, when sunlight is the least direct and color temperature can be evened out with filters. This was a good idea in theory, but the logistics of getting to the locations often pushed us into the wrong time of day, and we had to rely more on filtering and printing down the negative than would have been ideal.

Consistency has to be maintained in other areas of the photography.

Each lens length has its own character, its own mood within a certain scene. A long lens doesn't "spread" so much in the distance. Think of a shot from behind the catcher toward the outfield in a baseball park. A normal or wide-angle lens might be able to see both foul lines as they fan out and all the players on the field would be in the shot. A long lens would see only the catcher, pitcher and centerfielder. It would also shrink perspective and minimize motion, stacking the three players up and making the centerfielder roughly the same screen size as the pitcher and the catcher. When faced with an unmovable, undesirable element in the background behind one of your characters it is tempting to frame it out by switching to a longer lens. But though the image size of the character can be kept the same by moving the camera back, the shot will look "flatter" than the other shots around it made with shorter lenses and will be jarring to the audience. Haskell was careful not to make extreme changes in focal lengths within a scene, no matter what composition problems this might have solved.

The desire for consistency informed the decisions we'd make in planning the photographic attack on a scene, trying not to paint ourselves into a corner by beginning to shoot a sequence in a way impossible to maintain. Basic to this planning was making priority lists of shots we absolutely had to have, insuring that we'd get the essential coverage and then pick up whatever was helpful later. For the shoot-out, we began each day with some of the shots of the Baldwins approaching Sid and Cabell and of Joe running into town. As it turned out we never got to the part of the gunfight that takes place toward the train-station end of town, but because this was our lowest priority we still had enough to put the sequence together in the editing room. If we'd missed one of the setup shots, something like the side angle of Sid and Cabell and the Felts brothers coming to a stop and facing each other, there would have been a noticeable gap in the flow of events and we'd have been forced to do something tacky like cut away to birds fluttering off the roof of the coal dock.

Night shooting presents a number of decisions to be made. The conventions of moonlight in movies have changed over the years, but we still accept scenes where we know it's night but we can see pretty much everything that goes on. In *Matewan* we had night scenes in woods far away from any city or other source of manmade light, we had night scenes in a tent camp with cookfires burning, we had night scenes in a deserted railroad yard with a few electric lights hanging overhead. We treated night in different ways in these different situations. Because night shooting is more expensive and tiring, we tried shooting the ambush sequence in the woods as "day-for-night," using the natural sun-blocking of the tree canopy above to cut out most of the direct rays and later

"Hanging the moon" for a night shot of the tent camp

printing the film down to get true blacks in areas that were actually shaded daylight.* Day-for-night is an old technique and not a perfect one, but we tried to use it in a slightly less obvious way than usual, not throwing any supplemental light on the characters' faces. We wanted to portray the confusion and betrayal of the ambush, not to highlight individual reactions.

* "Printing the film down" is done during the "timing" of the cut negative of the edited movie. Each frame of negative is printed by shining light through it for a fixed duration — "timing" it.

In the sequence between Few Clothes and Joe where Few tries to carry out the execution, we shot in true night. The camp is a clearing with open sky overhead and the scene called for the men to sit by a fire, making day-for-night shooting impossible. Morris Flam, the gaffer, rigged up a firelight unit that threw flamelike illumination on the actors' faces from below the frame line, giving Haskell enough exposure to keep them in focus and read their expressions. When Few leads Joe into the woods, however, there is no longer a fire to provide an excuse for lighting and the day-for-night look would never have matched what we'd just seen in the camp. In this scene we did want to see the characters' faces and the only light available was whatever we could provide, so we had to "hang a moon." Stefan Czapsky, the key grip, devised an enormous grid of lights diffused inside a box of scrim, all suspended high overhead by a crane. This was swung over the edge of the woods and supplemented by side light from units just off screen. The effect still feels like night even though we see more than we actually could, which is the basic aim of psychological realism.

The interior sets were more controllable but created their own problems. In the night meetings in C.E.'s restaurant we wanted the feeling that the only light was from the oil lamps set low on the tables and floor so light wouldn't leak out through the shaded windows — a close, clan-

Interior C.E.'s restaurant, the miners vote to attack the scabs

destine feeling. We didn't have the time or budget to light the scene with thousands of candles like Stanley Kubrick did in *Barry Lyndon*, and Haskell had to improvise. Nora Chavooshian designed some cross-supports on the ceiling to hide some of the general illumination units, while other lights were kept low and hidden from the camera by miners' bodies. Giving texture to the room, creating hot spots and areas of shadow, took some time, but the only real difficulty came during Joe's speech to the miners the first night. We had started recording the scene with an "open" microphone (a microphone on a boom pole as opposed to radio microphones hidden on the actors' bodies) and it was fine for the relatively static beginning of the scene. But when Joe began to move through the room, the low ceiling hung with lighting units got in the way. There was no good angle from which to follow Joe with the microphone without casting boom shadows onto the scene. Switching to a radio microphone would have made for a very inconsistent sound match. The final solution was to compromise on all fronts — Haskell moved some lights, the boom operator changed her position and Chris Cooper altered his path and his head position as he said his lines.

The adjustment between the actor and the technicians is one repeated in varying degrees throughout the shooting. You want to give the actors enough breathing room to inhabit their characters physically, but you've established a look and need them to stay on screen and in focus. A narrow depth-of-field or overly intricate lighting setup can be a cage for an actor, nailing him to one spot or crowding his head with too many technical adjustments if he does move. On the other hand, you pay for your freedom — the more ground the actor covers, the more area the lighting has to cover, the more focus adjustment you'll need and the longer it will take to set all this up. If the actor moves inconsistently from take to take, the camera operator has to be psychic or you have to move back and loosen the shot a little.

The balance between actor freedom and photographic requirements is worked out shot by shot, situation by situation. A character study like *Raging Bull* or most of John Cassavetes's movies might opt for simplicity and lots of room for the actors, whereas *Star Wars*, with all its glass painting, projected backdrops and other effects, calls for extremely precise body placement. Actors differ in their tolerance for technical distraction and it can be helpful to give them more room for the most emotional scenes. It's tough to scream and shout and appear to be out of control while you're worrying about tape marks or sandbags on the floor. Everyone wants to do their best work and often the director's job is to set priorities and mediate between the actors, camera crew and sound department when something one party needs to do makes life difficult for the others.

The shooting process was made easier when Haskell convinced us to bring in Steve Apicella and his video-assist equipment. A very small unit is placed on top of the camera and "sees" through the camera lens itself. A video image is then sent to a monitor either by hard wire or radio signal. The rig was usually ready long before we were ready to roll and with a touch of a button Steve could print stills of the action appearing on his screen. Because the video assist can monitor while the camera is being set up, I could keep track of how the shot was shaping up without constantly butting in to peek through the eyepiece. Any adjustments I wanted could be made before lights started being set in place, saving the crew a lot of wasted effort. We could monitor and tape rehearsals without shooting film, so we could review and adjust any shots involving camera movement. Background action could be checked, hunches about possible problems tested. When pressed for time I never had to guess whether we had a usable take yet — I could see what we'd done right away. Steve also proved to be a valuable pair of eyes on the set, spotting things in the frame that were wrong or that could be better. His video stills were helpful in figuring out eyelines and in matching composition for shots meant to cut together that were shot days apart.* On location, where dailies lag a couple days behind shooting, the video sometimes helped us decide whether a sequence needed reshoots or if we could strike the set and go on to something new.

There are a lot of beautiful shots in *Matewan*, but the mark of Haskell's skill is that they are appropriately beautiful, never gratuitously drawing you away from the story with their look. Though often not able to do what he would or could have done given a more merciful schedule and more money for lights and equipment, he always managed to come up with something in tune with the feeling of the movie. In collaboration with me and Nora Chavooshian and the forces of nature, he took the story off the page and put it back into pictures.

## Sound Recording

Movie sound is something that we notice more when it's not right than when it is. Sound rarely has the breathtaking potential of the picture, but

---

* "Eyelines" refers to the direction and angle a character's eyes are looking in a scene. In a conversation between characters the eyelines must be consistent from shot to shot or the audience will become disoriented. If we are looking over Joe's left shoulder at Sephus in a two-shot, and Joe is to the left of the frame and Sephus is to the right of the frame, when we cut to the single close-ups Joe must be looking off to the right of the screen and Sephus must be looking to the left of the screen (as he was in the original shot). This can change only if we see Joe cross from one side of Sephus's vision to the other on camera. Keeping track of this stuff is one of the biggest pains in the ass of movie-making.

if it's out of synch or inappropriate for what's on the screen it pulls the audience out of the story. Sound on a movie has to be planned and built up as carefully as the picture.

It is easier to add the sounds you want together in the final mix than to subtract the ones you don't want. If sound were painting, the record-ist's job would be to supply all the colors and types of paint necessary, leaving the sound mixer to mix them together and apply them, layer by layer, to the scene being painted. Whenever possible you try to leave as many sound elements "unmarried" (cleanly recorded on separate tracks) as possible. This gives you the option of changing the relative levels of those elements in the mix rather than having to live with whatever existed while you were shooting. In the hill people confrontation scene the Baldwin agents jump in their car and drive away. We were careful to keep the sound of the car separate from any of Isaac's dialogue (by push-ing it from below frame rather than running the engine) so we could cut from angle to angle of him and the tent camp people without worrying about the sound level of the disappearing car. The engine sound was recorded clean without the camera and mixed in later underneath the voices in a gradual fade to distance. Later in the same scene, as Bridey runs up to help Joe off the ground, we asked the people standing in the background to whisper to each other but act as if they were talking in a normal voice. The whispers were not loud enough to be picked up by the microphone recording Joe and Bridey, and the extras didn't have to totally mime the scene, which often produces overly large gestures. These back-ground characters are far enough back that we can't tell exactly what they might be saying, and months later I got some women in Boston to record dialogue which we laid in over the extras' moving lips during the mix. Though this was very low in volume, almost inaudible, absence of sound would have been more disturbing.

Each location, exterior or interior, has its own "tone": it can be domi-nated by the rush of a nearby river, the hum of a refrigerator or just the particular acoustics of a "silent" room. John Sutton, our location sound mixer, would always get some room tone, a half minute or more of the sound of the location without camera or crew noise, before we left. This is used later in the sound mix to fill in holes in the track. If a character is speaking and in a space between words a car horn honks in the dis-tance, you can cut out the horn and fill the resulting dead spot in the track with the ambient room tone you have gotten.

Very often sounds not made by something on screen are important to a scene. Gunshots are added later, birds, crickets, ticking clocks, ap-proaching cars, wind howling, thunder, off-screen voices. Some of these are made by the sound editors or gotten from a sound effects library, but if you're shooting on a location with special characteristics it's best to

record them there. John would often follow up the shooting of a scene by getting some track of the sound elements that made it up, in close perspective, with no other sound covering each one. River tone, wind rustling, doors shutting, footsteps on the railroad ballast, steam engine farts and whistles, distant dogs — all these location wild tracks could be useful later to boost or replace the synch track. Some scenes were shot silent for reasons of expediency, and on these John's location wild tracks were especially important. He would try to think three-dimensionally, recording sounds that could later add "depth" to a scene by mixing them in different perspectives. He would record these as "flat" as possible, leaving frequency modulation, reverb and other treatments to the postproduction sound mixer, once again obeying the rule that it is easier to add sound than subtract it.

The main decision in recording dialogue is whether to use an open microphone hidden somewhere on the set or pointed on the end of a boom pole, or to use radio microphones hidden on the actors' bodies. Radio mikes have the advantage of staying with the actors whichever way they turn, eliminating the problem of lines going "off mike" and the difficulties of moving the boom pole under lights without casting shadows in the frame. The quality of the sound, however, is more one-dimensional than what you get with an open mike, since the voice is always close no matter where the character moves within the frame and there is no sense of "space" around the sound. This can be improved some by mixing in ambient sound of the location recorded with an open microphone. Radio mikes fail to pick up synch footsteps and clothing rustle, which then have to be made and added later. I prefer to use open microphones whenever possible, but often the logistics of this requires too much time or compromise and we have to wire everybody with radio mikes. John usually put the radio rigs on our actors while they were still getting dressed whether we planned to use them or not, saving time later if we had to suddenly stop using the boom.

Unlike picture, sound can be erased or added after you've left the set. Looping (actors redoing their lines in a studio after the picture is cut) is expensive and often it's difficult for the actors to match their original performance. So when there are sound problems on the set we'll get wild lines. We'll turn the camera off and bring all the actors in the scene close to the mike to do it again as if it's the radio version, trying to match their on-screen readings but careful not to let them overlap each other. These lines are usually preferable to looped lines and can make it possible to use your favorite acting take even if a truck rumbled past through part of it.

The negative side of the flexibility of sound compared to picture is that the sound people almost always are put in second place, having to adjust

their boom position and closeness to the demands of the picture frame, rather than the other way around. You can get very lax about sound during the heat of production, and you always pay for it later with the expense and time of making sound effects and room tone in postproduction. Early on I tried to establish that taking room tone was part of the normal routine, not an afterthought. The picture crew wants to get moving to the next setup when you finish the last take of an angle, and it's tough to freeze and listen to the house creak for a minute while the sound people record. But in an hour, when the rest of us are gone, the house creak won't sound the same and it won't do the sound crew any good to get tone then.

Sound people learn early in their careers they are doomed to be poor relations on the set, and the good ones develop strategies for doing their job well without bending everybody else out of shape. One of the main things John Sutton did was to get to the set first, to scope out what the problems in the scene might be throughout its coverage. If it became clear that one or two important angles were going to be impossible to boom, he'd be sure to use radio mikes right from the beginning. Though the audience can buy hearing sound from either kind of mike, switching from one type to the other in the middle of a scene is jarring. If we started with an open mike and came to the impossible scene, John would have to ask for adjustments in the blocking we might not want to do or spend a lot of valuable time hiding open microphones all over the place. Starting with the radio mikes means that this problem doesn't arise, and knowing my preferences John would always tell me why he was going that route. He was able to use the video assist to see what the frame line was, so his boom operator, Lisa Schnall, didn't have to keep bugging the camera operator to ask if he saw the mike. He also warned me when something was not going to sound good to the ear because he was purposely not treating it. Having been a postproduction sound mixer, he was well aware that his job was to be not the final word but the original supplier of sound, giving us as much ammunition to take into the final mix as he could.

## Shooting

### PRIORITIES

It's 1:45 in the afternoon and lunch is scheduled for 2:00. You're three shots behind what was planned for the morning. You're in the middle of an exterior shot and it looks like it might start raining in an hour or so. The actress is in the next shot scheduled as well, but she'll need a change

of hair and clothes that will take forty-five minutes. The one you're in now is very emotional, and it's taking quite a while to get her face back in shape after each take. The crew went into overtime last night, it's late in the week and they're tired and hungry. The only cover set if it does rain is an interior that needs an hour or more of prep by the art and props people, but you need them here for the next two shots. Another actor supposed to shoot in the afternoon has a plane to catch at 7:00, taking him to another movie commitment that will keep him away for a full two weeks. The leaves on the trees in the background, acres and acres of them, are supposed to all change color in the next day or so. The first shot tomorrow needs to be at sunrise and if you go into overtime tonight there won't be enough turnaround time to make it. The last take convinced you the shot would be better with a wider lens, but a wider lens will reveal the production trucks and craft services table set up at the other end of town and the unit manager's walkie-talkie is on the blink and a decision has to be made in the next ten minutes whether to rent the crane for that dawn shot tomorrow or not.

Who lives in the red house?

The number of variables and pressures that figure into a shooting day are like those word problems in math, only there is no correct answer. Each decision you make brings a whole new set of variables into play. This makes it doubly important to have your priorities set before you start shooting. Which sequences, which shots, are the most important? How far behind schedule can you afford to get? What comes next and how does what you're doing now affect it?

In a movie like *Matewan* believable acting was usually the highest priority. We would go a few extra takes in one scene to let the actors do their best, sometimes giving the lighting people very little time to set up for the next one. A camera move might be fine but not perfect and I'd have us move on because it was late in the day and I didn't want the actors to be hurried into a performance on the next scene. In a science fiction or horror-action movie the acting might be a lot less involved and camera moves and lighting would be given preference. A few times late in the production rest became the main priority — I might choose not to go into overtime not because we couldn't afford it but because it was clear we'd get much better work from everybody after a night's sleep.

It is hard to predict exactly which shots are going to give you the most trouble. You may have to retake a scene for reasons beyond your control — the sun comes out in the middle of a shot, a light burns out, an airplane comes overhead or the wind suddenly blows the set over. You may have to retake it because somebody messed up. When this happens it's important not to scapegoat whoever did it and to keep the cast and crew from scapegoating each other. Everybody wants to do their best work

Haskell Wexler indicates a medium close-up on Few Clothes.

and it doesn't help to have a lot of people on your back when you make a mistake. If you as director can chill out when members of the cast and crew mess up you can expect more support from them when *you* mess up.

## COVERAGE

Coverage refers to the number and type of shots you use to build a scene. A very standard, basic coverage of a conversation between two people at a dinner table would be a master shot wide enough to see both people in profile, a shot over person A's shoulder toward person B, and a reverse shot over person B's shoulder toward person A, each running the duration of the scene. With this coverage you could let the scene play in the master shot or you could break out of it and start cutting back and forth between the over-the-shoulder shots. Planning coverage is a little like listing all the adjectives and adverbs you might want to use in a paragraph you're going to write. The more of them you have the more arrangements you could come up with, but if the words aren't the right ones your sentences aren't going to make much sense or have much impact.

Different types of shots give you different feelings. The shower scene

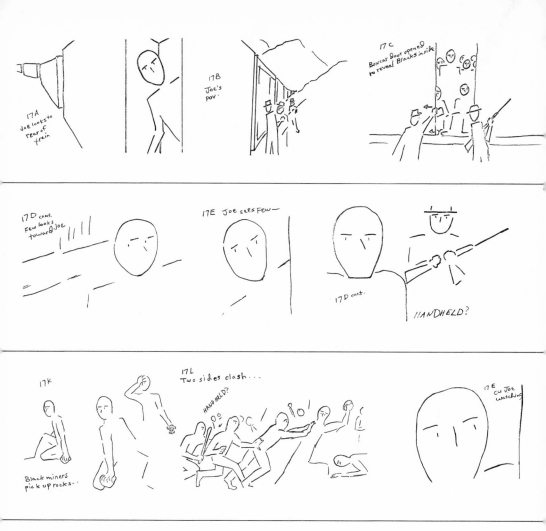

## Storyboards

A storyboard is a series of drawings indicating what coverage you're going to try to get in a scene. Laid out in comic strip form, a storyboard gives you something tangible to look at and to hand on to the various departments on the movie to help them plan what they're going to do. Camera movement and movement of the characters are suggested by arrows and other symbols. The crudeness of the drawing varies depending on who does it, but quality is less important than information in this case. Storyboards are often ignored or diverged from when you finally get on the set, but they provide a basis for planning the "attack" on the scene. If by lunch you've only shot five of the twenty angles planned for the day, you can go back to the storyboard and figure out which ones you could possibly do without and still put the sequence together. The storyboard panels here are taken from the beginning of the train fight sequence.

17C cont.

→

17D

Men climb about & are lined up by guards →

17D cont. Few steps into ru

HANDHELD

Rock thrown at
Few

17D cont.

HANDHELD

17F
Ludie
charges from
woods

17G

Shoot behind guards as
miners charge from
the woods —

17B  Joe's POV (conductor run?)

17H

HANDHELD?

Miner running
with club

(others in BG)

17I

HANDHELD?

Miner throwing rock
(others in BG)

17J
Miners come over
couplings behind
guards

Miners come over

in *Psycho* would play very differently if shot in a single master from the doorway. Sergio Leone's Westerns stripped of their extreme close-ups would lose a lot of their sweaty intensity. In planning the coverage for *Matewan* we tried to balance the practicalities of time and money against the desire to move the camera and to have lots of freedom in the editing room. Our one general decision was to stay away from self-conscious, authorial kinds of camera moves. As often as possible we wanted the characters and the action to lead the eye, rather than have the camera drag it around. Though bravura camera moves can add a lot to a certain kind of movie, establishing a grand style or an ironic distance from the story, we wanted the audience to be inside the story and to forget about the movie-makers as much as possible.

The one scene where we planned fairly elaborate coverage and managed to get most of it shot was the driftmouth confrontation. Though it doesn't take much screen time, it is the first major turning point in the movie and a scene where it's important to get close to several characters' reactions. Joe's hopes for the union are on the line, so we want to be with him a bit, and Danny is watching Joe by now so he's got to be there, and Few Clothes and Fausto have their decisions to make and C.E. Lively has predicted violence and the mine guards are tense — there's a lot of people to check in on. It would be possible to start with a high crane shot, looking down at the approaching scabs from above and behind the mine guards, then crane down as the miners appear and surround them, ending up with an angle over the machine-gunner's shoulder toward Few Clothes and the other men. This master shot would cover all the pertinent action but distance us from the individuals. In a Socialist-realist drama about the glory of the masses this might be appropriate, but at this moment in *Matewan* we have a bunch of individuals all straining to go in opposite directions, and we have to find a way to give a flow to the scene as a whole while touching base with each of them.

The sequence broke up into three sections — the scabs coming up the path and being surrounded by the miners; the confrontation and decision just in front of the driftmouth; and the return of the now united groups back down the path. Each section had its own character. For the entrance of the scabs we wanted a feeling of confusion, to graphically portray their position between a rock and a hard place. We started with shots of the mine guards in their machine gun nest hearing men approaching from downhill. The guards are lit from above, their faces thrown in shadow but the metal of their gun barrels highlighted. We then go to a shot from their point of view, looking out over the swiveling barrel of the machine gun as a group of miners bursts out of the trees in the distance and runs yelling toward the top of the pathway. We move to the top of the pathway and look left to another group of miners sprinting toward us in the dark,

rifles in hand. Then we move to their point of view, looking down the path as the scabs, marched in double file between armed mine guards, are led up toward us.

By the end of this shot the first miners have started down the path toward them, lining both sides of it, warily eyeing the guards. We go to a shot from the path upward as the rest of the miners arrive and wait on the upper lip of the path, the driftmouth and machine gun nest visible across an open yard behind them. The coverage so far is not personal in that it doesn't include any detailed close-ups, but it does give us a look at the three groups — mine guards, miners and scabs — and then gives us a look from the point of view of each. This establishes that we aren't meant to see this scene from just one group's perspective (nor from the omniscient distance of a static wide shot) but to consider how *everybody* feels in the situation.

We then move in closer for shots of the scabs as they pass some of our main characters, getting a quick glimpse of each nervous face as it goes by. We move back to a shot from the top of the path as the scabs approach and pass right in front of us, a miner's rifle framing the shot on the left. We return to the mine guard's point of view, a wide shot of the yard in

The miners and scabs brawl.

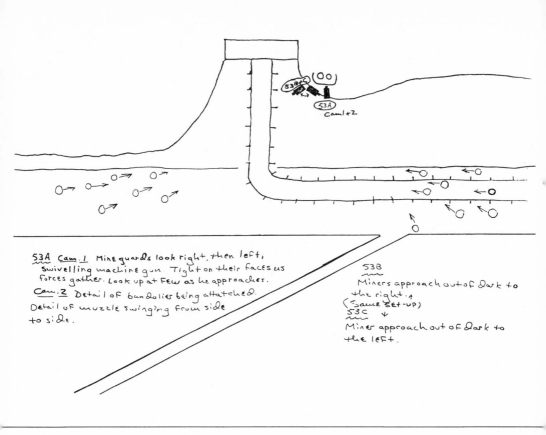

53A **Cam.1** Mine guards look right, then left, swivelling machine gun. Tight on their faces as forces gather. Look up at Few as he approaches.
**Cam.2** Detail of bandoliers being attatched. Detail of muzzle swinging from side to side.

53B
Miners approach out of Dark to the right. ↑
(Same set-up)
53C ↓
Miner approach out of Dark to the left.

## Ground Coverage Plan

Often in planning out extensive coverage it helps to map out how you're going to attack the entire sequence, trying to work things so you turn the camera around as little as possible and use your actors' time efficiently (shoot the SAG actors out first and end the day with the extras or shots involving no actors at all; try to finish the shots with the most people in them early so if there's overtime it isn't multiplied too many times). The first sheet here is one of many from the coverage of the driftmouth confrontation scene, showing the shots that will cover the arrival of the miners in the open yard in the company guards' line of fire. The next two are details from the planned coverage of the final shoot-out, with symbols for bullet direction that were used by the special effects coordinator in preparing his body squibs and the actors' clothing.

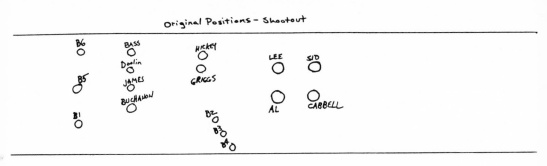

B6 ○   BASS ○   HICKEY ○
       Doolin          LEE ○   SID ○
B5 ○   JAMES ○   GRIGGS ○
       BUCHANON ○
                        AL ○   CABBELL ○
B1 ○
                  B2 ○
                   B3 ○
                    B4 ○

139 F

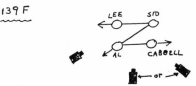

Al shoots Cabbell - entrance wound, stomach
Sid shoots Al - exit wound in hair behind ear (entrance wound
Sid shoots Lee - hat blows off backwards (exit + entrance wound

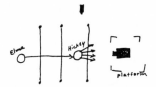

Elma                    Hickey

platform

142 B

Hickey faces Elma with sheets
aging between them, sheets
.hind Hickey. Elma blasts Hickey. (shotgun)
re sheets between them blowing upward
sheets pre-shot). Pellets exit from Hickey's
ack and go toward sheet behind him.

141  Tolbert and Ellix drag James
from house onto street, shoot down
at Wm - James out of frame.

147  Mrs. Elkins shoots into Griggs'
dead body over and over.

Hickey            Elma

front of the mine opening as the scabs uneasily begin to spread out into it, hemmed into the middle by armed miners. We move back to see Joe catching up with Sephus at their flank, then go in closer to see Fausto and Few Clothes settling to a stop, looking around uneasily. We see the machine gun from their point of view, swiveling to cover them. We move back to the most neutral shot so far, a wide master from behind telling us that all the scabs and miners are now in the yard and facing off.

This sets the stage for the second section. The purpose here is to build some tension, to give the characters and the audience some time to stew, waiting for whatever happens next. We use close shots of miners fingering their weapons, of scabs looking around tensely, of the mine superintendent and his guards watching, waiting to shoot. We see Danny and Hillard, we see C.E. Lively, we see Joe and Sephus. Sephus tells Joe to get ready to duck. All these shots contribute to making a frozen moment. Once again they encourage us to see through different people's eyes rather than concentrate on one point of view. If the movie were mostly a coming-of-age story about Danny we'd probably keep cutting back to him again and again, staying inside his head. But we're after more than that, and the number of cutaways will allow us to quicken the rhythm in the cutting to the point where Few Clothes starts to move. The guard follows him with his machine gun. Few walks right at us as we look over the gunner's shoulder (we can see the barrel pointed right at him) and he throws his shovel down. The mine superintendent reacts. Fausto throws his shovel down, turns to the men we see behind him in the wide shot and says in Italian, "Long live the strike!" We cut to Tom and Gianni, also with miners behind them, as they join in.

Now we move from clusters of scabs throwing down their tools to various characters reacting. We move back for a wider shot as Joe steps into the middle of the miners and takes charge. We see him as an important individual, but as one surrounded by supporters, more of a catalyst than a hero. Another scene in another movie might shoot him from a low angle as he climbed onto a barricade, separating him from the others and giving his action more weight, but we wanted to keep him tied to the miners here. Joe is at his happiest and most successful when he's among the men — it's when he is isolated from them that he's in danger. He tells the company men off and begins to lead the united miners away.

What we wanted from the third section was the feeling of different groups mingling, the high spirits of the men in their victory, and a note of concession from C.E. to Joe. We chose to shoot from the top of the pathway toward the driftmouth rather than continue from the over-the-machine-gun angle, gaining the energy of people coming toward us rather than fading away into the dark. We start with Fausto and Gianni as they begin to sing "Avanti Populo," then move back to let the men stream

past us, the tight formation of the scabs as they arrived now replaced by a jumble of black and white and Italian miners, some singing, some laughing and shouting. Sephus shakes Few Clothes's hand as they pass by. As they thin out we move to a shot with C.E. in the foreground and the yard and driftmouth out of focus in the background. As Joe passes he gives C.E. a small salute, then we change focus to the superintendent and guards as Joe looks toward them. We hold on them as he walks out of the frame, seeing them small and weak-looking across the yard (as opposed to their first, low-angle, menacing close-ups).

In practice, of course, we didn't shoot anywhere near in this sequence. We wanted the actors fresh for the few lines they have in the meat of the scene and shot the moment of Few Clothes throwing down his shovel and Joe taking charge first. You try to "turn around," go from shooting in one direction to shooting in the opposite, as few times as possible. Every time you turn around, all the lights and equipment that were off screen are now on screen and have to be moved. So we tried to shoot everything toward the driftmouth first, then turn around and shoot everything with the mine at our backs, facing the pathway. A lot of the shots of men coming up the pathway were similar in camera position to those of men going down the pathway, so we shot those together. Most of the shots of the mine guards and of Turley, the superintendent, don't have anybody else in them, so we shot those after everyone else had been broken for lunch. The low light level appropriate for the scene gave us a limited depth-of-field and made camera movement a difficult and time-consuming proposition, so we concentrated on getting lots of good coverage and relying on the movement within the frame and within the cutting to give the scene life.

In other scenes we weren't as successful getting everything that had been planned, but the basic attack usually included a fall-back position, a point at which we had enough in the can to make something out of the sequence even if we stopped shooting right then. Other times we'd have to do our falling back at lunch or the night before, realizing that the time and conditions weren't right to even start with our original plan. The important thing then was to keep our concentration and do a really good job of the shots that remained, finding ways to tell the story of the scene with less ammunition.

## DIRECTING ACTORS

A movie performance is a collaboration primarily between screenwriter, actor, editor and director. The ideal movie actor combines a solid sense of character with the flexibility to react to situations in many different ways. Unlike acting in theater, a movie performance is made of many

HICKEY

A few thoughts on the character of Hickey. Hickey is someone who volunteered for service in WW1, probably out of boredom, and was older than most of the cannon-fodder he found around him in the trenches. He was in some heavy, grisly hand-to-hand combat, saw people gassed and blown up, and his mind has not returned from the place where it's kill-or-be-killed. Hickey feeds on violence, or at least the atmosphere of violence, and everything he does is to control and shape that atmosphere. When he meets someone new he immediately starts to push to see if they'll push back and how much -- he's constantly filing information for future conflict. He wants people to be afraid of him, realizing that intimidation is often more effective than actual violence. He realizes he is a foreigner in a guerrilla conflict -- anyone, man, woman or child, could shoot him in the back at any time. Griggs is basically his button man, a more volatile killer that he unleashes when needed. Hickey has a dog-eat-dog world view and wants to be the big dog. Violence is a sickness with him, as opposed to C.E. who is pretty cool and professional about it. He is fully aware of the irony of being honored by his country for sticking a bayonet in people. In a way he has as much political analysis as Joe, it's just that he has taken the cynical rather than idealistic path and has sided with who he thinks the winners will be.

## Character Sheet

This is a character sheet, a rumination that I'd either mail to the actors in advance or give to them when they got to West Virginia. Since we didn't have time for rehearsal before shooting, these were meant to help the actors think about their characters and to be the basis for further discussions we might have.

pieces, shot from many angles and rarely in sequence. A movie actor is not projecting to a live audience but behaving in character in front of a camera. Each actor has his or her process for finding a character and performing, and the director's job often entails finding ways to make that process mesh with the practical concerns of getting the movie shot and with the processes of the other actors.

Some actors need to feel more of the emotion their characters are going through than others, need to stay away from the distractions of the set and stay in character all the time. Others are more technical, able to step in front of the camera, turn it on, then step away and turn it off immediately. It's not important to the movie how the actor arrives there as long as what goes on screen is right and doesn't mess up the other actors in the scene. As a director you try to learn each actor's process early on and help him or her adapt it to the production. With actors who feel they need warming up and exploration time I'll try to do some rehearsal while lights are being set and the camera position worked out. If the other actor in the scene is someone who gets bored and stale real fast I'll leave him out of the rehearsal and read the part myself. It's best not to do emotional scenes over and over, and when a scene calls for a lot of coverage it's best to do the close-ups first and then move back, or to rein the actors in a bit emotionally till you come close enough to have their heavy stuff really "read" on camera.

Before shooting starts I'll try to get together at least once with each actor to talk about who the character is and what his or her relation is to the other characters. This can be very philosophical and very technical. For *Matewan* we talked about how far up or down the hill the characters lived, about what their past experience with the coal company was, about their religious background and degree of suspicion of outsiders. We'd go over the dramatic progression of their characters through the movie, where they start and end up. A peripheral character like Ellix or Tolbert might not really change much throughout a movie and our conversation in their case was more about reactions to the specific situation of a scene. But with Joe and Danny and Elma and others there is an emotional progression that has to be understood and kept track of as we shoot out of sequence.

On the set we would go over the personal dynamics of the scene, then move on to more technical matters like physical business, blocking and the type of coverage planned. I'm not real fond of the idea of tricking actors into doing stuff, putting them personally through the emotions the character should be experiencing, and try to hire people who don't need or want to be tricked. I prefer to let the actors know as much about the scene and our plans for it as they think they need and use that

information however they want. Actors who feel too much information gets in their way tell you early on and you can leave them alone.

Once we'd shot a take we'd talk about adjustments to be made. They might be purely technical — talk louder or faster, try to finish pinning up the blue shirt before you finish the second line, pour the milk with your left hand — or they might be about the emotion of the scene — try to be more or less angry, sad, distracted, attracted, open with your emotions, closed with your emotions, whatever. What we then aim for is not a "perfect" take but a range of possibilities to bring into the editing room. This is especially true of a scene with several characters covered from a number of angles. Until you put the scene into sequence with the rest of the movie you can't be sure how you'll want to play it. The preceding scene may turn out so emotionally devastating that you want to back off a bit, or maybe you need to emphasize the comic possibilities in it, or have the dialogue play fast and furious to get the movie rolling again. This is hard to do if each take is nearly identical and played on the same note. It is possible to "bracket" a performance just as you bracket an exposure in photography, making sure that somewhere in the range of what you've tried you'll get what you need. Actors have to have confidence in the people who control their performance after the shooting stops — the director, the editor, in some cases the producers and studio heads and their demographic experts — or they won't be willing to bracket. It is not unusual to find that actors who have reached a certain level of success and who feel they've been burned a few times will set a certain performance in their heads and refuse to budge from it. Many of the reports of stormy weather on the set come from an actor's defensive posture running up against a director who wants to try something different. Sometimes the actors are right to be defensive, sometimes they aren't. When I disagree strongly with the way an actor wants to do something I try to make time so that we shoot a couple my way and then shoot a couple the actor's way. The actors know they still don't have final say, but at least they feel like they'll have a shot at it in the editing room.

I tend to resist doing a lot of acting rehearsal for movies. If there is difficult choreography between actor and camera we'll work on the move as long as we need to, but without acting. There is a freshness, a shock of the new to early takes that is very difficult to match if you've done the thing a dozen times before the camera starts rolling. I do encourage the actors to work with each other off screen, talking about their characters together, working out physical stuff, playing in character.

Ideally the actor is into the part deeply enough to stay in character no matter how the situation changes from take to take. I often write or make up lines and actions that come just before the scene we are shooting.

This can help the actors get some momentum going, and sometimes I'll like the run-up lines enough to keep them in the movie. The extended scene where C.E. is breaking down Bridey Mae with his story about Joe and duping her into betraying him was written to be moments in a longer conversation, with cutaways to Ludie's tent in between. Each time we came back to her cabin I wanted Bridey to be a little more shaken, a little further on the road to hysteria. Rather than have the actors play the pieces, stop, then ask them to imagine what went on in between and start up several emotional minutes later, I wrote connective dialogue. This was not as long as the full scene would have been, but did contain a kind of an emotional build, a way for Bridey to get from A to Z without having to do it all in one leap. See the following scene, which is what we shot, and compare it to the original script (page 120).

TRANSITION - C.E. AND BRIDEY

82   INT. BRIDEY'S CABIN - DAY
C.E. sits at a little table across from Bridey, a bottle of liquor and a pair of glasses between them --

                     C.E.

I talked to Ellix an he says your
phonograph machine gonna be fixed in a
couple days now.

                     BRIDEY

S'awful nice for you to do, Everett --

                     C.E.

Well, we gotta take care of our favorite
lady, don't we?

                     BRIDEY

You been so generous -- thinkin about me
when that Mr. Kenehan got you all so
busy with the union --

82   cont.

                              C.E.

          That Mr. Kenehan is what I come to talk
          to you about -- I got a suspicion he
          might not be what he says he is.


                              BRIDEY

          What do you mean?


                              C.E.

          Bridey -- did you send Kenehan some sort
          of letter?


We TRACK IN toward Bridey's stricken face as C.E.
pours liquor into her glass --


                              BRIDEY

          Well -- yeah --


                              C.E.

          What did you say in it?


                              BRIDEY

          It's kinda personal.


                              C.E.

          Not anymore it's not.


                              BRIDEY

          What?


C.E. is on his feet now --

82    cont.

                    C.E.

          (sighs)  This morning up at the tent
          camp Kenehan was readin it out loud like
          it was the Charleston newspaper --


                    BRIDEY

          No --


                    C.E.

          I heard him myself.


                    BRIDEY

          No.  He wouldn't.


                    C.E.

          They's a whole crowd of fellas around
          him, I see him laughin and wavin that
          letter an I come over to see what's so
          funny --


                    BRIDEY

          (despairing)  A lot of fellas?


C.E. puts a hand on Bridey's shoulder, in control
now--


                    C.E.

          You mind if I take a drink, honey?  It
          aint pretty what I got to say.


He pours himself a drink and sits next to Bridey on
the bed.  She takes a drink straight from the bottle
to steady herself --

82   cont.

                         C.E.

          He said some things, Bridey.  "She's
          been follerin me since I come here,"  he
          says, "--trailin after me like a dog in
          heat,"  he says, "sniffin round my legs
          like a brood bitch--"


                    BRIDEY

No!


                         C.E.

          "She don't wear no drawers,"  he says,
          "so's she can be ready for whatever
          stumbles down the pathway."


                    BRIDEY

Lyin bastard!


                    C.E.

He said you did it with one of the
colored.


                    BRIDEY

(crying)  Naw.  He didn't --


                    C.E.

Now Bridey -- I think it's worse than
that.  I think he might be a spy, in
with the coal operators.  But he's got
the fellas so turned around with all his
talk -- well, I need you to help me,
Bridey.  And sometimes you got to tell a
little bit of a lie to get the truth
acrost --

Unless we run out of film or sound tape in the middle of a take I encourage the actors to keep going even if there's a line flub or similar screw-up. If you're covering from more than one angle you don't need a perfect take of every angle, or even of any one angle. The first half of Take One might be great and the second half of Take Two might be great and as long as you can cut away to something in between you can use the good parts of both. Each time you call cut and have to reslate it costs you time, film stock and shooting momentum.

Every once in a while you'll enter the Twilight Zone with a shot, often not a very difficult one, and between actor mistakes, technical problems and antagonistic acts of God you're hitting Take 13 with no end in sight. If your brains haven't numbed out and you haven't copped the attitude that you're going to punish everybody by making them do it over and over till they get it right, the best thing to do is change the shot. There may be one specific thing you can change that makes it easier, or maybe the change is meaningless but the fact of moving the lights and camera to a slightly different position somehow breaks the spell and the camera assistant gets to say "Take One" instead of "Take Fourteen." Energy is very important in working with actors, and they get recharged not only from the director and the other actors but also from the crew.

We've never done much improvisation on any of the movies I've directed. It takes time, for one thing, and actors shouldn't be expected to be writers. Good actors can make something totally scripted *seem* improvised, and often we try for that feeling, but actual improvisation has been limited to background business and a few action scenes. In *Matewan*'s baseball and union-relief-day scenes, we set the actors up with a general idea of the action and then let them go and shot like it was a documentary. I had certain specific shots and moments in mind, Haskell Wexler had additional ideas, and we kept track of whether we caught them on camera or not. The home run that is scripted for Few Clothes becomes a double in the final movie because that's what he hit, and the action looks much better than anything we could have staged in the time we had. I do encourage actors to tell me if there are lines they don't understand or have trouble with, but we work that out before the shooting.

Judging acting is very subjective. I tend to get uncomfortable when the performance I'm watching seems to be based more on another performance the actor has seen or imagined and not on the life of the person being played. Some of this is about fully "inhabiting" a character, thinking and seeing the world the way the character would, as well as the more physical aspects of performance. Once an actor has gotten to the point of inhabiting the character we tend to work on playing the moment rather than playing more complicated psychological or historical wrinkles. Those should be internalized by the time you're really out there

Setting up the death of Griggs

dealing with the other characters, allowing you to make fairly simple, straightforward choices and reactions. If you have the character down the scene can really be about the moment and the movie camera is best at capturing the moment. I can often tell whether I'm buying a performance or not by watching the character listen. When a person is really listening he doesn't necessarily do anything different with his face, but you can feel the information going in, being thought about, and a reaction forming before the character answers. When an actor is too busy working on sense memories or mentally rehearsing a certain note he wants to hit, all you see is somebody waiting for his turn to talk. When good actors really lock into each other you get involved in the push and pull, you feel that unless the first one said what he did exactly the way he said it, the other one would never have answered the way *he* did, and each moment is up for grabs.

On *Matewan* we worked with a lot of people who had never acted before. They were cast by type and for their interest and energy, and they added a lot to the sense of people and place we were going for. In planning coverage for scenes with nonactors, I'll usually leave open the possibility of isolating them in a single shot for their lines. This is a safety net in case they tighten up once they're under the lights with the "real" actors. If you have an actor alone in the frame you can direct him line for line till you get the level needed to match the other people in the scene. Giving beginning actors something physical to do can also help, converting their nervous energy into muscle work and giving them something

natural to do with their hands and eyes. Choosing them for lines to be delivered at high volume is wise, as most people are better actors when they shout than in a normal tone of voice where you expect more inflection. Nonactors tend to do their best stuff in the first couple takes, when they're reacting to the situation and other characters for the first time, so I try not to rehearse them much. We have been lucky, though, in finding people with a sense of drama and timing who could have been actors if they'd had the interest or opportunity. Once you discover that kind of ability in nonactors you can loosen up in the coverage and include them in master shots, freed from the worry you'll need to cut around them in the editing room.

In *Matewan* we had a core group of extras who played the native, black and Italian miners, and they quickly got used to the camera in a good way. Within a few days I felt comfortable keeping them in the frame with the principal actors, giving them specific business to do and directing them pretty much the way I did the professionals. The hours of waiting around together helped make them seem like people who had grown up together, though many met while on the shoot. The focus and energy they provided was great for the principal actors to play to — Joe's speeches, the eviction and driftmouth scenes, the confrontation with the hill people all benefited from their interaction.

Movie actors often find themselves playing from the heart to a piece of gaffer's tape on a grip stand, or hugging a loved one while balanced on an apple box, or having to set off their own death wound without seeming to anticipate the shot. They can play Simon Says, looking up, down, left and right in the same take to provide quick cutaway shots and somehow stay in character and give each look some weight and meaning. There really is something magical when they can transcend the maze of technical requirements and make something human come alive on screen, and the director has to find whatever ways possible to help make that happen.

## THE POLITICS OF THE SET

You hear a lot of metaphors comparing a film crew to a small army. I never wanted to be in the army and I'm not at all interested in running one. The chain of command on a movie set is important as long as it relates to function, the efficient progress of what you're all trying to do together, and the rest is bullshit. It may be bullshit you have to put up with for one reason or another, but it is still bullshit. People get paid more or less depending on their relative importance to the movie (their irreplaceability) and the relative bargaining power of their agents, guilds and unions. It may not have much to do with how hard a person works

or what his or her final contribution is. On *Matewan everybody* was working really hard and we tried to be somewhat equitable in paying people but it didn't always work out ideally. Rank has its function on the set — the gaffers and grips take their cues from the director of photography, the art department workers from the production designer, the actors from the director, etc. Unlike the army, though, this rank is not meant to last beyond the shooting day. It often does, because the movie business is as concerned with status as any other, but we try to do everything we can to discourage this. Somebody who takes orders from you on the set is not your personal servant but another person making the movie, a partner, and should be treated that way.

A movie set is far from being a democracy, however. The decision-making is collaborative but very centralized, and things often work best when all the debate has been worked out before you get to the set. I'll often set up a shot that I'm not sure we'll ever use rather than hash out the pros and cons of it for a half hour, feeling that the momentum of the

Blocking a master shot for the driftmouth confrontation

shooting will suffer more from sitting around waiting for three people to make up their minds than from doing some work that may not end up in the final print. I've found that crew members, even ones with a surface attitude of cynical distance, are proud of what they do and just want to be given the chance to do it well. Though the speed and inventiveness of our grip and gaffing crews enabled us to get surprising amounts of coverage in a short time and reduced technical rehearsals and retakes to a minimum, they never got the kind of immediate positive feedback the actors did when they did something well. It's something I'm not especially good at doing, and I think they often had to settle for the quality of what was in the dailies (when they had the time or energy to see them) as their reward. But their attitude was very professional and supportive of the actors throughout, which always helps the focus and feel of a scene. This attitude came back from the actors and the time we spent with them was really about making the movie instead of about establishing beachheads for the ego.

What people do hate is to have their time wasted, and a lot of our efforts in running the set went toward minimizing waiting-around time and unnecessary duplication of work. You make sure you know where you want the lights before people set them all up, you try not to turn the camera around till you've shot the angle out completely, you don't do lots of gratuitous takes after it's clear things are not going to get better.

People have different styles and rhythms of working, different temperaments, and one department's work will often get in the way of or contradict another's. The assistant director has to do a lot of the mediating while on the set and the producers tend to do it for the big picture. Getting people to work with rather than in spite of each other can be difficult, and whenever possible we try to appeal to people's sense of collaborating on a shared project rather than retreat behind the safe formula of rank. Sometimes the props people *should* take precedence over the camera crew, sometimes the lead actor has to make an adjustment for the sound man and vice versa. It helps if you explain to the people involved why this is the case rather than just say do it, I'm the boss. This can take a bit more time now and then, but it's worth it in the long run. Nobody I've known who was in the army was very impressed with its efficiency in doing anything but making people miserable.

# EDITING

# Music

MOVIES HAVE a musical element before the first note is played. The edited images have a rhythm, a key, a sense of orchestration. Music added to the images can reinforce, underline, counterpoint or deny what is happening on the screen. Music can be treated as "source" or as "score," as something that comes from the world on screen or as something the movie-makers are adding from the outside, an editorial comment. When it works movie music is like a natural voice, like the only sound the picture up there could possibly make.

In *Matewan* we wanted music to be an important plot element as well as a visceral device. The three camps of miners — native white, black and Italian — are first seen cut off from each other by their racial and cultural differences as well as by armed company guards. But their music can float past those barriers, can go out and mix with the others in the night air. This nonverbal musical fusion is the first step in forming a union out of people initially suspicious of each other. Integration of musical groups has always been a factor in the spread of new musical forms, from country to swing to jazz and rock and roll, and that is why the music is usually labeled sinful and dangerous. There was a rich intermingling of music in the teens and twenties, as blacks moved north to work in factories and immigrants brought both classical and folk influences across with them.

Just as we chose a limited color scheme for the look of the movie, we were careful in choosing instruments to put across this idea of musical fusion. Our composer, Mason Daring, decided with me to characterize each type of music with only a few instruments — harmonica, mandolin, mountain fiddle, a mournful dobro — each capable of having an individ-

1-3      Int. coal mine - word spreads
Possible harmonica notes over int. mine - POST

3-5      Miners walking montage, Pappy VO
Song, "Fire in the Hole," instrumental leading to Hazel Dickens
vocal (voice in after Pappy VO ends) - Scratch PLAYBACK available
on set for tempo

5-7      Joe in train - black miners attacked

7-8      Joe and Bridey - Joe sees town
Poss. fiddle or harmonica notes - POST

9-11     Joe and Elma - Danny and Hillard return

11-13    Turley and blacks in shed

13-14    Elma's table - Sephus comes for Joe

14-16    Sephus and Joe to C.E.'s, grill Joe
Distant organ from church (maybe "Gathering Storm," maybe chorus)
POST if organ only, record on location if want O.S. chorus as
well

16-23    Miners bitch, Joe speech x-cut with Hardshell rap

23-28    Danny sermon x-cut with Hardshell rap

Solo mandolin, off screen - Written and rehearsed for shooting,
  poss. live or taped PLAYBACK
Italian voices singing - Poss. record on set but probably also
  get real Italians to do a version in POST
Picker and fiddler, on screen - Record on screen, then re-record
  during POST, using same players if poss.
Harmonica, on screen and off screen - Prerecord off screen,
  record on screen part on the set, re-record in POST
(Note - prerecording will take place in Boston or W.Va.,
  depending on the players)

## Music Cue Breakdown

This is a page from the list of possible and definite music cues I worked out
with Mason Daring. Besides the type of instrumentation and name of the cue
(if there is one) it indicates whether the music needs to be ready in a scratch
(with click track) version on the set for the shooting, or if it will be done
during the postproduction period.

ual voice, of expressing the player's feelings. Though banjo was commonly played in the hills in those days we felt its bounciness and attack were inappropriate to the mood of the story and kept it out of even the upbeat musical cues. As the movie progresses the instruments try to stretch. A country fiddle plays "Avanti Populo," a harmonica bends notes around an Italian mandolin melody, the players move closer to each other, all trying to pick up phrases of a new language.

My own tendency is to minimize the amount of scoring in a movie. The lush orchestrations of old Hollywood movies rarely move me and the formula scores of TV dramas are often more annoying than helpful. I like to hear the silences of the actors, like to let the breathing and wind rustling and crickets do their own work. On *Matewan*, however, we did feel there were times we could use an extra boost from music. The most obvious of these are the transitional montage sequences — the men walking out of the mine, the building of the tent camp, the organizing and baseball montages. Each of these sequences has a kind of positive energy, each of them has expository narration from Danny as an old man. Obvious scored music sticks out less here, as the sequences are already omniscient and authorial in their point of view and execution. The songs picked — a union fighting song, a down-home instrumental of "Avanti Populo," an old Italian workers' song — all could exist as source music within the story and all have a feeling of communal energy and high spirits.

Throughout the movie we laid in harmonica and dobro underscoring to help set a mood or punctuate a transition from scene to scene. We were able to get John Hammond to do the harmonica, watching a cassette of the movie and playing to it in a 1920s delta style. This harmonica is sometimes a kind of editorial comment, sometimes the sound of a character's emotional state, sometimes the mood of the shot made into sound. Working with John was similar to working with an actor — our discussions were about feelings and colors of emotion rather than musical technicalities, and his playing "breathed" with the movie rather than forcing itself upon it.

The order of the process of recording music with Mason depended on the nature of the music cue. Mason wrote "Fire in the Hole" and "The Gathering Storm" to specifications we had worked out together. One is a marching anthem, the other a mournful lament with overtones of Old Testament retribution. Though they were based on the style and instrumentation of existing mountain songs, writing our own pieces made for more flexibility in length and rhythm (as well as eliminating the expense of buying rights) when it came time to cut. Both songs were written and recorded in a scratch version (to a click track to keep the beat constant)

before the shooting started.* We were able to shoot the montage of the men walking out with the rhythm of "Fire in the Hole" in mind, careful not to let the shots drag too slow. The final element with both songs was bringing in Hazel Dickens to do the vocals. Hazel plays the mountain woman who sings "The Gathering Storm" at Hillard's funeral, and her a cappella performance on the synch track is everything you can't get in the usual lip-synched movie musical.

The segueway between the scab miners turning back at the drift-mouth, with the Italians singing "Avanti Populo," and the mountain fiddle rendition that follows over the tent building was planned carefully. We picked a tempo for the song and recorded it with fiddle and click track, then Mason worked with the actors before we shot the scene, getting them to sing along with a tape and internalize the rhythm as well as learn the words. We were lucky in that Joe Grifasi, who plays Fausto and starts singing the song, is also a singer. He was able to start people on the right key and tempo take after take. We wanted a ragged, almost mocking sound to it and as the night wore on that took care of itself. When it came time to shoot and cut the tent-raising scene we had the scratch track of the instrumental to work with and could have cast and crew listen to it before starting their movement.

Joe's first walk through town was a trickier sequence. The footage we had, a man walking past people who don't pay much attention to him, seemed a bit flat, like not much of a story was being told. We wanted the audience to get oriented in town a bit, but also to start seeing through Joe's eyes — shots of the town and Joe walking through it are intercut with closer shots of Joe looking. What he sees is neither foreboding nor joyous, and to help the scene we had to find music that conveyed "looking" rather than something dark or bright. As each new cut of the sequence was ready we'd send Mason a cassette of it and he'd do test recordings with different instruments and send them back to us. A standard fiddle song seemed too jarring, and mixing a guitar in with it gave a bouncy, buckboard-and-calico feeling we didn't want. The harmonica was too evocative of the deep South and another try with something slower on the fiddle was too lugubrious and menacing. Finally Mason got hold of a dobro, an instrument that in the twenties was made from a guitar with a metal pie plate set in as a resonator (it later evolved into Hawaiian steel guitar, then into the pedal steel). A little less southern

---

* A "scratch" version of a song is a recording in which the elements will eventually be changed. Until a week before the final sound mix we cut the walking-out montage to the rhythm of a recording of "Fire in the Hole" with Mason singing the vocal. In the final version Hazel Dickens sings it. Both Mason and Hazel sang while listening to the same "click track," a metronomic beat that kept them in tempo. The singer or musician listens to the click over headsets so it is not recorded on the resulting track.

and bluesy sounding than slide guitar, the dobro turned out to be the right voice for the scene. The notes have a clean, liquid attack but bend into a question at the end, sort of a *boinnnng!* What gives here? Who are these people? What happens next?

Mason and I both wanted to get Hazel Dickens involved from the beginning. Hazel grew up in West Virginia coal country hearing the songs and sermons, and her voice carries all the mournfulness and strength of the hill tradition. We wanted to build a very spare, evocative sound from just a few elements, and Hazel's voice was central to that plan. When she sings at Hillard's funeral it is not only background sound but an important action in the story. There is a sense of tragic destiny in many hill ballads, and the expression of that resignation to doom is as palpable an antagonist to Joe as the Baldwin-Felts agents are. As he stands at the graveside and Hazel sings we wonder how can he go against fate — how can he fight all that?

The power of the music went beyond what ended up on the sound-track. "Beautiful Hills of Galilee" was a traditional ballad Hazel had recorded long before we shot *Matewan*. The first time I heard it I knew it should go over the final credits, and I had actors listen to it before we'd talk about who their characters were. During the darkest hours of the long fund-raising haul, when we'd be thrown back to square one without a dime, we'd take out the album and listen to Hazel sing and remember why we were going through all this stuff to make a movie.

Deep into the shooting schedule, when exhaustion was a memory and a kind of numbness had set in, we found ourselves out on a drizzly night with dozens of our local extras climbing the steep, slippery path to the driftmouth again and again. People were willing but very tired and it looked like the night would go on and on. We broke for "lunch" at two A.M. or so, and the rain got a little heavier. As the shuttle van crawled along the narrow mud road to the catering tent we heard music. One of the native miners was picking a banjo, another singing in that high, nasal mountain way, and around them were our actors and extras in their headlamps and coal-darkened overalls — black, white, Italian — joining in when they knew the words. It was so much a scene from the movie, a feeling from the movie, that we hooked back in to why we were there, what we were doing up on that dark mountain in the middle of nowhere, and when we tore ourselves away to go back to work the night didn't seem so long anymore.

# Editing

## Tension and Release

Most generic movies depend on a cycle of tension and release for their impact. The classic American Western, such as *Shane* or *High Noon*, is a series of escalating violent incidents leading to a final, cleansing shoot-out. The monster movie and the haunted-house movie both work in cycles of tension, each attack another step toward the final confrontation between hero and creature. Perhaps the purest form of this cycle is seen in the melodrama of professional wrestling. A pro-wrestling card is an evening-long series of reversals, with the good guys winning through skill and virtue and the bad ones through cheating. Each match has its frozen moments of tension ("Will the abdominal claw paralyze Chief Strongbow?") and sudden release ("But no! He miraculously kicks free!"). The results of the matches are staggered so that rarely do the bad guys win more than two in a row and rarely do the good guys win more than one in a row. The psychic scorecard of the audience builds up a tension for justice that needs to be released in the main event at the end of the card. A promoter with a piece of the concessions will often put off the climax a bit by matching two "scientific" (boringly fair) wrestlers for the next-to-last fight, sending fans running for a final round of beer and hot dogs before the stands close. The final bout is usually the most emotional if not the most physically spectacular, and the outcome is chosen based on the situation of the promoter. If the good guys win there will be happy, satisfied people in the parking lot and lots fewer broken bottles and fist fights than you get with a boxing crowd. But if there's a chance for a sequel, a rematch of the same wrestlers in the near future, the bad guy

will win and promise to do the same next week, grabbing the microphone to specify time, date and arena.

A movie may be more subtle than this, but the technique is the same. The audience is made to expect or fear something, the event draws nearer and tension builds, then the thing happens and the tension is released. The event can be a gunfight, a moment of extreme success or defeat, a kid finding his lost dog, whatever. Even in genres where a happy ending is mandatory the tension can be built, putting off the release to give it greater impact.

*Matewan* is built around tension and release, around confrontations that threaten or spill over into violence. Applying the psychic scorecard, the train brawl is a draw, the eviction scene a victory for Sid, the tent-camp shooting a victory for the Baldwins, the hill people confrontation a defeat for the Baldwins and a small victory for Joe, the ambush a defeat for the miners, the aborted execution of Joe a victory narrowly snatched from defeat for the miners, and the final shoot-out — whether anybody wins there is one of the important questions of the movie. The upper hand is constantly changing, the *chi* of victory switching from one side to the other. In editing these sequences and planning the rhythm of the movie as a whole we wanted not only to maintain the tension throughout but to stretch the story beyond generic expectations. In each case of a showdown that stops short of killing we wanted the possibility that shots *will* be fired, that maybe Hillard won't get there in time to stop Few Clothes from killing Joe. The tension has to be maintained throughout the movie by never totally satisfying the audience at the points of release. Yes, the miners got out of that one, but the Baldwins are still in town, C.E. Lively is still undiscovered, the system of oppression still exists and it's only a matter of time before the Empire strikes back.

The danger of the subplot of Joe's near execution by his own men is that it is so strong it threatens to make any action after it anticlimactic. This is why I wrote the montage showing the strikers organizing, an attempt to let some psychological time pass, to give the audience time to wipe the slate clean and start the last section of the movie with a new burst of energy. In the editing we left the sequences of the night before the shoot-out long, with very few cuts within them, trying to linger with the sense of dread awhile before plunging into the final confrontation.

The cutting of the driftmouth sequence is similar. The first section of the movie points to the question of whether the blacks and Italians will walk out and join the other miners or not. In an earlier draft I let the natural rhythm of work shifts inform the structure of the story. Joe and the black miners arrive one day and he pitches the idea of a union to them that night. The blacks and Italians get together and debate the question underground on their shift the next day, and the confrontation

takes place the *next* morning as they walk to the mine. This made literal sense but took too long. I found myself writing other scenes just to tread water until that third day could come around. The second morning seemed too soon, giving the scabs no time on camera to decide. Then I got interested in setting the confrontation at night to heighten the dramatic feel and look of it, and realized I could have them be marched in for a night shift on the second night (surprise shifts were sometimes used to avoid strikers). The rhythm still seemed a little abrupt, a little arbitrary and quick, and so we tried to slow things down in the shooting and editing. The walk of the scabs through the waiting, armed miners is seen from several angles, slowing it down, building anticipation with each frightened or grim face. The scabs stop in front of the driftmouth. We see faces, waiting. The company machine-gunner stands ready. Few Clothes decides.

He moves.

The sequence as cut together becomes a visual microcosm of the situation that led up to it, the blacks and Italians caught between armed miners and armed company men, likely to get shot from either or both sides, looking to their leaders Few Clothes and Fausto. The audience tension at this point should be not only about whether shooting will start or not but about *which decision* the scabs will make. So we let Few Clothes take some time stepping forward, poker-faced till he throws his shovel down, making us wait for the release.

What works or doesn't work in a sequence is affected by the scenes that have gone before. We found in cutting Danny's sermons that the punch lines were much stronger when we cut back to him with an angle that was different or closer than the one before we cut away. A new or closer angle can add heat to a performance, even if that performance is interrupted by another whole scene. Cutting back to a different angle can also help create the feeling of time progression, can tell us that we're getting further along in this speech we keep coming back to. The sequence where the hill people save Joe from the Baldwins would play very differently if we hadn't already seen the eviction sequence. Some of its comic edge comes from seeing Hickey and Griggs denied *again* by an outside protector, and some of its importance to the story lies in comparing Joe's method of resistance to Sid's in the earlier eviction scene.

We moved scenes around in the editing to make the build to a release stronger and more organic. The scene of Sid loading his guns alone in his office was originally written for the night of Joe's near execution, but in the final movie it comes on the night before the shoot-out. The same exact scene, done in a single master shot, has a very different weight and feeling there. It's no longer a cutaway used only for mood and pacing but a real moment alone with Sid before he faces the doom he's been predict-

ing for so long. The further you get into the editing of the movie the harder it gets to move things around without upsetting the story's ecology. I think this is why last-minute studio cuts are so often obvious and damaging. For the sake of a few minutes' running time or a trend of coughing and squirming during the market test screenings, scenes are omitted or altered for reasons that don't relate to the story as a whole.

# Pace

Audience members vary widely in their attention spans, and five minutes without an explosion or a stabbing is an eternity for some. The movie-maker has to be aware of this but also has to maintain the proper pace for the specific story being told. Rhythms change over the years. Watch a silent movie and see how long the scenes are sustained after you've gotten the point three or four times. Movies took a leap forward in pace after ground-breakers like Godard's *Breathless* introduced a kind of action shorthand to the screen, while rock videos and roller coaster action movies like *Raiders of the Lost Ark* may be a sign that audience rhythm is clicking into an even higher gear. For *Matewan*, however, we wanted the movie to reflect the pace of the time and the people. Coal-country people are rarely fast talkers. Ask a question and they'll think about it a bit before their mouths start running, a refreshing change if you're used to working in New York or L.A. There is a quiet, dry sense of humor hidden in their talk that takes a moment to recognize. The pace of coal-mining life in 1920 was that of relentless hard work, steady and grinding, punctuated by the sudden violence of mine accidents or armed conflict. In cutting *Matewan* we let most of the dialogue stand as it was played, rarely compressing or overlapping it to speed things up. We used the natural cycle of day to night to give the movie a more organic pace, often adding fades to black to end the night scenes. We rarely cut out the natural silences in the middle of scenes, keeping the reticence of the mountain people, their lack of glibness. All this helped to counter the snowballing effect of packing so many scenes and so much plot into one movie. Though never as stately and "large" as a David Lean kind of epic like *Dr. Zhivago*, *Matewan* does have some of the pace of a long, sad mountain ballad, a song of fate and revenge and transcendence.

# Trial and Error

On *Matewan* I worked with editor Sonya Polonsky, who had also cut *Baby, It's You* with me. The form of this collaboration is like the one between director and actor. With an actor you discuss what the scene is

about and how you want to approach it, then the actor goes out and does a take. You discuss the results, ask for some changes, and the actor goes out again. Take Two. Very often the process with Sonya is like that, a series of refinements and discussions of a scene. The editing is the final draft of a movie, the version where things either work or they don't. No matter how carefully you plan and how closely you stick to the script in shooting, scenes have a different impact when you start cutting them together. An actor can say the same lines and evoke a different feeling on each take and an editor can use the same footage and cut it into extremely different scenes. The important thing is the through-line. What is the story we're trying to tell and how do we tell it best?

On some scenes I'd have very fixed, specific ideas and pick exact takes and cutting points for Sonya to try or, when time was a factor, make a first-draft cut myself. On other scenes the directions were more general, maybe a few preferred acting moments to work in, a word or two about pace or mood, and I'd wait to see what she came up with. The director's hope in working with an editor is that when you have specific ideas the editor will make them work exactly the way you want or better, and when your ideas are more general the editor will build something you'd never have thought of yourself but that works just the same.

## Process

On a movie with a budget ceiling like *Matewan* there is a lot of time pressure. Each day you rent the cutting room and equipment, each day you hire the editing crew, adds to the cost of the picture. Because the basic technique of editing is trial and error and this takes time, you have to establish priorities, you have to put deadlines on decisions. Having a lot of coverage of a scene opens up a lot of possibilities for cutting, but this can be a liability. The more angles, the more takes, the more screening time to view the footage, the more possible permutations, the more incentive to linger on a single scene. On our budget we couldn't afford to shoot a huge block of footage and carve it into a tiny, well-formed statue of a story. Neither could we take the finite amount of footage we did have and speculate with it endlessly, hoping the perfect cut would reveal itself. We started with the script, trying to cut each scene as written, and refined things from there. The script provides a basic structure to hang the editing around till you can build stronger supports, get rid of the deadwood. Once the script version of the scene was done we could go back to the core questions — What is this scene about? What should the audience learn or feel when they see it? How does it relate to the central questions of the story? To the structure of the section?

Rather than doing an "assembly," laying loosely cut scenes end to end, I prefer to cut each scene pretty tight as we go along, giving it its full day in court before deciding to cut it down or cut it out.* The opening sequence of Sephus working at the coal face and Danny bringing word through the mine began to change almost immediately. Because of the difficulties of shooting underground and the time pressures we were under the days we were in there, some shots hadn't been gotten, some didn't work at all and some worked to a different effect than planned. So we went back to the basic purpose of the sequence. We wanted the audience to spend some time underground, to get just a taste of the work and conditions the men were striking about. We wanted some sense of urgency, of something about to happen, as Danny ran through the mine. We wanted the exposition that the company had just lowered wages and the miners were about to do something about it.

By intercutting the shots of Danny running with those of Sephus working we got some sense of urgency, and a few cutaways to the burning fuse increased this. The shots of Sephus were essentially nondramatic, documentary coverage of him picking an undercut into the coal face, drilling a shot hole, loading the shot and lighting a fuse. We wanted these to have a sense of real time without taking up too much real time, without lulling the audience too much at the very beginning of the movie. When we got to the point where the shots couldn't get any shorter without losing their weight, they still seemed to drag a little on the cutaways to Danny's run. We decided to move some of the opening credits from the black space preceding Sephus's first appearance and put them over the sequence itself. A credit over a shot can tend to speed it up a bit, splitting your attention and giving the visual information less time to register. Tibor Kalman, who designed our titles, tried to keep them visually "quiet" so they wouldn't overwhelm the shots. We placed them where the audience could ignore them if they wanted or read them if they were interested, and where they wouldn't block the on-screen action.

Having an editor on location as you're shooting is a nice luxury if you can afford it. As the production went on and the schedule tightened with reshoots and bumped scenes, I had less and less time and energy to see dailies every night. An important part of Sonya's job was to watch the footage as it came back from the lab and warn me when the coverage of a sequence seemed inadequate or off the mark. Akira Kurosawa allegedly stays up after a day's shooting and cuts yesterday's footage together, and

---

* To cut a scene "tight" or to "fine cut" it is to cut it with the detail and pace you'll want in the final version. An "assembly" is a much less detailed combining of scenes, sometimes only cutting together all the master shots in sequence to get a feel for the overall flow of the story.

all I can guess is that he's transcended the need for sleep. By week two I was missing dailies half the time in order to prep for the next day's shooting and get a few hours of rest before going to the set again. So I concentrated on sequences we thought had possible acting and editing problems. We'd talk, Sonya would do a rough cut and we'd either relax about it or schedule some reshoots. On this picture there was no going back to West Virginia for a couple pickup shots after we wrapped, we either got it in the weeks allotted or we didn't get it at all.

As the editing evolved we saw that the strength of the characters was able to carry some of the burden usually carried by cutting alone. The performances were so good, so fully inhabited, that we didn't have to do as much cutting away to check in with principal characters as is usual. We could "lose" a character for longer periods of time and be confident the audience would still be in synch with him when he reappeared. Will Oldham's acting ability as Danny allowed us to cut down on his watching-from-the-sidelines close-ups. We just had to establish him on the premises and let the audience's identification with him take it from there. In a movie with lots of important characters this was a big help, smoothing the flow of the cutting in mass confrontation scenes.

As a screenwriter you often try to enter a scene as late as possible in the course of its unfolding and let the viewer figure out what went before from its context. In the editing you try to cut even closer to the bone. The accumulation and juxtaposition of scenes and images build an enormous stock of context, and you find you need less and less dialogue and visual exposition to get the point across as the story progresses. Though we've never seen the stairwell at Elma's boarding house or the interior of Hickey's room before, we know right where we are when we cut to Danny walking up and in carrying a pile of sheets, because of the associations that have built up between Danny, Hickey and Griggs and the boarding house. We were able to cut scenes in half, to trim them at beginning and end and lose some altogether, tightening so that the incidences of real time and frozen moments of tension that were left would stand out more, have greater impact. You're always looking for a balance between getting to the point and letting the scene breathe a little, giving the characters some space.

## Parallel Action

Ideally, parallel action serves several purposes. You can skip lots of the legwork of a scene by cutting away, then cutting back for the next important development. The TV series *Mission: Impossible* always ended with an extended parallel action sequence, with each of the members of

the team making contributions to the scam of the week in separate places but closely synchronized with the others. We never watched the electronics expert do all his wiring work, only the part where he tensely screwed the two connectors together to trigger an important mechanism at the last possible moment. In movie time a cutaway can represent an hour later or seconds later, and parallel action gives you a lot of possibilities with time. A complex plot and lots of characters can be fit into a short format, soap operas being the most extreme example of this. Parallel action can help you build tension when two events are related to each other, when things are coming together. If you have someone in a car crossing the railroad tracks and all of a sudden a train comes along and smashes into them it might be shocking, but it's less suspenseful than if you cut back and forth between the approaching train and the stalled car a few times. The danger in parallel action is that it can get too complex, it can cut off the flow of the movie and lose the audience. In *Matewan* we condensed some of the parallel action in the editing and left some as written. In the script the cross-cutting of Joe's first night out was —

1. Joe at C.E.'s restaurant — miners air grievances
2. Hardshell church — Few peeks in window, preacher works the congregation up
3. Main Street — Few walks past Sid Hatfield
4. C.E.'s — miners air grievances
5. Church — Hardshell preacher turns on Danny
6. C.E.'s — Few arrives, Joe gives his unity speech
7. Church — Danny starts his sermon
8. Exterior coal camp — Joe and Sephus hide, watching guard pass exterior of Fausto's house, start in
9. Church — Danny continues his sermon
10. Exterior coal camp — picker and fiddler try to play with distant mandolin, hear harmonica player
11. Black section of coal camp — harmonica player plays as guard passes, Few tells Tom that Joe is coming to talk union
12. Church — Danny continues sermon
13. Interior Fausto's house — Joe explains union to the Italians
14. Church — Danny finishes his sermon, is chased by the preacher
15. Exterior Elma's house — Joe meets Sid on the steps

The original intent was to have the parallel action tie the locations together geographically (Few peeking in the church, walking through town, ending at the restaurant) and to compare the three main speakers — Joe, Hardshell and Danny. When we cut all the scenes together the amount of cross-cutting was disorienting and the shorter cutaways didn't

have time to make their points before they were gone. We shifted and combined scenes, trying to give the night a more definite shape. I had written dialogue extensions that connected the various sections of Danny's sermon, so we weren't limited in where we could cut in and out of it. The configuration in the final cut was this —

1. C.E.'s — miners air grievances
2. Church — Hardshell preacher works up the congregation, then turns on Danny
3. Main Street — Few walks past Sid
4. C.E.'s — miners air grievances, Few arrives, Joe makes his unity speech
5. Church — Danny begins his sermon
6. Coal camp — a guard passes outside Fausto's house, Joe explains union to the Italians inside, the guard passes in the opposite direction
7. Exterior coal camp — the picker and fiddler play with the mandolin, hear the harmonica
8. Exterior black section of camp — harmonica player plays as the guard passes, Few tells Tom that Joe is coming to talk
9. Church — Danny finishes sermon, is chased by Hardshell
10. Elma's — Joe meets Sid on the steps

There is still parallel action but it has been compressed. Danny's sermon is now in two pieces rather than four. Few Clothes doesn't peek in the window and Joe and Sephus no longer talk in hiding outside Fausto's house. The geography of buildings is replaced by a racial and ethnic geography — we are either in native, black or Italian territory and company men with guns are patrolling the boundaries between them.

In a later parallel-action sequence, Joe's near execution, we made only minor changes in scene order. We did pull out a cutaway to Bridey Mae crying and one of Sephus running in the woods and moved a scene with Sid loading his guns to later in the picture. This left us with Joe and Few at the campfire and Danny with the miners in church, simplifying the cross-cutting between them. The cutting in the scenes between Joe and Few is fairly leisurely. Since both we and Few know that Joe is supposed to be killed, it gives an undercurrent of tension and a certain amount of resonance to everything Joe says precisely because he is unaware of what is going on. As Joe keeps talking he is helping to save his own life without even knowing it, and we have time to see Few wrestle with his conscience. Down in the church the rhythm is much quicker, since Danny knows he is racing against time.

# Sound Editing

WHEN THE picture editing is down to the fine-tuning stages the sound editing begins. Besides the foreground tasks of cleaning up dialogue and splitting it into separate tracks for the sound mix, there is a whole body of background tones and effects that have to be built up.

We shot the driftmouth confrontation in two long nights. Shots that are cut together in sequence were often taken hours apart or on a different night, and their background tones can be drastically different (in this case the number and pitch of the serenading crickets). Skip Lievsay and his sound editing crew separate and extend the background tones for each shot so they can be controlled in the mix. The mixer then has the ability to blend several different cricket tones into one that runs consistently for the length of the scene and can be turned up or down in volume. It can also be used as a musical element, getting louder or shriller as the tension mounts, backing off when it breaks.

Sound editing can greatly enhance the sense of three-dimensionality in a movie. Layers of sound with different perspectives help establish depth. In scenes at the tent camp we could add distant voices and work sounds to give a feeling of more people, more tents, more activity beyond what the eye could see or we could afford to put there. Sound can also help bridge separate scenes. When Bridey dictates a letter to her friend Luann the scene opens with dogs baying in the distance. The next scene opens with those dogs heard up close, having cornered the wounded Sephus by a tree, tying the two scenes together in time and space.

Sometimes sound can substitute for picture. The sound of the Baldwins' automobile is used several times as a signal of impending violence. We played the ambush scene in the woods in the shadows rather than

the bright patches (if you're a miner laying out to kill someone you tend to avoid light) and the whole scene leans heavily on sound — the car approaching, rifles cocking, gunshots ringing out, screamed cries and directions, men crashing through underbrush.

The conversations Sonya and I had with Skip were both general and specific. In reviewing a reel with him we might talk about giving a scene a "busy" or "sparse" quality of sound, but also talk about laying in a specific cough or chair creak. Skip and his assistants take things several steps further on their own, laying in coughs, creaks, birds, bugs, wind, water, crickets, clothes rustle, wherever they might be needed. These sounds are on separate tracks unmarried to anything else and available to use or not use in the final mix. In choosing these sounds Skip considers the psychological as well as the literal action of each scene. One scene might call for crows in the background, another for nightingales, though in neither case are the birds on screen.

## Sound Mix

The sound editing comes to fruition during the mix. Voices are equalized and given the proper perspective, background tones made level, effects added and smoothed over, music laid in. We worked with postproduction mixer Tom Fleischman, who had mixed both *Baby, It's You* and *The Brother from Another Planet* with us. Tom sits at a huge sound board in front of a screen on which the picture is shown in synch with all the various dialogue, effects and music tracks. Our suggestions to him are on the order of "Can you make it sound closer, or farther off, more echoey, louder, less strident, less sibilant?" and Tom knows from decibels and frequency and pitch and a half-dozen other variables and can treat each sound as it comes up.

The sequence of Joe's first night out organizing is a good example of the importance of the mix in telling the story. We start with a shot of a guard passing the exterior of Fausto's house. We hear his feet crunching on the railroad ballast, hear crickets in the woods and hear, not too far off, a mandolin playing an Italian melody. We cut to the inside of Fausto's house. We still hear the mandolin, though a bit muffled, helping us realize this is the interior of the exterior we just saw the guard pass. The characters begin to speak. In recording, the position of the microphone might have been off slightly or the character may have turned away from it, or he may have been sitting in the liveliest or deadest spot in the room. If his voice sounds too much different from the others in the scene it takes away from the flow, makes us aware of the machinery in the room just as the sound of the camera whirring might if we didn't mix

that out. The mixer can add or reduce volume, bass and treble, can limit or increase reverberation, can compress the range and reduce sibilance in a voice. Since the voices are split onto separate tracks the mixer can treat each differently, "equalizing" them to the audience's ear. If the camera noise, often unavoidable in a room with hard, flat walls, is still audible underneath the voices it can often be lessened or eliminated with a band-pass filter. Since the human voice ranges over several frequencies and most machine noise exists on a specific, narrow frequency, a filter that blocks only sound on that frequency will cancel out the machine and leave the voice relatively unchanged.

During the course of the scene in Fausto's house we can play with the volume of the mandolin. Human perception of sound is psychological as well as physical: a faucet can be dripping for weeks but we only hear it the night we can't get to sleep. When we first cut to Fausto's interior we leave the volume of the mandolin up a bit, reminding the audience it is just outside, then mix it down as the dialogue starts so it won't compete. At the end of the scene we can sneak it back up again to make the cut to outside smoother. Since we want to know what is being said in the room, this accomplishes what our brain would do given a bit more time — to gradually filter out the less essential sound information.

We cut outside to the guard passing in the opposite direction, still hearing the mandolin nearby. Then, in the distance, we hear a fiddle and guitar join in. We cut to a camp-house porch and there they are, the picker and fiddler trying to play along, and the mandolin is now distant. The sound overlap bridges the cut, leading us from one to the other, and gives us a sense of distance by the relative perspective of volume and echo. At the end of this shot a harmonica player chimes in from the distance, then we cut to the black section of the coal camp to see the player. As he plays on screen we can still faintly hear the mandolin he is listening to, as well as the tentative, distant notes of the picker and fiddler. Once again the cut is anticipated and the sense of distance conveyed. We cut to the inside of the house and can hear the harmonica outside, close but muffled, the minute the door closes behind Tom. The music throughout this sequence helps give a three-dimensional feeling to what we see, helps us feel like we are moving through space because we have a changing sound perspective as a reference.

The mixer makes the sound more organic to the picture by evening it out, giving it shape and perspective and removing the sense of camera and tape recorder. Each new sound presents another flock of decisions — volume, echo, perspective, whatever — that have to be worked out to give each moment its maximum impact.

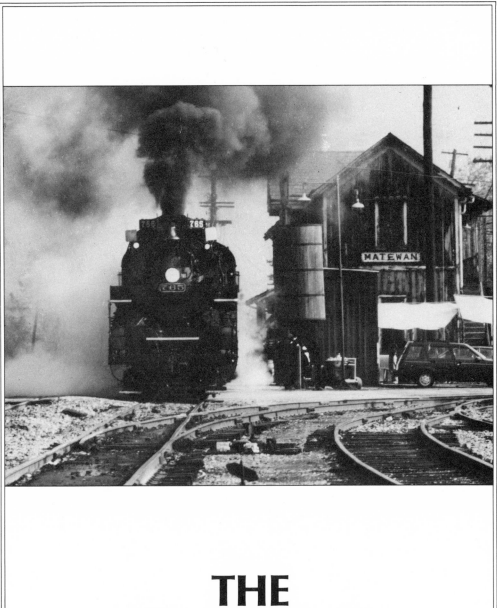

# THE
# BIG PICTURE

I'VE LEARNED when I write movies for other people to make that it's best not to visualize the ideal movie in my head after I hand in the script. This can only lead to disorientation and disappointment when you finally see the picture. You give it your best shot, wish them luck, and hope for the best. When I work on a movie as writer and director and control the cutting, the visualization is a constant process involving many people. The original idea may be very explicit but I know that it won't take its real shape until we've all done our work on it.

It's like there's this house you want to build and you know certain specifications you want, sometimes very specific, like the kitchen counter should be forty-five inches high, and others more vague, like the living room should be comfortable and, you know — have a lot of light or something. You raise a certain amount of money to build this house and maybe you draw a picture of it or tell somebody who can draw what to put down, and then you hire people who know about plumbing and wiring and roofing and windows and all that. You know you want the tub here and the sink here and maybe the plumber tells you it would work much better here and here and maybe you do it his way or maybe yours. When the house is finished you hope it feels like the one you imagined way back when, but of course the oak was too expensive and you had to go with yellow pine and they don't make kitchen counters that height and customizing was out of the question, but then the woman who put in the windows had this great idea, you never would have thought of it in a million years. The closet on the second floor is always going to be a problem and you try not to think about it when you think about the house. After a bit the house takes on its own character,

and though you had a lot to do with how it is, it exists as this *thing* and it's hard to imagine it any other way.

*Matewan* in script form was one thing, a potential for action, a story waiting to get told. During the shooting it was more amorphous, a thousand situations and relationships constantly changing that produced this half-cooked material on film stock. It was still mostly potential, but certain bridges were burned each day, certain forks in the road chosen. Other people's ideas began to pump into the story, characters got faces, names on a page became three-dimensional. During the editing, the material shot in production was collected and shaped, the story refined from it. Possibilities became choices, choices became inevitabilities. You can't imagine another actor playing a character, the four takes you have of a shot, the three angles you have of a scene, become finite worlds. The scene as written may no longer be possible given the footage you have, or it may no longer be desirable now that you've seen it played out. As you "lock" each reel of the picture it becomes a thing, with its own character that won't change anymore. If you stay away from the movie long enough you may even forget where you were standing when a certain shot was taken, may forget the trouble you had leveling the dolly track in the mud and the bees that attacked the catering table at lunch that day. Whole scenes that were shot and edited and finally cut from the movie seem to no longer exist, like a wall that once stood between your living room and hallway.

This book tries to be very rational about how a movie gets made and so leaves out a lot of what the process of making *Matewan* was about. You work that hard for that long with people and the production isn't just what you do for a living, it becomes your life, the people working with you become your community. The strangest and nicest thing during shooting was that even though all of us were neck-deep in the technical demands of making the movie, of creating the illusions that would eventually tell the story, the story would sometimes just pull us out of all that and make us pay attention and think about what had brought us all together. It might be a shot in dailies or the look of an extra when he walked down the tracks covered in coal dust or an actor really connecting with an emotion during a take or maybe just walking into the tent camp at night with the mist hanging low, but the movie was already asserting its character, letting us know what it was supposed to be, like it was out there all the time just waiting, waiting up in those hills for us to find it.

# Credits

FRONT CREDITS

CINECOM PICTURES AND FILM GALLERY PRESENT A RED DOG FILMS PRODUCTION

EXECUTIVE PRODUCERS
Amir Jacob Malin
Mark Balsam
Jerry Silva

ASSOCIATE PRODUCERS
Ira Deutchman
James Dudelson
Ned Kendall

Barbara Shapiro

CASTING
Mason Daring

MUSIC
Cynthia Flynt

COSTUME DESIGNER
Nora Chavooshian

PRODUCTION DESIGNER
Sonya Polonsky

EDITED BY
Haskell Wexler

DIRECTOR OF PHOTOGRAPHY
Peggy Rajski and
Maggie Renzi

PRODUCED BY
John Sayles

WRITTEN AND DIRECTED BY

(All credits listed above are single card.)

Chris Cooper as Joe

James Earl Jones as Few Clothes

Mary McDonnell as Elma

Will Oldham as Danny

David Strathairn as Sid

Ken Jenkins as Sephus

Gordon Clapp and Kevin Tighe as Griggs and Hickey

John Sayles as the Hardshell preacher

Bob Gunton as C.E.

Josh Mostel as Cabell

Nancy Mette as Bridey Mae

## THE REST OF THE CAST

| | |
|---|---|
| HILLARD ELKINS | Jace Alexander |
| FAUSTO | Joe Grifasi |
| MRS. ELKINS | Jo Henderson |
| LUDIE | Gary McCleery |
| ROSARIA | Maggie Renzi |
| TOM | Tom Wright |
| | |
| ELLIX | Michael Preston |
| TURLEY | Thomas A. Carlin |
| DOOLIN | Michael A. Mantel |
| LUANN | Jenni Cline |
| | |
| PAPPY'S VOICE | J.K. Kent Lilly |
| MRS. KNIGHTES | Ida Williams |
| TOLBERT | James Kizer |
| STENNIS | Ronnie Stapleton |
| GIANNI | Davide Ferrario |
| OLD MINER | Frank Payne Jr. |
| SINGER | Hazel Dickens |
| SHEB | Charles Haywood |
| ISAAC | Neale Clark |
| MISTER | Mitch Scott |
| MISSUS | Hazel Pearl |
| LEE FELTS | Michael Frasher |
| AL FELTS | Frank Hoyt Taylor |
| JAMES | Fred Decker |
| BASS | Bill Morris |
| CONDUCTOR | Delmas Lawhorn |
| BROKER | William Dean |
| BROKER | P. Michael Munsey |
| BOXCAR GUARD | Hal Phillips |
| REDNECK MINER | Stephen C. Hall |
| BLACK MINER | Percy Fruit |
| INJURED BLACK MINER | Thomas Poore |
| MINER'S WIFE | Tara Williams |
| FIDDLER | Gerald Milnes |
| PICKER | Mason Daring |
| MANDOLIN PLAYER | Jim Costa |
| HARMONICA PLAYER | Phil Wiggins |

## THE CREW

| | |
|---|---|
| PRODUCTION MANAGER | Peggy Rajski |
| ASSISTANT PRODUCTION MANAGER | Sarah Green |
| FIRST ASSISTANT DIRECTOR | Matia Karrell |
| SECOND ASSISTANT DIRECTOR | Benita Allen |
| | |
| AUDITOR | Barbara-Ann Stein |
| ASSISTANT AUDITOR | Robert Grindrod |
| | |
| ART DIRECTOR | Dan Bishop |
| SET DECORATORS | Anamarie Michnevich |
| | Leslie Pope |
| HEAD SET DRESSER | Leigh Kyle |
| SET DRESSER | Nancy Gilmore |
| SET DRESSER ASSISTANT | Daniel Boxer |
| SET DECORATOR ASSISTANT | Leigh Johnson |
| PROPERTY MASTER | Ann Edgeworth |
| PROPERTY ASSISTANT | Jem Cohen |
| CHARGEMAN SCENIC ARTIST | Roland Brooks |
| SCENIC ARTISTS | Pat McClinch |
| | Joel Ossenfort |

| | |
|---|---|
| CONSTRUCTION COORDINATOR | Tony Dunne |
| SET BUILDERS | William Lehne |
| | Ken Nelson |
| | Brent Haywood |
| CARPENTER | John Robinson |
| | |
| UNIT MANAGER | Diana Pokorny |
| LOCATION MANAGER | Paul Marcus |
| LOCATION ASSISTANT | Bob Bailey |
| | |
| KEY GRIP | Stefan Czapsky |
| GRIPS | Arthur Blum |
| | Robert Feldman |
| | Lee Shapira |
| GRIP ASSISTANTS | Clai Lashley |
| | Luke Latino |
| | Sean Garrett |
| | Erica Gelczis |
| GAFFER | Morris Flam |
| BEST BOY | Lynn Breschel |
| ELECTRICIANS | Robert Bruce |
| | Louisa Heyward |
| | |
| CAMERA OPERATOR | Mitch Dubin |
| FIRST ASSISTANT CAMERA | Scott Sakamoto |
| SECOND ASSISTANT CAMERA | Debbie Sarjeant |
| VIDEO ASSIST | Steve Apicella, Axis Video |
| STILLS | Bob Marshak |
| | |
| SOUND MIXER | John Sutton |
| BOOM | Lisa Schnall |
| | |
| SCRIPT | John Tintori |
| | |
| HAIR AND MAKEUP | James Sarzotti |
| HAIR AND MAKEUP CONSULTANT | David Halsey |
| ASSISTANT TO THE COSTUME DESIGNER | Susan Lyall |
| WARDROBE SUPERVISOR | Heidi Shulman |
| WARDROBE ASSISTANT | Lorna Scott |
| | |
| ADDITIONAL CASTING | Avy Kaufman |
| CASTING ASSISTANTS | Eve Battaglia |
| | Pam Flam |
| | Julie Hutchinson |
| | |
| ASSISTANT EDITOR | Geraldine Peroni |
| APPRENTICE EDITOR | David Leonard |
| SUPERVISING SOUND EDITOR | Skip Lievsav |
| SOUND EDITOR | Phil Stockton |
| ASSISTANT SOUND EDITORS | Marissa Littlefield |
| | Bruce Pross |
| | Christopher Weir |
| | |
| PRODUCTION OFFICE COORDINATOR | Cilista Eberle |
| ASSISTANT OFFICE COORDINATOR | Pat McCarthy |
| | |
| STUNT COORDINATOR | Edgard Mourino |
| STUNT PLAYERS | Danny Aiello III |
| | Lenny De Virgilio |
| | |
| SPECIAL EFFECTS COORDINATOR | Peter Kunz |
| SPECIAL EFFECTS | Shirley Belwood |
| | |
| | Russell Berg |
| | Todd Wolfeil |

| | |
|---|---|
| SECOND UNIT DIRECTOR OF PHOTOGRAPHY | Tom Sigel |
| SECOND UNIT COORDINATOR | Paul Marcus |
| SECOND UNIT ASSISTANT CAMERA | Claudia Bailey |
| DRIVERS | Sonny Adkins |
| | Roscoe Thomas |
| GENERATOR DRIVER | Mark Moore |
| CRAFT SERVICES | Sandy Cox |
| ART DEPARTMENT TROUBLE-SHOOTER | Howard J. Calvert Jr. |
| PROPERTY PRODUCTION ASSISTANT | Jeff Butcher |
| SET DRESSING PRODUCTION ASSISTANTS | Daniel Fisher |
| | Bill McKinney |
| | David Smith |
| | Nell Stokes |
| ART DEPARTMENT PRODUCTION ASSISTANTS | James Dean |
| | Chris Gibbin |
| | Archie Lambert |
| | Kim Parsons |
| | Almer Shuttle |
| OFFICE PRODUCTION ASSISTANTS | Beth Bernstein |
| | Libby Bika |
| SET PRODUCTION ASSISTANTS | Kevin Ball |
| | Rachel Bower |
| | Buddy Brewer |
| | Billy Chapman |
| | Greg Jacobs |
| | Ralph Renzi |
| | Brian Wenk |
| WARDROBE PRODUCTION ASSISTANTS | Gabriele Campbell |
| | Connie Lucas |
| | Holly Scarborough |
| INTERNS | Vince Gratzer |
| | Andrea Gustke |
| ITALIAN DIALOGUE COACH | Davide Ferrario |
| | Sara Malossini |
| PROMOTIONS | Gary Rosenblatt |
| PUBLICITY | STEVE SEIFERT ASSOCIATES |
| LEGAL COUNSEL | David Hollander |
| | John Sloss |
| CATERER | SEAFOOD HUT CATERING |
| TITLES | Tibor Kalman, M. & COMPANY |
| OPTICALS | EFX UNLIMITED, INC. |
| PROCESSING | DUART FILM LABORATORIES, INC. |
| EQUIPMENT SUPPLIED BY | PRODUCTION SERVICES ATLANTA |
| NEGATIVE CUTTER | J.G. FILMS, INC. |
| COMPLETION BOND | FILM FINANCES, INC. |
| SOUND MIX | TOM FLEISCHMAN, SOUND ONE, INC. |
| MUSIC ENGINEER | Leanne Unger |

# THE
# SHOOTING
# SCRIPT

## Reading the Script

A few abbreviations are used in the screenplay and are explained below. Scene numbers will sometimes repeat out of sequence. This is because the number indicates a shooting unit, rather than a merely sequential shot. A numbered scene has the same set, props and actors and is shot at the same time, though parts of it may be separated by other scenes in the final cut. Capitalization of names and other words is an aid to various departments in breaking the script down, helping them pick out pertinent elements more easily. The first time a character appears in the script, his or her name is capitalized, helping the production manager get a quick idea of the number of speaking parts in the movie. At times I capitalize just for emphasis, as in the *Batman* school of *BIFF, BAM* and *KAPOW!*

ABBREVIATIONS

| | |
|---|---|
| INT. | Interior |
| EXT. | Exterior |
| CU | Close-up |
| cont. | Continued |
| VO | Voice-over (voice on the track from a speaker outside of the story) |
| (off) | Off-screen speaker |
| POV | Point of view |

1     INT. COAL MINE - DAY - HEADLAMP BEAM

Blackness.  We SUPERIMPOSE the title --


                    MATEWAN


The title FADES and a HEADLAMP BEAM swings around into
the lens, then passes us.  We FOLLOW, the headlamp
becoming our eyes in the dark.  We FOLLOW as it scans
the floor, ribs and roof of a damp, narrow room.  The
roof is slate, dripping with condensation, supported
here and there by wooden posts, never more than four
and a half feet high.  The ribs are glossy black coal
carved by pick and shovel.  We FOLLOW the beam along
the tracks on the ground till they end.  The beam
TILTS ahead to illuminate a foot-deep puddle banked up
against the scored coal face that dead-ends the
tunnel.  We hear the labored BREATHING of the miner
who is wearing the headlamp as he comes up to the face
-- his lungs are in bad shape.  The headlamp studies
the puddle --


                    SEPHUS   (off)

          (softly)  Damn.


We hear the puddle RIPPLING as the man kneels in it.
The beam focuses on the base of the coal face where it
disappears into water.  WHACK!  A pick swings into
frame, taking a chunk out of the face.  Water
SPLASHES.  WHACK!  WHACK!  In the light that bounces
off the face from his lamp we see SEPHUS PURCELL, a
grizzled miner in his forties, grimly hacking at the
face with his pick as he kneels in the puddle, black
water spattering his face and body with every swing --


2     INT. COAL MINE - DAY - ANOTHER ROOM

BLACKNESS again at first, then we hear PANTING then
DANNY RADNOR, a trapper boy of fourteen, pops into
CLOSE-UP right in front of us, breathing hard,
excited.  He looks around, then puts his fingers in
his mouth and WHISTLES a code.  A HEADLAMP BEAM
appears from around a corner far in the BACKGROUND,
the WHISTLE answered.  Danny hurries toward it --


                    1

1     cont.  SEPHUS'S ROOM

We PAN from where a long drill is turning in the coal
face (lit by a headlamp) along the shaft to Sephus,
bracing it with his shoulder --


3     INT. COAL MINE - DAY - ANOTHER ROOM - GONDOLA
      CAR - STENNIS

STENNIS stoops to lift chunks of blasted coat with his
shovel and heave them over the side of a gondola car
parked at the edge of the track in his room.  There is
hardly space to fit the shovel --

      CU STENNIS

He heaves another couple shovels full.  A hand grabs
hold of the shovel to stop him.  We WIDEN to include
Danny, who stretches up to whisper furtively in
Stennis's ear --


1     cont.  SEPHUS'S ROOM

Sephus takes a squib of black powder with a long fuse
and tamps it into the hole he's drilled, using a long
iron rod --


4     INT. COAL MINE - DAY - MAIN HALLWAY - MULE

A litter wider and higher than the other rooms, the
roof strung with electric lightbulbs every twenty
feet.  We START on the face of a stationary MULE, then
PAN back to see the skinner, TOLBERT, leaning down
from the seat of his gondola car getting the final
whisper from Danny.  Danny runs AWAY FROM CAM, and
Tolbert, troubled, clicks to the mule and snaps the
reins --


1     cont.  SEPHUS'S ROOM - CU MATCH

Struck, flaming, then brought down to ignite the end
of a short fuse that leads into a hole bored into a
coal face.  It SIZZLES --

1     cont.  CU SEPHUS

Sephus looks both ways, lamp arcing through darkness,
as he hollers --


                         SEPHUS

          Shootin coal!  Shootin coal!


5     MINE SHAFT

Sephus's headlamp bobs toward us as he walks calmly
from the face.  He crouches at the base of a pillar,
back to the face.  We hear the fuse SIZZLING.  We hear
WATER DRIPPING.  We hear someone RUNNING away from the
face.  Danny trots up and slides down, startling
Sephus.  His teeth shine white from his coal-blackened
face as he grins --


                         SEPHUS

          Danny, what in God's name you doin?  I
          got a shot set up back there!


                         DANNY

          The word come down from Turley.


                         SEPHUS

          Tonnage rate?


                         DANNY

          They brung it down to ninety cent a ton.


                         SEPHUS

          Down?


                              3

5     cont.

                    DANNY

          They got them dagoes holdin fast in
          Number Three -- he says take it or leave
          it.


Sephus looks angry and weary --


                    DANNY

          Sephus?  What we gonna do?


Sephus spits a stream of tobacco juice into the
puddle --


1     cont.  CU FUSE

Sizzling a fraction of an inch from the face, then
disappearing inside -- KABOOM!!!  There is an enormous
EXPLOSION --


A6    INT. COAL MINE - DAY

MUSIC BEGINS as we ride toward the light at the end of
the tunnel, the RATTLE of the gondola car beneath us.
The VOICE of an old man, PAPPY, begins to reminisce --


                    PAPPY (VO)

          Hit were 1920 in the southwest field and
          things was tough.  The miners was trying
          to bring in the union to West Virginia
          and the coal operators and their gun
          thugs was set on keepin em out.  Them
          was hand-loading days -- they paid you
          by the ton and they didn't care no more
          for a man than they done for a draft
          mule.


4

A6    cont.

We blast out into the burning white light of a sunny
day --


6     MINERS' FACES

Smeared with coal dust.  They shield their eyes from
the light --


                    PAPPY (VO, cont.)

               Them was hard people, your coal miners
               then, they wudn't nobody you wanted to
               cross.


We PAN over to the side of the driftmouth where a pair
of mine guards man a sandbagged machine gun.  They are
shocked to see the miners coming out --


                    PAPPY (VO, cont.)

               So push come to shove and pretty soon we
               had us a war down there --


7     EXT. DRIFTMOUTH - DAY - SHIFT BOARD

Miners' hands switch their name tags from the IN
column to the OUT column as they file past --


                    PAPPY (VO, cont.)

               -- in Mingo County, which in them days
               were known as "Bloody Mingo."


8     EXT. DIRT ROAD - DAY

Looking down a steep hill, the coal tipple silhouetted
against the sky at the top of it.  Clusters of miners

8     cont.

pass by us on their way down.  Danny brings up the
rear, smiling --


                    PAPPY (VO, cont.)

               And that's where it all come to a head,
               there on the Tug Fork, in the town of
               Matewan.


9     EXT. BRIDEY'S CABIN - DAY

A VOCAL BEGINS in the MUSIC, a haunting mountain
ballad.  Miners trudge past a tiny shack built on the
side of the steep, wooded pathway.  We PAN to BRIDEY
MAE, a pretty woman in her early thirties, standing on
her porch wondering why the men are out --


10    EXT. MAIN ST. - DAY

We look up over the shoulder of the town's mayor,
CABELL TESTERMAN, as he watches the miners winding
down the hill in the distance.  He looks at his watch,
worried --


11    EXT. RAILROAD YARD - DAY

The miners cross through a maze of coal cars on side
tracks, some empty, some brimming with coal.  A MINE
GUARD steps into the shot in the foreground, realizes
what's up and runs off past camera --


12    EXT. COMPANY STORE - DAY

MINERS' WIVES step out of the company store as the men
file past, followed by the STORE MANAGER and the guard
we just saw.  The manager hangs a CLOSED sign on the
door and locks it behind him, looking grim.  We PAN as
the men pass to a CU of SID HATFIELD in the
foreground.  Sid is the chief of police, his badge
glinting in the afternoon sun.  He looks grim too --


                         6

13   EXT. ITALIAN CAMP, STREET - DAY

The miners, fewer of them now, walk past the wives and
children of the Italian miners who have stayed on the
job.  The women and kids stand on their porches
staring, dressed in what will soon be rags, scared.
We HOLD on ROSARIA MAGGDINO, who hugs her two little
children closer to her as one of the passing miners
glares in her direction --


14   EXT. BOARDING HOUSE - DAY - ELMA

ELMA RADNOR, a strong-looking woman in her thirties,
stands at the bottom step of her boarding house porch
as the miners go by.  Danny, her son, comes and stands
grinning before her as the SONG ENDS --


                    DANNY

          We done it, Ma.  We're gonna have the
          union.


15   EXT. RAILROAD TRACKS - DAY

The WHEELS of a steam engine rush past us --


16   INT. PASSENGER CAR - DAY

JOE KENEHAN sits by a window, steep-sided hills
flashing by him.  He is in his mid to late twenties,
good-looking, and seems nervous as he hears the two
COAL BROKERS sitting in front of him --


                    BROKER 1

          Hooper there, what runs the Stone
          Mountain store, he says they got more
          ordnance floatin around the country than
          people know what to do with --


7

                    BROKER 2

          Hit's the Boleshevists is what.  Some a
          these fellas went over to the war there
          and they come back Red.  Hit's like a
          disease, hit just spreads --


A CONDUCTOR passes by Joe as the train slows to a
halt --


                    CONDUCTOR

          Just gonna stop for a little repair,
          here.  Sorry for the inconvenience.


                    BROKER 1

          They shipped in all kinds of Italians,
          right off the boat, so they still
          bringing coal outa there --


                    BROKER 2

          I'd hate to get a whiff a that mine
          shaft.


The two laugh.  The train stops, and Joe, suspicious,
gets up.  We FOLLOW to the door.  He opens and looks
out --


17    EXT. TRAIN - DAY - JOE'S POV

The conductor stands two cars down with a pair of coal
company GUARDS, unlocking the door of a boxcar --

17   cont.

BOXCAR

The conductor heaves and the door slides open.  A
group of young BLACK MEN peer out, apprehensive --


                    GUARD

          Step on down here, gennlemen.  This
          here's your new home.


The men begin to hop down from the car.  They are
poorly dressed, hungry-looking, straw from the boxcar
floor sticking to their clothes.  Some carry bundles,
others are empty-handed.  The guards start to form
them into a double row for marching --


     FEW CLOTHES

A hugh man, chest bare under a tattered vest, looks
around warily.  He and Joe lock eyes for a moment,
both suspicious, then break off --


                    FEW

          Why aint we stoppin in town?


                    GUARD

          Just get in line.


Few moves to join the others when -- WHACK!  A rock
whizzes past his head and smashes against the boxcar.
A VOICE hollers from the trees --


                    VOICE

          Goddam scabbin sonsabitches!

17    cont.

The guards step forward and are immediately pelted by
rocks from the woods.  Miners dash out from under the
train behind them, grabbing for their guns, then
others stream out of the trees to attack the black
men.  The miners carry tree limbs and baseball bats
while the black men have only their fists and rocks
from the railway bed.  The conductor races to Joe's
door, leaps up past him and yells to the engineer --


                    CONDUCTOR

          Let's move it!


The train chugs into motion.  Joe looks out as Few
Clothes is running toward him, pursued by two miners
with clubs.  He pivots and rolls, cutting one down
with a cross-body block, then springs up to
clothesline the other with a massive arm.  The train
pulls away, leaving the battling men on the tracks
behind it --


18    INT. PASSENGER CAR - DAY - JOE

Steps back inside to look at the conductor, who is
scared and breathless --


                    JOE

          When do we get to Matewan?


                    CONDUCTOR

          You don't want to get off there, Mister.
          It aint nothing but crazy people.


19    EXT. TRAIN STATION - DAY

Joe stands alone, the only passenger to get off.  He
looks around.  Bridey Mae sits on a bench, waiting.
She smiles at Joe --


                        10

                         BRIDEY MAE

Hi.


                              JOE

Hi.


                    BRIDEY

Everybody was here, then they got word
and gone up the line a ways.  Some kinda
union business.


                         JOE

I saw.


                    BRIDEY

You'd best steer clear of it.  (smiles)
My name's Bridey Mae Tolliver.


                         JOE

Joe Kenehan.  You know Radnor's boarding
house?


                    BRIDEY

Big white house on past the coal dock.
(points)  She's a real sourpuss though,
Elma Radnor.


                         JOE

Thank you.


                         11

                         BRIDEY

          You gonna be in town long?


                           JOE

          It depends.


                         BRIDEY

          Well, you just don't take sides.
          People's all excited.


                           JOE

          (smiles)  Oh, I never take sides.  See
          you around.


                         BRIDEY

          I hope so.


Joe takes his bag and heads into town.  Bridey watches
him go --


20    EXT. MAIN STREET - DAY - JOE

Looking around as he walks --


     HILLS, TOWN - JOE'S POV

Beautiful steep-sided wooded hills under a morning
mist.  The coal tipple stands against the sky at the
far end of town.  The main street is parallel to the
railroad tracks, which is parallel to the river.  The
buildings are square, simple brick and wood --

21   EXT. BOARDING HOUSE - DAY

Elma sullenly sweeps dirt off the front porch as Joe
approaches --

                         JOE

          Mrs. Radnor?


                         ELMA

          Yuh?


                         JOE

          My name's Joe Kenehan and I'm gonna be
          in town a bit, and your place here was
          recommended --


                         ELMA

          (suspicious)  What do you do?


                         JOE

          Oh -- I guess I'm lookin for work --


                         ELMA

          You with the compny?


                         JOE

          The company?

21    cont.

ELMA

          You aint with the compny there aint no
          work.  Lookit, Mister, don't act the
          lamb with me -- what's your business
          here?


Danny rushes up leading Hillard, whose nose is mashed
and bleeding --


                             DANNY

          Mama!  Mama!  It's Hillard!  They bust
          his nose!


They arrive, Danny breathless, blood pouring down
Hillard's face onto his chest --


                             DANNY

          Them scabs done it, Mama!  Up the line a
          mile.  They was all colored this time
          and they bust Hillard's nose!


                             ELMA

          I aint a doctor, Danny, I don't know
          what I can do --


                             JOE

          You got any ice?


                             ELMA

          Ice?  What --


                               14

                    DANNY

Moreland brung some this mornin, the
milk is settin in it --


                    JOE

You fetch me two chunks, bout this big,
and a piece of rag --


                    DANNY

(running off)  Sure thing --


                    ELMA

You a doctor?


                    JOE

I seen my share of broken noses.  (to
Hillard)  You just point it up in the
air, buddy, like you're watchin the
clouds.  We'll get that bleedin stopped.


                    HILLARD

(gagging) I ga my liggid --


                    JOE

Say what?


                    ELMA

(bitter)  He said he got his licks in.
Seems to be all the men around here care

                           ELMA (cont.)

            about.  Wives and kids is starvin but as
            long as they get their licks in --


                           JOE

            It's just frustration, is all.  When
            you can't take care of them you care
            about --


                           ELMA

            (softening)  I know.  It aint their
            fault.

Danny hurries back with the ice and rag --


                           DANNY

            Here you go.


Joe wraps one chunk in the rag and holds it to the
back of Hillard's skull.  He presses the other lightly
against his lip --


                           JOE

            This freezes up all them little veins in
            their, so's they close up and don't let
            any more blood out.


                           DANNY

            You a doctor?

                    JOE

          (looks to Elma)  Nope.  Just a guy
          looking for a place to stay.


                    ELMA

          (grudging)  Five dollars a week, cash.
          That includes dinner and clean sheets.
          Hope I'm not making a mistake.


                    JOE

     Name's Joe Kenehan.


He smiles and offers his hand to her.  Elma shakes,
then looks at the blood Joe has left on her hand.


22    INT. SUPPLY ROOM - DAY - CU TOM

TOM, one of the blacks from the train fight, pulls
away a piece of rag that he's wrapped around his fist
to examine his scraped knuckles.  In the background we
hear the voice of TURLEY, the mine manager, droning
on --


                    TURLEY

          These picks and shovels are to be
          considered a loan from the Stone
          Mountain Coal Company -- their cost will
          be deducted from your first month's pay.


Tom looks over and we do a short PAN with his gaze to
a CU of Few Clothes.  He gives TOM a "here it comes"
look--

22     cont.

                         TURLEY

              Tool-sharpening provided by the company,
              twenty-five cents a month --


The black miners pass picks and shovels to each other
as Turley wearily walks among them, giving them the
run-down --


                         TURLEY

                   --use of the wash house, seventy-five
                   cents a month, medical doctor provided
                   by the company, two dollars a month,
                   special procedures extra.  Your train
                   ride here, provided by the company, will
                   be deducted from your first pay at the
                   end of the month --


The men begin to look to Few Clothes, alarmed at the
mounting costs of being allowed to dig coal --


                         TURLEY

                   Your pay will be issued in company
                   scrip, redeemable for goods and services
                   at the Stone Mountain company store.
                   Purchase of items available at the
                   company store from outside merchants
                   will result in firing without pay --


                         FEW

                   What's to keep y'all from jackin up them
                   prices in your store?


Turley looks at Few drily for a moment --

22    cont.

                    TURLEY

          Name?


                    FEW

          Johnson, They call me Few Clothes.


Turley nods and continues his drone --


                    TURLEY

          Powder, fuses, lamps, headgear and
          appropriate clothing are all available
          at the company store and Stone Mountain
          will generously advance you one month's
          supply of these items, payment to be
          deducted.  I'm going to take you over to
          the camp where you'll be living --
          there's some Italian gentlemen who are
          very eager to meet you --


He steps out the door to lead them, still spouting --


                    TURLEY

          Rental for a single room is two-fifty a
          month, company rule no more than two to
          a room including children.  Electricity
          for those units so equipped is one
          dollar a month, coal for heating --


23    INT. ELMA'S DINING ROOM - NIGHT

Cornbread, navy beans, greens, ham and a pitcher of
milk.  Joe sits with Elma, Danny and a very old woman,
MRS. KNIGHTES.  Danny is very taken with Joe --

                    JOE

Oh-- mostly I worked for the railroads
laying track.  Kansas, Missouri -- went
out west for a bit, worked in a lumber
camp.  Little a whatever pays an honest
dollar.


                  DANNY

(proudly)  I'm a coal miner.  Least till
we come out I was.  Had me over in
Section Three.  I was a trapper boy.


                    JOE

Aren't you a little young?


                  DANNY

I'm omost fourteen.  There's some in
there younger'n me.  Course with the
strike now, I mostly work on runnin this
place.


                  ELMA

(teasing)  I help a little, don't I?


                  DANNY

Hit's gonna be a long one.  That
superintendant at Stone Mountain he said
he'd go broke afore he'd let one union
sumbitch so much as step into his coal
mines --


                    20

                    ELMA

        Danny --


                    DANNY

        Sorry, M'am.  But that's what he said.


                MRS. KNIGHTES

        Daniel's a preacher.


                    JOE

        That so?


                MRS. KNIGHTES

        He got the callin.  Boy his age --
        oughta hear him testify.


                    JOE

        What church you with?


                    DANNY

        Round here there's the Missionary folks,
        they's the Hardshell Baptists -- and
        then there's the Freewill folks, which
        is your Softshell Baptists.  Right now I
        preach for both.


There is a loud KNOCK on the door.  Danny runs to open
it --


                    21

23    cont.

                              MRS. KNIGHTES

                    Daniel's gonna preach tonight.  Over to
                    the Missionary.


                              JOE

                    I never been religious, myself --


                              DANNY

                    Hit's Sephus, Mama.


We MOVE the camera to see Sephus enter, looking
directly at Joe --


                              SEPHUS

                    Lo Elma.  Mrs. Knightes.


                              ELMA

                    Lo Sephus.


                              SEPHUS

                    I come to have a word with your new
                    boarder.  If he don't mind.


All look at Joe --

24    EXT. MAIN STREET - NIGHT

Joe and Sephus hug the shadows as they move down the
street trying not to be seen.  They cut into an
alleyway between a pair of buildings and we HOLD a
moment until once more Sid Hatfield steps into the
foreground of the shot in a CU, watching --

                              22

25    EXT. RESTAURANT - NIGHT

Sephus pulls Joe into the shadows behind a little
restaurant back porch.  He knocks a code onto the back
door and after a moment C.E. LIVELY steps out.   C.E.
is a thick-bodied man in his fifties who looks as
tough as Sephus.  He holds a gun under Joe's nose and
hardeyes him.  Joe hardeyes him back.  The men speak
softly ---


                    SEPHUS

          Says he's the fella the union promised
          us.


                    C.E.

          You prove it?


Joe reaches for ID but C.E. stops his hand --


                    C.E.

          Don't take nothin to have a card printed
          up.


                    JOE

          I guess you'll just have to trust me.


C.E. and Sephus scrutinize him silently for a
moment --


                    C.E.

          Who wrote The Iron Heel?


                    23

                        JOE

        Jack London.


                        SEPHUS

        Where's Joe Hill buried?


                        JOE

        All over the world.  They scattered his
        ashes.


                        C.E.

        Which eye is Big Bull Heywood missing?


Joe thinks for a moment, covers one of his eyes to
check --


                        JOE

        Left one.


                        SEPHUS

        How'd Frank Little die?


                        JOE

        Butte, Montana.  They hung him from a
        railroad trestle.


C.E. and Sephus exchange a look --

                    C.E.

        If you're a spy you know your stuff.


                    JOE

        I was with the Wobblies.


                    SEPHUS

        Me too.   Back when it meant something.


                    JOE

        (grins)   One Big Union.


                    C.E.

        Not around here, buddy.


C.E. puts the gun down and offers his hand, a tight
smile on his face --


                    C.E.

        C.E. Lively.   This is my restaurant.
        The fellas'r waitin --


26    INT. RESTAURANT - NIGHT

A man who has spent half his life underground stands
speaking in the dim-lit room --

26    cont.

                    OLD MINER

          They had us pullin pillars with the roof
          all working like it does right before it
          comes down?


     INT. C.E.'S - JOE

Flanked by Sephus and C.E., Joe faces an angry,
suspicious group of miners.  The room is lit only with
a few candles, windows draped in black cloth, Hillard
stationed by the front windows peeking out to see if
anyone is coming --


                    OLD MINER

          If you say "Nosir, I aint adyin in here"
          and you walk away the'll stick you down
          in some damn puddle with a two-foot seam
          an no air to breathe.  You can't mine no
          coal like that.  They just pushin a man
          where he can't go no further.


     STENNIS

Younger, angrier --


                    STENNIS

          The checkweighman he'll take fifty pound
          off your load for slate when there aint
          a pebble in it.  Hit's down in the
          bottom, he'll say, where there aint no
          lookin for it --


     LUDIE

Angrier still --

                         LUDIE

          Then they raise up the prices at the
          compny store the same damn week they
          lower the tonnage rate --


                         TOLBERT

          (off)  Any they still aint rock-dusted
          that damn hole --


27    EXT. MISSIONARY CHURCH - NIGHT

We FOLLOW as Few crawls through some bush, then makes
a dash to the side of a church building, crouching
below the window line, breathing hard.  We MOVE UP to
look through the lit window and see a HARDSHELL
PREACHER performing for his flock --


28    INT. CHURCH - NIGHT - HARDSHELL

Sweating, shouting, bringing it to his congregation --


                         HARDSHELL

          I'm talking about Je-sus!  Do you know
          His name?  Have you seen His glory?


          CONGREGATION

Not huge but very enthusiastic.  They are hooked into
the preacher, all but Danny, who sits calmly waiting
his turn --


                         HARDSHELL (off)

          Have you felt the warming comfort of His
          precious love?


                           27

28    cont.  HARDSHELL

A grim look on his face, he brings his voice down to a
near whisper, speaking as if the wrong somebody might
overhear --

                    HARDSHELL

          Listen to me now.  The Prince of
          Darkness is upon the land.
          He takes on many guises.
          He'll say he's your best friend.
          He'll say he's your Savior.


     DANNY

Listening, wondering where this will lead --


                    HARDSHELL (off)

          (whispers)  But he's come here to
          de<u>stroy</u>.


29    EXT. MAIN STREET - NIGHT

Few walking in the open now, down a sidewalk on the
main street, nervous.  Someone steps out in front of
the camera in the foreground, partially blocking the
shot with his back.  Few sees him, but keeps coming.
Few gives a nod as he passes, acting cool.  The man
turns to watch him go -- Sid Hatfield.


30    INT. RESTAURANT - NIGHT - TOLBERT

On his feet, flushed with anger and excitement --


                    TOLBERT

          The first thing we got to have is alla
          these niggers and alla these dagoes that

30    cont.

                    TOLBERT (cont.)

          come in here to take our jobs thrown
          outa the mines --


     JOE

Listening, not happy with this turn in the mood --


                    LUDIE (off)

          Mines, hell!  They got em in our <u>houses</u>!


     LUDIE


                    LUDIE

          They're sittin at our tables right now
          an sleepin in our beds while we're out
          livin under a piece of canvas at the
          back of the holler!


28    cont.  INT. CHURCH - NIGHT - HARDSHELL

The congregation totally with him now, ready for the
revelation --


                    HARDSHELL

          In the Bible his name is Beelzebub.
          Lord of the Flies.
          On earth today his name is <u>Bole</u>shevist!
          <u>Social</u>ist!
          <u>Comm</u>unist!
          <u>Un</u>ion man!


                         29

28    cont.

DANNY

Rage in his eyes --


                    HARDSHELL (off)

             Lord of Untruth!


HARDSHELL


                    HARDSHELL

             Sower of the evil seed!
             Enemy of all that is good and pure and
             this Creature walks among us!


30    cont.  INT. RESTAURANT - NIGHT

C.E. is up fanning the flames --


                      C.E.

             I been a union man my whole life and I
             know the story with these coal operators
             and their gun thugs!  The only thing
             they understand is the bad end of a
             bullet!


     JOE

Seeing that things are about to blow --


                    C.E. (off)

             And if we shown em we'd just as soon
             blow up their damn mines as see em


                         30

                    C.E. (off, cont.)

        worked by a bunch of scabs, then they're
        gonna <u>listen</u>.


    MINERS

Shouting agreement, forgetting the secrecy of the
meeting in their passion.  Suddenly --


                HILLARD (off)

        Someone's comin!


    HILLARD

Turning from his position at the window --


                HILLARD

        Hit's Ellix!  He got someone!


Hillard goes to the door, unlocks it, and opens it
quickly.  Few steps in, followed by ELLIX, a young
miner holding a sawed-off shotgun at his back --


    CU FEW

Trying to keep his cool as he faces the hostile
crowd --


    MINERS - FEW'S POV

Hard faces, violence in their eyes.  C.E. takes a step
forward --

30     cont.

                              C.E.

                    Where'd you find him?


         FEW, ELLIX


                              ELLIX

                    He come right up on the steps --


                              FEW

                    They tole me C.E. Lively's is where the
                    union men meets.


         ROOM

C.E. steps toward Few, the tight smile twisting his
face --


                              C.E.

         So?


                              FEW

                    I got bidness with the union.


                              C.E.

                    That so?   What's your name, son?


                              FEW

                    They calls me Few Clothes.


                              32

30   cont.

There is a snicker from the miners --

                         FEW

          I didn't come here lookin for no
          trouble.  A man get to eat --


                         TOLBERT

          So whynt you go eat back where you come
          from?


                         FEW

          They told us there was jobs here --


                         MINER (off)

          Go home, nigger!


                         ELLIX

          Goddam scab!


     FEW

He's had it with being careful --


                         FEW

               Watch you mouth, peckerwood!  I been
               called nigger and I can't help that, the
               way white fokes is, but I aint never
               been called no scab and I aint startin
               up now!  I go ton for ton loadin coal
               with any man here an when I do I spect
               the same dollar for the same work!


                         33

                    C.E.

          You get outa this holler alive, son,
          you'll be doin pretty good for yourself.


Few and C.E. stare at each other, tension at the
breaking point, when Joe calls from the back of the
room --


                    JOE

          Union men, my ass!


We PAN to see Joe as he takes stage for the first
time, wading into the midst of the miners, voice full
of fire --


                    JOE

          You want to be treated like men?
          You want to be treated fair?
          Well you aint men to that coal company,
          you're equipment, like a shovel or a
          gondola car or a hunk of wood brace.
          They'll use you till you wear out or you
          break down or you're buried under a
          slate fall and then they'll get a new
          one, and they don't care what color it
          is or where it comes from.


Joe moves among the men, looking into their faces --


                    JOE

          It doesn't matter how much coal you can
          load or how long your family's lived on
          this land -- if you stand alone you're
          just so much shit to those people!

30    cont.

Joe points to Few Clothes --


                    JOE

          You think this man is your enemy?   Huh?
          This is a <u>worker</u>!  Any union keeps this
          man out aint a union it's a goddam <u>club</u>!
          They got you fightin white against
          colored, native against foreign, hollow
          against hollow, when you <u>know</u> there aint
          but two sides in this world -- them that
          <u>work</u> and them that <u>don't</u>.  You work,
          <u>they</u> don't.  That's all you get to know
          about the enemy.


The miners are listening now, Joe focuses their
anger --


                    JOE

          And you say you've got guns.  Well I
          know you're all brave men and I know you
          could shoot it out with the company if
          you had to.  But the coal company don't
          want this union, the <u>state</u> government
          don't want it, the <u>federal</u> government
          don't want it and they're all of em just
          waitin for an excuse to come down and
          crush us to nothing!  You don't go
          shootin the solid if you can undermine
          the face, do you?  So we got to pick
          away at it, we got to plan it and prop
          it and keep an ear out for how it's
          working and we got to work together --
          <u>together</u> -- till they can't get their
          coal out of the ground without us cause
          we're a <u>union</u>, cause we're the <u>work</u>ers
          dammit and we take care of each other!


There is a silence.  Joe has them thinking, but
they're still wary of him --


                    35

                         LUDIE

        How can we shut the mines down if we
        don't dynamite em?


                          JOE

        The men walk out.  <u>All</u> of em.


                         C.E.

        Fat chance.


Joe looks at Few --


                          JOE

        And every man that walks out on his own
        steam we take into the union.


Joe looks to the men --


                          JOE

        That a deal?


     MINERS

We PAN across their faces.  This isn't an easy thing
for them to accept --


                        SEPHUS

        All the dagoes and all the colored?

30    cont.  ROOM

Joe deadpans the lot of them --


                    JOE

          That's what a union is, fellas.  Better
          get used to it.


31   INT. CHURCH - NIGHT

Danny stands at the head of the congregation, a
natural storyteller --


                    DANNY

          So this fella owns a vineyard goes out
          first thing one morning, an he hires
          some workers.  Says he'll give em a
          dollar for the day, which was decent
          wages in Biblical times.  Then he's at
          the marketplace an he sees some other
          fellas an he hires them an some more at
          noon an some at two an some at five --
          an every time hit's the same deal, a
          dollar for the day.


32   EXT. ITALIAN CAMP - NIGHT

A mine guard strolls sentrylike, rifle slung low,
above the Italian section of the coal camp.  We can
see a few lantern-lit porches below and hear MANDOLIN
MUSIC and Italian voices SINGING ALONG.  The guard
passes by and we TRACK IN as Joe and Sephus stick
their heads up from the brush where they've been
hiding --


                    SEPHUS

          They keep the dagoes sealed off from the
          rest of the camp.  Even have em working
          a different section of the mine.

32    cont.

                    JOE

          They got a leader?


                    SEPHUS

          Fella name of Fawsto somethin.   Tough
          little monkey.


31    cont.   INT. CHURCH - NIGHT - DANNY


                    DANNY

          Sun goes down an he send for his foreman
          and he says to go pay off the workers,
          startin with the fellas he picked up
          just an hour ago, and to pay ever one of
          them the same dollar a day.  Of course
          the fellas that went out first is roped
          off about this --


33    EXT. NATIVE'S CAMP - NIGHT

Two young mountain men, FIDDLER and PICKER, listen in
the shadows to the distant MANDOLIN MUSIC.  Picker
fingers a guitar, trying to match the chords to the
mandolin --


                    FIDDLER

          What is he playin?


                    PICKER

          Shhh.


A HARMONICA begins to PLAY from the other direction,
improvising bent notes around the Italian melody --

33    cont.

FIDDLER

Now who's that?


34    EXT. BLACK CAMP - NIGHT

We hear LAUGHTER, the HARMONICA playing, as a guard
strolls by the porch of a company house.  Tom sits
sprawled on the steps, smiling at him.  He nods to the
guard, who nods back.  When the guard is past, Tom
goes up the steps, past the harmonica player, and we
FOLLOW him into the house.  A group of black miners
cluster around Few Clothes on the floor, lit by a
single, low-flamed kerosene lantern --


TOM

Peckerwood's gone past.


FEW

(nods)  Union man be over in a few
minutes.


TOM

What we listenin to him for?


FEW

You want to walk back to Alabama?


31    cont. INT. CHURCH - NIGHT - DANNY


DANNY

So they get to agitatin, complaining so
loud that the owner come up an he says

39

31    cont.

                              DANNY (cont.)

                "Lookit, we dealt for a dollar an that's
                what you get an what I pay anybody else
                is none of you lookout.  So <u>there</u>."


35    INT. FAUSTO'S HOUSE - NIGHT - JOE

The interior lit by a sole kerosene lamp, Joe looks
around as he sits on a rickety wooden chair --


        INT. HOUSE - JOE'S POV

The coal camp houses are tiny wooden boxes, equipped
with a coal-burning grate for a stove, a cold-water
pump over a basin that doubles as the bathtub and a
few sticks of plain pine furniture.  We see into the
other room, a half-dozen pallets on the floor.  Four
small, ragged children stare up at Joe.  Sephus stands
by the door, uncomfortable.  GIANNI PALMA sits on a
crate with his wife, GEMMA, who holds an infant in her
arms.  At the little table sit Roasria, Gianni's
sister, and her husband, FAUSTO.  Fausto stares across
at Joe, all business --


                              JOE

                Now I know you people got it hard --
                comin to a new country, don't know the
                rules, don't know how things work --


                              SEPHUS

                They don't know shit from coal minin,
                that's for sure.  Been dyin like flies
                in that Number Three hole --


Joe stops him with a look --


                                  40

                         JOE

          But how it is, you don't have a whole
          lot of choice in this thing.


                       ROSARIA

          (Italian)  Fausto, what's he talking
          about?


                         JOE

          You know what a union is?


                        FAUSTO

          (nods)  Sindacato.


                       ROSARIA

          (reacting, worried)  Sindacato?


                         JOE

          Well, what the situation is --


                        FAUSTO

          We join the une, they shoot us.  We don'
          join the une, you shoot us.


Joe and Sephus exchange a look --


                         JOE

          That's one way of looking at it.

35    cont.

                    ROSARIA

          (Italian)  Fausto!   What does he want?


                    FAUSTO

          (Italian)  He wants us all to join the
          union.


                    ROSARIA

          (Italian, crossing herself)  Christ help
          us, the union!  Again with the union!


31    cont.   INT. CHURCH - NIGHT - DANNY

Finishing up the Gospel --


                    DANNY

          Now that's all that the Gospel story
          says, except for the moral that Jesus
          drew out of it.


     ELMA

Proud of her son as she watches --


                    DANNY

          And so Jesus says, "Thus it will be in
          the Kingdom of Heaven -- the first'll be
          last and the last'll be first."


     DANNY

31     cont.

                              DANNY

                Now it's clear from this parable that
                Jesus hadn't heard <u>noth</u>in about the
                union.


A rumble from the pews --


                              DANNY

                If He was walking the earth today an
                seen the situation we got with these
                coal operators He'd of changed His tune.


        HARDSHELL

Rising from his seat, incensed --


                              DANNY

                "A man deserveth an hourly wage,"  He'd
                say, "for though the pit be gassy and
                the face fulla slate a man still toileth
                by the sweat of his brow and want a
                better deal here on earth --"


        DANNY

Edging away from the platform, knowing he's about to
get the hook --


                              DANNY

                "--no matter what I got in store for him
                in the hereafter."  Praise Jesus!


                                43

31    cont.

He runs from the pulpit as the Hardshell minister
bears down on him --


                    MRS. KNIGHTES

          Praise Jesus!


36    EXT. BOARDING HOUSE - NIGHT

Joe is returning, just about to climb up Elma's steps,
when Sid Hatfield steps out above him.  Sid is wearing
his badge and has a gun slung on his hip --


                    SID

          Kenehan.


Joe looks at the badge, then steps up to face the
lawman --


                    SID

          Out kind of late, aren't you?


                    JOE

          I met some people.  We got to talkin.


                    SID

          Talkin.


                    JOE

          Yeah.  Who are you?


                         44

36    cont.

                            SID

            Name's Sid Hatfield.    I'm chief of
            police here.


                            JOE

            Oh.   Aint against the law to talk, is
            it?


                            SID

            Depends.


Sid steps out into the porch light so Joe can see his
eyes.   They are cold and hard --


                            SID

            I take care of my people.    You bring em
            trouble and you're a dead man.


Sid spits tobacco past Joe, then steps down past
him --


                            SID

            Sleep tight, Kenehan.


We HOLD on Joe as Sid strolls off into the night --


37    INT. RESTAURANT - NIGHT

Somebody is writing furtively by lamplight.   We make
out only the phrases "I'm sure he is a <u>Red</u>" and "Send
help immediately."   The note is folded so we can't see

                            45

37    cont.

the signature, then stuffed in an envelope.  We get a
glimpse of the address on the envelope --


          Baldwin-Felts Detective Agency
          Bluefield, W. Va.


38   EXT. TRAIN STATION - DAY

Two men, HICKEY and GRIGGS, have just stepped off the
train.  They look like killers.  Bridey Mae is in her
usual seat.  She smiles at them --


                    BRIDEY

          Hi.


                    HICKEY

               Lookit this, Griggsy, they got up a
               reception committee for us.  Watcher
               name, honey?


                    BRIDEY

          Bridey Mae.


He stoops to look into her eyes.  His voice is smooth
and menacing --


                    HICKEY

               You like to watch the trains come and
               go, Bridey Mae?


                         46

                    BRIDEY

          (shy)  Yeah.  And the people what come
          into town.


                    HICKEY

          There been a lot of new people come here
          lately?


                    BRIDEY

          A few.


                    GRIGGS

          Fella name Joe Kenehan show up?


                    BRIDEY

          (scared now)  Maybe -- I forget.


                    HICKEY

          (sighs, smiles)  You married, honey?


                    BRIDEY

          I was.  He got kilt in the mine.


                    HICKEY

          Awww.  That's too bad.  He got kilt in
          the mine, Griggsy.

38     cont.

                         GRIGGS

         It's a shame.


                         HICKEY

         Was your husband a union man when he was
         living?


                         BRIDEY

         No -- he said it wouldn't never take
         hold down here.


                         HICKEY

         Sounds like a smart fella.  (smiles)  I
         think you're real pretty, you know that,
         Bridey Mae?


                         BRIDEY

         Thank you.


                         HICKEY

         Int she pretty, Griggsy?  Best lookin
         mountain trash I seen in a long while.


Hickey grips her face in his hand, threatening --


                         HICKEY

         We'll see you around, honey.

38    cont.

He and Griggs start away, leaving Bridey in tears --


                    HICKEY

          Let's roll, Griggsy.  Sooner we get done
          with this shithole the better.


39    EXT. BOARDING HOUSE - DAY

Joe tries to talk to Elma as she briskly hangs wet
linen out to dry --


                    ELMA

          (impassive)  Hit took two days to dig
          through, an then when they brung them up
          you couldn't tell which was which.  They
          found blood on the walls from fellas
          trying to claw their way out.  Mrs.
          Elkins, Mrs. Mounts, Bridey Mae -- me --
          we all lost our men in that fire.  Danny
          were seven then.  Now he's back in the
          same hole.


                    JOE

How'd it start?


                    ELMA

The coal dust gets hanging in the air
down there, and there's a spark -- they
could spray the walls down but the
compny says that'd cost too much.


                    JOE

Was Sid Hatfield ever a miner?


                    49

                              ELMA

            Naw.  He don't like to be closed in,
            Sid.  He was always real friendly,
            Smilin Sid, and then the war come --
            Cabell Testerman got to be mayor and he
            made Sid chief of police.  Then the girl
            Cabell married -- well --


There is a pause --


                              ELMA

            I don't want you usin Danny on no crazy
            union business.


                              JOE

            A man has to stand up for what he
            believes.


                              ELMA

            Danny aint no man.  Look, Mister, you
            gonna be movin on.  Win or lose, you'll
            be walking outa this holler.  We got to
            stay here.


                              JOE

            I intend to leave a union when I go.


                              ELMA

            My husband used to talk union.  I see
            where it got him.

39    cont.

We hear Danny CALLING from the front.  Elma flops a
bundle of wet sheets into Joe's arms and exits frame.
Joe holds them a moment, then drops them into the
basket and starts after Elma --


40    EXT. BOARDING HOUSE - DAY

Elma faces Hickey and Griggs, blocking their way up
the steps as Danny looks on tensely --


                    GRIGGS

          I don't see where you got much say in
          the matter --


                    DANNY

          My mama says you can't stay here then
          you can't, that's all.


                    ELMA

          Keep outa this, Danny.  Look, I only got
          one room left --


                    HICKEY

          Then somebody's got to go, don't they?
          Let me see your register --


Joe arrives and watches for a moment --


                    ELMA

You aint seein nothin.


                         51

                         GRIGGS

          Lady, we're here as guests of the Stone
          Mountain Coal Company.  They <u>own</u> this
          house --


                         JOE

          (cheerful, steps past them)  <u>Good</u>
          mornin.  You fellas movin in?


                         GRIGGS

     Yeah.


                         ELMA

     No.


                         JOE

          Well you won't find a better night's
          sleep anywheres in town.  It's a shame I
          got to move over to the hotel.
          Business, you know.  (to Elma)  You mind
          if I settle my bill, M'am?


Hickey and Griggs look at Elma smugly.  She sighs,
gives Joe a look --


                         ELMA

          Danny, you sign these two gentlemen in.


The two step past Elma.  Danny takes their bags
grudgingly --

40     cont.

                    GRIGGS

          Don't think the company isn't gonna hear
          about this.


When they're inside Elma faces Joe --


                    JOE

          Sometimes you got to bend so's you don't
          break.


                    ELMA

          Food's awful at the hotel.  The
          mattresses got lumps.  Probly cooties,
          too.


                    JOE

          I'll be all right.  I'll get my things.


Joe starts inside --


                    ELMA

          Thank you.


41   INT. COAL MINE - DAY - FEW CLOTHES AND FAUSTO

Crouching under a support in a five-foot section of
the seam.  Few has a length of two-by-four and is
sounding the roof ahead of them, reaching out to tap
at it with the board while holding the fingers of his
free hand up on the slate to feel the vibrations.
Fausto looks on, uneasy underground --

41    cont.

                         FEW

          You get a ringin sound you all set --
          got a nice solid top over your head.  If
          it's a kinda holler sound, like a drum,
          then that slate's hangin a bit and you
          wants to put up another post.


                       FAUSTO

          You dig coals a long time?


                         FEW

          Been goin underground since I's ten.
          You?


                       FAUSTO

          We make a shoe.  Evabod inna same
          fabbrica, a Milano, make a shoe.


                         FEW

   Shoes.


Few gives the roof ahead a slightly harder thump and a
big chunk of slate comes crashing down.  Few looks to
the frightened Italian --


                         FEW

          You make-a shoes.


42    INT. RESTAURANT - DAY

Morning sunlight slants in as C.E. takes chairs off of
the tables.  He brings us to Joe and Sephus talking


                          54

42     cont.

strategy at one of the tables and we HOLD on them as
he moves by --


                         JOE

          -- they had strikebreaker written all
          over them.


                    SEPHUS

          Down here hit's the Baldwin-Felts that
          they use.  They's just gun thugs,
          though.


                         JOE

          They'll have the chief of police
          deputize them and all the company's mine
          guards -- so we won't just have to fight
          the operators, we'll have to fight the
          law --


                    SEPHUS

Not Sid.


                         JOE

          I never known a small-town bull that
          wasn't in their pocket.


                    SEPHUS

          (adamant)  Not Sid.


There is a KNOCK at the front door.  Sephus and Joe
stiffen, and we PAN to C.E. as he looks through the
front window --

                         55

                         C.E.

              It's all right.


He opens the door a crack and we see Bridey Mae on the
front steps.  C.E. says something to her and steps out
of the frame.  Bridey peeks into the room --


        CU JOE

Meeting her eyes --


        BRIDEY

Smiling at Joe.  C.E. steps back into the frame, gives
her a sack of food, then closes the door on her --


        CU JOE

Curious, attracted --


                    SEPHUS (off)

              Won't nobody starve in this holler if
              they got friends or family.


We PAN to include SEPHUS in the shot --


                    SEPHUS

              Bridey Mae got lots of friends.


                    JOE

              (smiles)  I bet she does.


                         56

42    cont.

C.E. steps into the shot, cut off at the waist --


                    C.E.

          I'd steer clear of that if I was you,
          Kenehan --


Standing over them, a small, framed picture in his
hand --


                    C.E.

          Bridey ever had a baby they'd have to
          name it Coal Camp Number Nine.


He lays the picture on the table --


                    C.E.

          Take a look at this.


        CU PHOTOGRAPH

A photo of C.E. standing beside old Mother Jones in
her granny dress and spectacles --


                    JOE (off)

          Mother Jones.


                    C.E. (off)

          Had that took with her up to Kanawha
          County couple years back.


                    57

42    cont.

     C.E., JOE

Looking down at the photo --


                    C.E.

          If that lady was here there wouldn't be
          a scab left by nightfall.


43    INT. COAL MINE - DAY - BLACK MINERS

They sit with their backs against a wall of coal,
wolfing down coaldust-smudged sandwiches --


                    MINER

          Soon as they get their union they'll
          send us packin.


                    TOM

          Could be.  But you try to leave here
          now, you be owin all that money like
          they say, compny shoot you for a thief.
          We just some slaves up here, man.  They
          owns our black asses.


Few Clothes appears from the dark to sit with them --


                    FEW

          Gennlemen --


                    TOM

          Hey Few, I got a question --


                    58

43    cont.

                            FEW

        Yeah?


                            TOM

        We join the union, they gonna make us
        work with those Eye-talian people?


44    INT. COAL MINE - DAY

Dozens of miner's headlamps illuminate the scene.  A
secret meeting of the Italians is in progress.  They
speak in hushed tones, IN ITALIAN.  We see only HANDS
gesturing in the headlamp beams --


                         GIANNI

        The bosses have got the guns.


                         FAUSTO

        The mountain people have got guns,
        too --


                         CLEMENTE

        I just want to feed my family.  We came
        here because it was going to be better
        than home.


                         RENATO

        They have families, too --


                         FAUSTO

        Let's have a vote -- Renato?


                           59

44    cont.    HEADLAMP POV

We FOLLOW Fausto's headlamp as it moves from hand to
hand.  Renato's hand appears -- thumbs up.


                    FAUSTO

          Clemente?


The headlamp PANS and Clemente's hand appears, thumbs
down.  The headlamp PANS again --


                    FAUSTO

          Gianni?


Gianni's hand appears and waves side to side --
undecided.


45    EXT. BRIDEY'S CABIN - DAY

Four walls and a chimney sitting on the side of a dirt
path leading up a hill through the woods.  Bridey Mae
sits in a chair out front, her feet curled under her.
Joe climbs into view --


                    BRIDEY

          Takin a walk?


                    JOE

          Hi.  I'm goin up to the coal camp, meet
          those new fellas when they come off
          their shift.

45      cont.

                              BRIDEY

                You doin union bidness, aint you?


Joe shrugs --


                              BRIDEY

                How you like Radnor's?


                               JOE

                Wasn't room.  I'm at the hotel now.


                              BRIDEY

                Int she a sourpuss, though?


                         HILLARD (off)

                (calling)  Mr. Kenehan!  Mr. Kenehan!


Hillard comes running up the hill after Joe and
arrives huffing --


                             HILLARD

                They's evictin in town, Mr. Kenehan.
                Hit's Baldwins!


46   EXT. NATIVE'S CAMP - DAY - LITTLE GIRL

Holding a doll, scared.  We PAN to her brothers and
sisters, then to her parents, who look on, stonefaced.
We PULL BACK to see a pair of mine guards carrying
furniture out onto the street, supervised by Hickey

                               61

46    cont.

and Griggs.  Townspeople crowd around, watching
silently.  Turley stands to one side --


        JOE

Clearing his way through the crowd.  Sephus and some
of the other miners are there already.  Joe and
Hillard stop at the edge of the crowd as Cabell steps
out to confront the Baldwins, still wearing his
druggist's apron --



                CABELL

        This here is town property, you know.



                HICKEY

    Who are you?



                CABELL

    I'm the mayor.



                HICKEY

    (smiles)  Pleased to meet you.  Name's
    Bill Hickey and this here's Tom Griggs.
    We're carryin out some evictions for
    Stone Mountain.



                CABELL

    You can do what you want up at the coal
    camp, but this is town property.

46    cont.

                    TURLEY

          Stone Mountain holds deeds on these
          houses, Cabell.


                     SID

          (from the crowd)  You need a writ for
          eviction.


Sid steps out from the crowd.  He wears a gun on each
hip --


                   HICKEY

          You the law here?


Sid nods --


                   HICKEY

          Good.  You can help us.  These people
          been trespassin on Company property --
          they signed a contract sayin they
          wouldn't join no unions, and then --


                     SID

          You Baldwin-Felts Agency?


                   HICKEY

          That's right.

                    TURLEY

          Presently employed by the Stone Mountain
          Coal Company


Hickey pulls out a pair of letters.  Sid glances at
them --


                    HICKEY

          We got this from Mr. Turley here, and
          this from our boss, Mr. Thomas Felts.


                    SID

          I've met Mr. Felts.


                    HICKEY

          (smiles)  Well then, we don't have any
          problem --


                    SID

          I wouldn't pee on him if his heart was
          on fire.  Neither of these'll do for a
          writ.  You'll have to see the judge in
          Charleston.


                    GRIGGS

          (threatening)  What if we aint got time
          to go to Charleston?


                    SID

          You'd better find some.  I can't do
          nothin bout what you pull outside the

                         SID (cont.)

          town limits, but you bother people under
          my jurisdiction I'll put you under
          arrest.


                         HICKEY

          (laughs)  You and whose army, tinhorn?


Sid gives him a cold look, turns to the crowd --


     WIDER SHOT - SID, CROWD, BALDWINS


                         SID

          (to crowd)  Alla you fellas own a gun,
          go home and get it.  You're deputies as
          of now.


Almost every man in the crowd goes running.  The
guards stop hauling furniture and look to Turley,
nervously touching their guns --


                         SID

          The rest of you people stick close.
          We'll need witnesses.


          JOE

Smiling --


     SID, HICKEY AND GRIGGS

Sid turns back to the Baldwins --

                          SID

               I'm giving you ten minutes to get those
               people's belonging back in their house.


                        GRIGGS

               If the rest of the boys was here you
               wouldn't be so cocky.


                          SID

               If the rest of the boys was here I'd
               give you five minutes.  Now move it.


     JOE

Watching, tense --


     DANNY

Watching --


     CABELL

Sweat breaking out on his forehead --


     SID AND HICKEY

Eyeballing each other.  Hickey looks to Turley in the
background.  Turley shakes his head.  Hickey looks to
Sid --


                        HICKEY

               You can't win, you know.  It's gonna
               happen with you or without you.  You
               can't hold it back.  (turns to guards)

46    cont.

                              HICKEY (cont.)

          Okay, boys, put it back in.  This aint
          our day.


A CHEER goes up from the crowd.  Joe approaches Sid as
the guards begin to load the furniture back in --


                         JOE

          I never seen a lawman buck a company gun
          before.


Sid stares at Joe and walks away.  Danny comes up --


                         DANNY

          He's mostly a real nice feller, Sid.


Cabell passes, muttering to himself --


                         CABELL

          Gonna get everybody kilt, I just know
          it.  Gonna get everybody kilt.


                         DANNY

          Contention makes him nervous though.


47    INT. RESTAURANT - NIGHT

Once again the miners meet by candlelight, windows
covered --

47      cont.

                         SEPHUS

              We got a motion on the floor here.   Mr.
              Kenehan --


      CU JOE


                         SEPHUS (cont., off)

              -- has put in his say for givin the
              scabs another day to make up their
              minds, while Mr. Lively --


      CU C.E.


                         SEPHUS (cont., off)

              -- has pointed out that with them
              Baldwins in town we got to move fast or
              find ourselves on the outside lookin in.


      ROOM, SEPHUS


                         SEPHUS

              So we're gonna put it to a vote now.
              (looks to Joe and C.E.)  This is coal
              miners only.  Alla them in favor of us
              keepin them scabs outa the mine tomorrow
              morning, usin whatever force hit looks
              like is necessary, raise their hands.


          MINERS

      Almost all raise their hands --

47    cont.

SEPHUS, JOE

Sephus looks at Joe.  Joe tries to be stoic about his
defeat --


                         SEPHUS

              Hit's settled, then --


48    INT. BOARDING HOUSE - NIGHT

Elma, Danny and Mrs. Knightes sit eating with Hickey
and Griggs.  Lots of tension at the table --


                         HICKEY

              Pass them peas, boy.


Danny glares at him --


                         ELMA

              Pass the peas, Danny.


Danny ignores her, keeps eating --


                         GRIGGS

              The boy deaf or dumb or what?


                    MRS. KNIGHTES

              (proudly)  Daniel aint dumb.  Daniel's a
              preacher.


                           69

48     cont.

                         HICKEY

             (teasing)  That right, boy?  You a
             preacher?


Danny reddens, doesn't answer --


                         GRIGGS

             Who you preach to, boy, the squirrels?


                       MRS. KNIGHTES

             Daniel preached at the meetin last
             night.  Was a good number of souls
             there.


                         HICKEY

             You a soul-saver, boy?  You want to have
             a go at me and Griggsy here.  We ought
             to be a challenge.


                         GRIGGS

             He's a squirrel preacher is what.
             Stands up on a stump in the woods and
             testifies to the Holy Rodent --


Danny jumps up with a table knife in hand --


                         ELMA

             Danny!

48    cont.

Griggs has his gun up from under the table, leveled at
Danny.  They stare at each other a long, tense
moment --


                    GRIGGS

        You in a hurry to meet your maker, boy?


                    MRS. KNIGHTES

        Aint no guns allowed at table!


                    ELMA

        (scared)  You sit down, Danny.


                    HICKEY

        Do what your pretty mama says, Preacher.


Danny sits --


                    MRS. KNIGHTES

        Guns at table!  My daddy would of
        horsewhipped you!


                    ELMA

        You put that away now, Mister.


                    HICKEY

        Pack it away, Griggsy.  Look, we're
        gonna be here for a while, little lady.


                        71

48    cont.

                    HICKEY (cont.)

          It can be the easy way or the <u>hard</u> way.
          (to Danny)  Now how bout them peas?


     DANNY

He jumps to his feet and we HOLD on the table as he
slams out of the house --


49   EXT. MAIN STREET - NIGHT

Danny slows, kicks the dirt angrily, then looks up in
the hills --


A51  HILLS - DANNY'S POV

We see a string of headlamps snaking up the hillside
in the distance, flickering like fireflies through the
trees --


     DANNY


                    DANNY

          (sees)  Oh Lord --


Danny runs down the street toward C.E.'s --


50, 51  DELETED


B51  INT. C.E.'S RESTAURANT - NIGHT

The meeting is breaking up, miners milling around as
Joe still tries to sway Sephus and C.E. at the back of
the room --

                    JOE

          They told me they'd talk to their
          fellas.


                    SEPHUS

          I saw their faces last night, Joe.   They
          wasn't buyin it.


A hubbub at the front door --


                    JOE

          We're playing right into the company's
          plans --


                    C.E.

          The men voted, Joe, what more do you
          want?


                    DANNY (off)

          Sephus!


Danny comes through the miners, breathing hard --


                    DANNY

          I seen lights on the hill, Sephus.
          They're sneaking em in for a night
          shift.

                         SEPHUS

                (grim) Let's go, fellas!


52   EXT. WOODS - NIGHT

Joe hustles to keep up with Danny and the other miners
as they run up a rough path through the dark woods --


                         DANNY

              Hillard tole me you was sent from the
              union.


                          JOE

              Un-huh.


                         DANNY

              You probably been in hundreds a strikes.


                          JOE

              Yuh.


                         DANNY

              (proud)  I got throwed clear outa the
              Missionary the other night.  Talkin
              union from the pulpit.


                          JOE

              (winded)  Yuh.  We gettin close?


                           74

53    EXT. DRIFTMOUTH - NIGHT - CU BANDOLIER

Of machine-gun bullets, bumping on the ground as
someone carries them along.  We PULL BACK as a mine
guard steps into the bunker guarding the driftmouth.
His partner helps him attach the ammunition to the
machine gun trained down the hill.  One of them sees
something down the hill, taps the other and points --


        WOODS, GUARDS' POV

On one side of the track leading to the driftmouth,
striking miners are stepping out of the woods and
lining the path, all wearing their headlamps --


        GUARDS

The two look at each other, then swing the muzzle of
the machine gun around --


        WOODS - CLOSER

The men out out in twos and threes, shooting glances
at Joe, who arrives with Danny, and at C.E. and
Sephus.  Ludie shouts --


                    LUDIE

            Here they come!


We MOVE to see the strikebreakers being marched in two
columns by rifle-bearing mine guards, the blacks and
Italians separated.  Some of the strikers run to the
other side of the tracks to flank them as they climb
to the driftmouth.  The mine guards raise their
lanterns to see what lies ahead --


        MACHINE-GUN MUZZLE

Swinging from side to side as if to decide who to
shoot --


                    75

53 cont.

GUARDS

Manning the machine-gun, scared, their faces tight --


STRIKEBREAKERS

More scared faces as they walk into the gauntlet of
strikers --


STRIKERS

We PAN from face to face, dull hatred in their eyes --


GUARD

One of the escort guards, finger on the trigger, rifle
held at chest level, walking like he's in a mine
field --


JOE

Searching the strikebreakers' faces for a clue --


FAUSTO

Turns his eyes away as he passes Joe --


JOE

Sephus comes up by him and pats a bulge under his
jacket --


                        JOE

        You didn't give me enough time.

                    SEPHUS

          When our fellas put their headlamps out,
          you just hit the dirt.


     FEW CLOTHES

Face deadpan as he passes, leading the blacks'
column --


          DANNY

Eyes wide, at the edge of the track.  He bends down
and grabs a big chunk of coal for a weapon, holding it
behind his back --


          LONG SHOT

The miners fall in a few yards behind the marching
strikebreakers.  Guards drop back to protect their
rear, rifles ready --


          TRACKS

Looking down over the shoulders of the guards at the
machine gun.  We TRACK IN tight as Few Clothes steps
up to the muzzle of the gun and looks down on the
guards --


                         FEW

               This here belongs to you.


He sticks his shovel into the dirt at his feet, turns
and faces his men.  Fausto steps up by him, raising
his shovel in the air --


                    FAUSTO

          Viva il sciopero!

                    77

53     cont.

He throws the shovel down --


          ITALIANS AND BLACKS

Staring at their leaders.  The time has come to shit
or get off the pot.  Gianni steps forward and throws
his shovel down --


                    GIANNI

               Viva il sciopero.


Tom tosses his down, looking at Gianni --


                    TOM

          Yeah.  I'm with him.


     GROUND

Shovels begin to fall left and right --


     JOE

A smile spreading on his face --


     GROUND

Shovels piling up --


     TURLEY

Stepping out into the light from behind the machine-
gun nest, grim --

53    cont.

   BLACKS AND ITALIANS

All throwing their tools down now, picks and shovels
clanging together in a heap --


   GUARDS

Trying to herd the men back into the driftmouth --


   JOE

Stepping out on the pathway to call out --


                    JOE

         Alla you union men!   Let's welcome our
         new brothers!


The native miners form a protective phalanx behind
which the blacks and Italians begin to move as they
get around the mine guards --


   ITALIANS

Gianni gives Fausto an ironic smile, then begins to
whistle "Avanti Populo."  A few of the others laugh
and pick it up, SINGING the words as they move down
the hill --


   BLACKS

Sephus steps forward and offers his hand to Few as the
blacks joint the white miners --


                 SEPHUS

         Gentlemen -- glad you could join us.

53   cont.

    JOE

Staring across the path at Turley --


    TURLEY

Returning a look of rage --


    JOE

Turns to the men, Danny looking up at him worship-
fully --


                    JOE

            From now on Stone Mountain don't move
            one piece of coal unless it's a union
            man that moves it!


There is a CHEER from the men --


                    JOE

            Let's get out of here.


Joe starts down the hill and the other miners fall in.
We HOLD on C.E.  He gives Joe a smile and a little
salute as he passes --


    WIDE SHOT - MINERS

They stream down the hill, blacks, whites, Italians
mixed in together, the Italians still singing a loose
version of "Avanti Populo" that blends into a FIDDLE
version as we --

DISSOLVE TO:


54    EXT. TENT CAMP - DAY

Whack!  Whack!  Whack!  A tent peg is driven into the
ground.  We PULL BACK to see miners and their families
beginning to lay out a tent camp in a little clearing
on the side of a hill --


                         PAPPY (VO)

              In them days the coal company owned your
              camp houses, they owned your land, they
              owned most of the town and the people
              who run it.


         BLACK MINERS

Nailing together wooden siding for a tent --


                         PAPPY (VO, cont.)

              If you wasn't for the company there
              wasn't too many places you could go that
              was still on the map.


         HANDS

Cutting the ties off a bundle of canvas --


         JOE

Carrying a ground plot, he leads a knot of native
miners and their families past the roped-off tent
sections --


                         PAPPY (VO, cont.)

              The union didn't have too much they
              could give to the people back then --


                              81

54    cont.

HANDS

Black and white mixed, pulling on a tent rope --


TENT

The canvas rising --


                              PAPPY (VO, cont.)

                    "All we got in common is our misery,"
                    Joe Kenehan used to say, "and the least
                    we can do is share it."


TENT CAMP - LONG SHOT

Families standing back as various groups of miners
pull up tents --


55    EXT. TENT CAMP - DAY

Hillard Elkins and his mother move their belongings
into a tent.  Mrs. Elkins stares suspiciously over at
her new neighbor, Rosaria, who is making a little
shrine in front of her tent for her statute of the
Virgin, talking to it all the while.  She notices Mrs.
Elkins watching --


                    ROSARIA

          (in Italian)  What are you staring at?


                    MRS. ELKINS

          (turns away, whispers)  She got the evil
          eye, that one --

                    HILLARD

          Aw, Mama --


                    MRS. ELKINS

          Don't let me catch you peekin over
          there, Hillard.  She got the evil eye if
          I ever seen it.


Joe comes by, checking up --


                    JOE

          You folks all set?


                    HILLARD

          Just fine, Mr. Kenehan.


We FOLLOW Joe past a few more tents till he comes upon
Danny and Elma staggering in laden with sacks of flour
and beans.  Danny is grinning while Elma looks
uncomfortable to be there --


                    JOE

          Whatta we got here?


                    DANNY

          We brung you some food.  Mama stole it
          from the compny.

                         ELMA

          Quiet, Danny --


                         JOE

          We can use anything you've got.


                         ELMA

          You people are crazy.   You aint never
          gonna win this thing.


                         JOE

          Then what are you helpin us for?


Elma puts the sacks down and starts away --


                         ELMA

          I got work to do --


                         JOE

          (calling)  We appreciate your help --


Danny looks around at the tents and the people,
beaming --


                         DANNY

          I aint never seen everbody all together
          like this.  Compny don't stand a <u>chance</u>.

56    EXT. MAIN ST. - DAY

Sid walks down the main street.  He stops in front of
the apothecary, adjusts his guns, takes a deep breath
and enters --


57    INT. DRUG STORE - DAY


Hickey and Griggs sit across the soda fountain from
Cabell and his young, pretty wife JESSIE.  Sid steps
in, first locking eyes with Jessie.  She stares back
at him till Cabell notices, than looks away.  Sid sits
a few stools down from Hickey.  Cabell gives Jessie a
nod and she makes herself scarce --


                    SID

          What's the pitch?


                    HICKEY

          I was just saying to the mayor how we're
          all just trying to do our jobs here.
          You, me, him.  And aint none of us
          gettin paid enough to be dodging no
          bullets for it.  Now Mr. Felts has
          authorized me to make it more attractive
          for you gentlemen to cooperate --


                    CABELL

          Town aint for sale, Mister.


                    HICKEY

          (to Sid)  How bout you?  I figure that
          little show you put on the other day was
          just for bargaining power.  Or are you
          gonna be stupid, too?

                        SID

            Either of you shithogs lift a finger in
            the town limits I'll put you away.


                      GRIGGS

            Damn hillbillies always got to do it the
            hard way --


The Baldwins get up, Hickey leaning close to Sid --


                      HICKEY

            You're goin up against some big people
            here.  Don't push your luck.


They walk out.  Sid and Cabell look at each other.
Sid is much better at hiding his fear --


                        SID

            How's Jessie these days?


                      CABELL

            She's okay.  Sid?  You think they're
            bluffing?


                        SID

            No.  Neither am I.

58    EXT. TENT CAMP - NIGHT

Ellix stands sentry.  Behind him we see a few fires in
front of tents, a few lanterns hung.  We hear MANDOLIN
MUSIC --


59    INT. TENT - NIGHT

Joe sits with Sephus, Ludie, C.E. and some of the
other native miners, lit by kerosene lanterns.  Few
Clothes and Fausto sit to one side, uncomfortable --


                         JOE

               So I report to the strike committee and
               they evaluate the progress we're makin
               here and the political situation, and
               then they release the strike fund --


                         LUDIE

               You mean they'd cut us off?


                         JOE

               The amount we get is based on --


                         SEPHUS

               What if they think we're gonna lose?


                         JOE

               The strike committee considers what's
               best for the union as a whole.  But that
               doesn't --


                              87

59    cont.

                        C.E.

            Politics, boys.  You gonna play union,
            you got to play politics.  (pats Joe's
            back)  I'm sure Joe don't like it no
            more than you do.


60    EXT. TENT CAMP - NIGHT - FIRESIDE

The Italian MANDOLIN player is PLAYING something
complicated and mournful.  A few other Italians sit by
him, looking homesick.  Gradually they become aware
that other instruments have joined in -- a country
FIDDLE and a GUITAR come from the darkness.  The
mandolin player stops -- the others stop too.  He
calls softly in Italian --


                        PLAYER

            Come.  Come closer.


Picker and Fiddler step shyly into the light.  The
mandolin player starts up against and the two join in,
standing, and watch his fingers work.  After a moment
we hear a HARMONICA pipe in from a far section of the
camp.  The players notice but keep going --


A60   CU HARMONICA PLAYER

The black miner sits PLAYING blues riffs around the
ballad the other men are laying down, as if the two
musics are calling to each other --


61    INT. TENT - NIGHT

As the other men argue, we watch Few Clothes pick up
the sound of the music and go to the opening flap to
look out --

61    cont.

                    STENNIS

          I didn't get into this thing so's I
          could have one more boss to tell me what
          to do.


                    JOE

          The union isn't your <u>boss</u>, it's <u>you</u>,
          it's all of us --


                    LUDIE

          Then why we got to wait for some Hunkies
          up in Pittsburgh to give us the word to
          move?


                    JOE

          Cause it's a democracy.  You know, like
          the United States is a democracy?


                    SEPHUS

          That's a joke.


                    FEW

          Quiet!


Few's call shuts them up.  He listens at the tent
flap.  The MUSIC has STOPPED and we can hear a CAR
ENGINE WHINING up the hill.  It stops.  A tense
moment, then -- SMASH!  A rifle bullet rips in and
shatters the kerosene lamp next to Joe, plunging the
tent into near-darkness.  Few dives for the floor --


                    89

61    cont.

                    FEW

          Get down!  They shootin!


The men dive to the floor as bullets whistle in from
all directions.  We hear SCREAMS from throughout the
camp --


                  SEPHUS

          I'm gettin my gun --


                    JOE

          Stay put, they'll cut you down --


Sephus is walking out of the tent, pissed --


                  SEPHUS

          The hell with that.


Sephus steps out of the tent as a volley of bullets
tears into the spot where he'd been lying.  C.E.
crawls over by Joe, who hugs the ground --


                  C.E.

          Just keep your head down, son.  They're
          gonna make a night of it.


62    EXT. RIVERSIDE - DAY

Women washing bloody shirts in the river --

63    EXT. TENT CAMP - DAY

A woman patches a section of tent ripped open by
gunfire --


     MANDOLIN PLAYER

Trying to figure out how to patch a hole blown in the
gourd of his instrument --


     TENT CAMP

A group of miners' wives and daughters have set up an
aid station.  Elma, Bridey and LUANN, a teenage friend
of Bridey's, have joined them.  Elma treats a black
miner who has been shot in the face while Bridey and
Luann tear a linen sheet into strips for bandages.  A
woman with a squalling baby cut by glass and other
wounded lie about being treated as best as possible --


                    ELMA

          Compny doctor said he wouldn't come out
          but there's a fella in Pikeville on the
          Kentucky side that'll treat union men on
          the sly.  He'll be here by noon.


                    MAN

          He treat colored?


                    ELMA

          If he treats union he'll treat colored.


She calls to Danny as he zips by --


                    ELMA

          More water, Danny!

63     cont.

                    DANNY

          Yes, M'am!


Joe wanders up, pale, looking at the wounded --


                    JOE

          You seen any of the men?


                    ELMA

          Only them that's wounded.


                    JOE

          (looks around him)  Nobody got killed.


                    ELMA

          No thanks to you.


Bridey gives her a sharp look, then looks to Joe --


                    BRIDEY

          Mornin, Joe.


                    JOE

          (distracted)  Hey, Bridey.


Joe walks away, worried about where the men have gone.
Bridey watches after him --

63    cont.

                    LUANN

        He's real nice lookin.


                    BRIDEY

        I can tell he likes me.


                    LUANN

    How?


                    BRIDEY

        I just know men, that's all.



Elma, overhearing, gives a snort of derision.  Bridey
gives her an angry look --


                    BRIDEY

            Least I haven't shriveled up and died
            like some people.


64    EXT. TENT CAMP - DAY - JOE

Walking past the tents, miners' wives out surveying
the damage.  He hears a COMMOTION up ahead and we
FOLLOW as he runs to see what's up.  Rosaria and Mrs.
Elkins stand by a cookfire arguing over a sack of
cornmeal.  They speak at the same time, not
understanding each other --


                    MRS. ELKINS

            Now lady -- lady -- you want to make
            that kinda slop for dinner you're
            welcome to go on back home and <u>make</u> it.

64    cont.

MRS. ELKINS (cont.)

But this is the United States here, and
we do things different.  Lady -- listen
to me now lady -- you can learn somethin
here -- oh Lord, she don't understand
the first thing I'm sayin --


ROSARIA

(Italian) Let go, you crazy old witch!
You cook for dogs!  No, even dogs won't
eat what you cook.  You make poison,
you'll kill us all with that food.  How
do you people survive, eating this slop?


Joe arrives --


JOE

Ladies, what's the problem here?


ROSARIA

(Italian)  I'm trying to make polenta
but this idiot won't let me!


MRS. ELKINS

I figured she's gonna make cornbread
with it but you should see the mess she
come up with.


ROSARIA

(Italian)  She wants to poison her
people, that's her business, but half
that cornmeal is mine!

64     cont.

                              JOE

              People got their own way of doin things,
              Mrs. Elkins --


                          MRS. ELKINS

              Waste of good cornmeal, you ask me.  She
              makes up some kinder porridgely stuff, I
              wouldn't feed it to pigs.


Rosaria stiffens, hearing --


                          ROSARIA

              (Italian)  Listen!  The soldiers are
              coming --


We can hear the same ENGINE WHINING up the hill.
Rosaria crosses herself --


                          ROSARIA

              (Italian)  They're coming back to kill
              us!


                          MRS. ELKINS

              (scared)  Where's all the men gone to?


65   EXT. RESTAURANT - DAY

Ellix nervously looks both ways, then ducks inside --

66    INT. RESTAURANT - DAY

Most of the native miners are inside, as well as Few,
Fausto and many of the black and Italian miners.  C.E.
has the floor --


                    C.E.

          -- I'm sayin is, unions is fine for some
          things, but for others a man's got to go
          on his own.  Course, that's up to you --


                    SEPHUS

          (crossing to Fausto)  Fawsto?


Fausto thinks for a moment.  His countrymen look at
him --


                    FAUSTO

          You make sindacato, you do what
          sindacato decide.  I listen to Joe.


                    SEPHUS

          (nods)  Few Clothes?


                    FEW

          Gonna be shooting white fokes, right?


                    SEPHUS

          That's the idea.


                         96

66    cont.

                    FEW

          People hear about black people shootin
          white people, no matter what it's for,
          there gonna be hell to pay.


                    SEPHUS

          You got a point.  Well then.   If you
          gentlemen will excuse us?


Few and Fausto lead their miners out.  C.E. calls
after them --


                    C.E.

          You fellas best stay in your tents
          tonight.   I feel somethin in the air --


67    EXT. TENT CAMP - DAY

Hickey and Griggs step out of their open car, two
rifle-bearing mine guards flanking them, as the tent
people line up to see.  Hickey steps forward to
shout --


                    HICKEY

          You people been put out of the Stone
          Mountain mine housing -- and some of you
          seen fit to take along --


    ELMA

Trying to get lost in the crowd so the Baldwins won't
see her --

67    cont.

                    HICKEY (off)

          -- certain items of furniture and
          clothing and food -- that belong to the
          company.  As of the day the strike
          begun --


     JOE

Standing with the wives and children, listening --


                    HICKEY (off)

          -- your company scrip ceased to be legal
          tender.  Meanin that any item of
          furniture, food or clothing not paid for
          in cash money has got to be handed over
          to me and my deputies.  I suggest you
          all cooperate -- my boys didn't get much
          sleep last night and they're kinda
          jumpy.  Besides, we got the law on our
          side.


                    HILLARD (off)

          You aint no law!


     HILLARD, BALDWINS

Hillard comes out of the crowd, hopping mad --


                    HILLARD

          You got to slip around the real law, you
          just got guns, that's all --


Whap!  Hickey slaps Hillard in the face.  Hillard
doesn't know what to do.  The two guards have their
rifles leveled at the crowd, laughing at Hillard.
Griggs has his gun out --

                         98

67    cont.

                        HICKEY

          Maybe you're right, sonny.  We just got
          guns.  You still got to hand over them
          goods.


                        HILLARD

          Yellow scab-herder --


Whap!  Hickey cracks Hillard again, knocking him into
a patch of mud.  The guards laugh.  Mrs. Elkins comes
out to her son as Joe steps forward to face Hickey --


                     MRS. ELKINS

          Hillard!  You get up from there!


                         JOE

          You got a list of goods?


                       GRIGGS

          Don't need one.


                         JOE

          How you gonna know what belongs to the
          company and what don't?


                       GRIGGS

          He's the Red, Hickey.  He's the
          agitator.

67    cont.

Joe raises his arms to his sides, turns to the
crowd --


                        JOE

          Everybody see I don't have a gun on me?


                        HICKEY

          What do you think that'll do for you,
          Red?


                        JOE

          (shrugs)  If you shoot me folks'll know
          it was murder.


                        HICKEY

          That's some cold comfort.


Hickey slaps at Joe, who blocks the blow and pushes
Hickey back.  Instantly Griggs cracks Joe from behind
with his gun butt and one of the guards whomps him in
the stomach with his rifle.  Joe falls to his knees,
the wind knocked out of him.  There is a SHOT --


     MEN

Four men, hill people, stand at the edge of the
clearing, long rifles leveled at the Baldwin agents.
The oldest speaks --


                        ISAAC

          We was huntin.  You folks making an
          awful lotter commotion.


                        100

                        SHEB

         You scairt all the game away.


                        ISAAC

         (indicates car)  Who's machine?


                        HICKEY

         Ours.


                        ISAAC

         Heard it last night, too.  Hit's an
         offense to the ear.


                        GRIGGS

         Hold on, Pops, you're talking to the
         law, here --


Sheb swings the gun to point at Griggs --


                        SHEB

         He ask you anything?


                        GRIGGS

         (false bravado)  Where'd you get that
         thing, Pops, the Spanish War?


Sheb gives a little smile and raises the muzzle to
Griggs's head --

                              SHEB

        Naawp.  War between the States.


                              ISAAC

        Now you all get in that machine and get
        back into town where you belong.  Haint
        but one law here, an that's the law a
        nature.


Hickey signals and the others grudgingly follow him
into the car.  The hill people watch it rumble off --


                              ISAAC

        You folks try an keep the noise down
        here, you'll do fine.  Help yourself to
        the bird and rabbit, but you see any
        hogs they's probly ours and we'd
        preciate it if you'd leave em be.  Good
        day to you --


He nods and the men follow him back into the woods --


        JOE

Still on his knees, getting his breath back.  Bridey
stoops over him, worried, while in the background Mrs.
Elkins tends to Hillard --


                         BRIDEY

        You okay, Joe?

                              JOE

          Be fine if it wunt for my ribs.  Who
          were those people?


                         MRS. ELKINS

          Rossums, mostly, and a Shuttleworth.


                              JOE

          They miners?


                         MRS. ELKINS

          Never find them folks near a hole.  They
          had most their land stole by the compny.


                            BRIDEY

          They's hill people.


                         MRS. ELKINS

          Foothill people, really.  Your genuwine
          hill people, they can be dangerous.


68    INT. RESTAURANT - NIGHT

C.E. kneels with Danny, tamping black blasting powder
down into a lead pipe --


                             C.E.

          What you got to remember, son, is your
          fuse burns a foot per minute.  Make it
          too long and they might see it and have
          time to put it out.  Make it too short

68    cont.

                        C.E. (cont.)
            and we'll all meet you on the other
            side --


They look up as there is a BANGING noise from
outside --


69    EXT. RESTAURANT - NIGHT

Joe bangs on the shuttered front door.  It is dark
inside, everybody gone.  He bangs again in
frustration --


69    cont.  INT. RESTAURANT - NIGHT

C.E. hands the pipe bomb to Danny --


                        C.E.
            The air shaft on Number Four.  Go out
            the back way.


He gives Danny a pat on the back as the boy hurries
away --


69    cont.  EXT. RESTAURANT - NIGHT

Joe gives up banging, then looks out onto the deserted
street --


70    INT. ELMA'S DINING ROOM - NIGHT

Elma sits across from Hickey and Griggs, picking at
her food as they wolf theirs down.  Griggs whispers
something to Hickey and they snicker --

70   cont.

                              HICKEY

          Where's our other friends tonight, Miss
          Elma?  Get tired of the chuck or what?


                              GRIGGS

          I think that old biddy went on strike.
          Laid her teeth down in protest.


                              ELMA

          They're just particular bout who they
          eat with.


                              HICKEY

          And how bout you, Miss Elma?  You
          particular?


                              ELMA

          If Stone Mountain didn't hold the lease
          here --


                              GRIGGS

          If Stone Mountain didn't hold the lease
          here you'd be peddlin poontang down in
          Cinder Bottom, so just shut your mouth
          about it!


Elma looks back at her plate for a moment, furious but
trying to hold it in --


                              HICKEY

          Where's the little preacher tonight?

70    cont.

Elma gets up from the table and walks out --


                    GRIGGS

        Bitch got no table manners.


71    EXT. BOARDING HOUSE - NIGHT - JOE

Walking past Elma's, he sees her sitting on a bench in
a dark corner of her porch --


        CU ELMA

She stares blankly out into the street, so spaced that
Joe is right beside her before she notices --


                    JOE

        (softly)  Elma?


                    ELMA

        You know where Danny is?


                    JOE

        (sits by her)  I don't know where
        anybody is.  Nobody wants to tell me,
        either.


He looks at her --


                    Joe

        You okay?


                    106

71    cont.

                    ELMA

          Just tired, is all.  I been workin all
          day.  This place --


Elma is starting to shake, the tension she's been
under catching up with her --


                    ELMA

          I been workin -- the day they buried my
          husband I started and I been workin --
          it don't never stop and I'm so tired
          sometimes and there aint nobody --


She starts to cry and Joe reflexively puts his arms
around her --


                    JOE

          It's hard, being on your own --


                    ELMA

          You don't know nothin about it.


Joe nods, shaken.  We TRACK AROUND them as they hold
on to each other, Elma's face softening, Joe unsure of
what comes next.  KABOOM!  What comes next is a hugh
EXPLOSION from the hills.  Elma and Joe break apart as
Hickey and Griggs burst out the front door, too
hurried to notice them in the corner --


                    HICKEY

          We're in business, buddy.  Get the
          boys --

72    EXT. HILLS - NIGHT

A fire visible through the trees in the distance --


72A  EXT. MAIN ST. - NIGHT - SID

Standing at the edge of town, looking up at the hills
darkly --


73    EXT. MAIN ST. - NIGHT - JOE

Running down the street till he sees Cabell step out
from his drug store --


                         JOE

             What is it?


                        CABELL

             Sounds like dynamite at the mine --


A car races by them with Hickey, Griggs and a bunch of
mine guards inside.  Cabell watches it sadly --


                        CABELL

             Nothin you can do now.


74    EXT. TENT CAMP - NIGHT - STRIKERS

Standing outside their tents, listening like foxes.
We see Fausto and Rosaria.  We hear Mrs. Elkins
wandering the camp, asking again and again --

74    cont.

                    MRS. ELKINS

          You seen my boy?  Anybody seen my boy
          Hillard?


We hear the CAR as it approaches, passes and fades
away.  An older woman speaks from the crowd --


                    WOMAN

          That'll be the Baldwins.


Mrs. Elkins wanders into the shot, distraught --


                    MRS. ELKINS

          Anybody seen my Hillard?


A75  EXT. HILLS - NIGHT - GAS FIRE

Crackling up from an air shaft on the hillside.  Danny
runs into the shot in the foreground, looks back at
the fire, then runs off --


75   CU HILLARD

Laid out behind a tree, facing downhill, rifle braced
against his shoulder.  One side of his face is lit by
the fire --


     CU SEPHUS

Armed and waiting --


                       109

75    cont.

CU LUDIE

Waiting --


CU C.E.

Waiting --


CU SEPHUS

Perking up as we hear the CAR APPROACHING, winding up
the mountain road toward them.  It comes closer,
closer -- then SHUTS OFF.  Sephus is puzzled.  He
peers down the road, raises himself slightly --
THWACK!  He is hit by a bullet from behind --


WOODS

Behind the men.  We see FLASHES as rifles fire --


                    HICKEY

          (in the dark)  Shoot low, boys!  Cut
          them grass tops!


SEPHUS

On his belly, fires a found back into the woods --


                    SEPHUS

          You fellas git outa here, I'll hold em
          back --


MEN

Bullets whizzing around them, running crouched through
the tall grass among the crest of the hill.  One of


                    110

75    cont.

the miners, Hadley, is hit and goes down a few yards
from Sephus --


          SEPHUS

We FOLLOW him as he shoots, rolls to another position,
shoots, rolls to another position, shoots -- WHAP!  He
takes a bullet in the shoulder, still rolling, wincing
in pain, comes up, shoots again -- WHAP!  WHAP!  He is
hit twice, rifle shocked from his hands, and goes
rolling backward down the hill --


          SEPHUS

Sliding, tumbling, sliding again -- he comes to rest
wedged under a fallen tree --


          CU SEPHUS

Scraped, bleeding, he grits his teeth and tries to
work himself further out of sight under the tree.  We
hear footsteps, men running and sliding down the face
of the hill, voices --


                    MEN

          Watch out, he'll be dangerous!
          He dropped his rifle --
          They allus carry a sidearm --
          Couldn't of gone far --


                    GRIGGS

          Hey, over here!  I got him, boys!


We hear a SCUFFLE --

                    C.E. (off)

         Hold it!  Hold it, boys, it's me!


                    GRIGGS (off)

         Hold your fire, boys!


Sephus strains to hear the men talking -- we can't
make out the words.  Sephus lifts his head to see --


     MEN - SEPHUS'S POV

Looking downhill we see the men surrounding somebody,
then breaking to let him trot away.  It's C.E. Lively.
The men start searching again --


     CU SEPHUS

Laying his head down --


                    SEPHUS

         Judas.


76   INT. TENT - NIGHT

Ludie is laid out on a cot, his leg shot up with
pellets.  Rosaria and Mrs. Elkins work as a team,
picking the shot out and keeping the blood flow down.
Hillard holds a lantern close.  Joe leans into the
light --


                    JOE

         What happened?


                    112

                    LUDIE

          We was sold.  Them Baldwins come at us
          from behind and known right where we was
          layin out --


                    HILLARD

          They known when the men was out of camp
          today, too --


C.E. Lively enters, a scowl on his face --


                    C.E.

          How's she feelin, buddy?


                    LUDIE

          You made it!  I thought we'd lost you
          back there --


                    C.E.

          Buried myself under the leaves.  I seen
          Reece Hadley go down though.  Sephus get
          back?


                    LUDIE

          I don't think so.


                    Joe

          See what happens?  You pick up a gun --

76    cont.

                    LUDIE

          All I see is them niggers and dagoes
          wunt there tonight and we was <u>sold</u>!


He glares up at Joe --


                    LUDIE

          And somebody gonna <u>pay</u>.


77   INT. BRIDEY'S CABIN - NIGHT


                    LUANN

          Somethin bad's happenin out there.


                    BRIDEY

          Huntin party, that's all.   Where was I?


                    LUANN

          (reads)  "-- time to put all shyness --"


                    BRIDEY

          (dictates)  "-- time to put all shyness
          aside and admit to our heartfelt
          attraction --"


                    LUANN

          I'm not sure how to spell "attraction."


                    114

77    cont.

                    BRIDEY

        How bout "heartfelt desires"?


                    LUANN

        You sure you wanna do this?


                    BRIDEY

        (recites)  "-- our heartfelt desires,
        dearest Joseph --"


78    EXT. HILLS - NIGHT

Skinny hounds growl and tug at something in the
bushes.  MISTER and MISSUS appear, Missus with a
lantern and Mister with a rifle.  They shoo away the
dogs and we TRACK IN as they bend over -- it's
Sephus --


                    MISSUS

        Lookit that.  Just acovered with gore.


                    MISTER

        Dogs dint do all that.  (pokes Sephus)
        You drawin breath, son?


We see Sephus's face in the lantern light --


                    SEPHUS

        (weakly)  Baldwins.  We was sold --
        they --


                    115

78    cont.

                    MISTER

          What's your name?


                    SEPHUS

          Bosephus -- Sephus Purcell --


                    MISTER

          Kin to Nimrod Purcell?


                    SEPHUS

          Daddy's uncle --


                    MISSUS

          That cousin Esker's Nimrod?


                    MISTER

          Say some Baldwin agents took you?


                    SEPHUS

          From behind --


                    MISTER

          Noner them Purcells ever <u>was</u> too bright.
          Grab his ankles, Missus, and mind you
          dress.  E's ableedin like a stuck pig.


                    116

79    EXT. HILLS - DAY - CORPSE

Tolbert rolls it over with his foot.  It is Hadley,
the back of his head shot away, leaves sticking to his
face.  Other miners search in the background --


          JOE

Looking down, sickened.  He turns away.  Sid comes
down the slope, squats to examine the dead man --


                    SID

          You got yourself a martyr.


                    JOE

          I tried to stop this.


Sid ignores him --


                    JOE

          Any sign of Sephus?


                    SID

          (shrugs)  We'll maybe smell him before
          we see him.


80    EXT. HILLS - DAY - C.E.

Watching from up the hill.  Luann comes by him --


                    LUANN

          They find somebody?

80    cont.

                         C.E.

          You just stay right here, honey.  Don't
          wanna look at that mess.


                         LUANN

          I got somethin for Mr. Kenehan.


C.E. sees the letter she's holding --


                         C.E.

          I don't think he's in no mood to be
          bothered right now.  I'll see he gets
          it.


C.E. plucks the letter from Luann as she stares at the
miners lifting the lifeless body --


                         LUANN

          Who is it?


                         C.E.

          Oh, just some poor coal miner whose
          troubles is finally done.  Don't you
          look, honey.


81    EXT. HILLSIDE GRAVEYARD - AFTERNOON

The funeral is over, Ellix and Stennis shovel dirt
into Hadley's open grave --

81    cont.

JOE AND DANNY

Sitting on the hill, watching --

                    DANNY

          I always figure it's like goin down into
          the mine.  Dyin.


                    JOE

          I never been underground.


                    DANNY

          (surprised)  No?


Joe shakes his head --


                    DANNY

          There aint no darkness like it.  You
          watch that little speck of light at the
          entrance get smaller and smaller -- the
          air smells dead, and all the sounds
          change -- you hear your heart poundin,
          hear the blood arunnin through your
          veins.  You go in deeper and it gets
          cold.  Sometimes your light'll go out
          and you're alone and you're numb and
          it's so dark -- you touch youself but
          you can't tell if it's flesh you feel or
          only just a dream of it, that you've
          gone and died down there and it's just a
          dream of bein alive, gettin smaller and
          smaller --


They watch the men shoveling for a moment --

DANNY

Old Reece won't have to do that no more.


82    INT. BRIDEY'S CABIN - DAY

C.E. sits at a little table across from Bridey, a
bottle of liquor and a pair of glasses between them --


C.E.

I talked to Ellix an he says your
phonograph machine gonna be fixed in a
couple days now.


BRIDEY

S'awful nice for you to do, Everett --


C.E.

Well, we gotta take care of our favorite
lady, don't we?


BRIDEY

You been so generous -- thinkin about me
when that Mr. Kenehan got you all so
busy with the union --


C.E.

That Mr. Kenehan is what I come to talk
to you about -- I got a suspicion he
might not be what he says he is.

82    cont.

                         BRIDEY

              What do you mean?


                          C.E.

              Bridey -- did you send Kenehan some sort
              of letter?


We TRACK IN toward Bridey's stricken face as C.E.
pours liquor into her glass --


83    EXT. TENT CAMP - DAY

Joe leads Fausto and Few through the native miners'
section, a few of the miners eyeing them suspiciously.
They turn into a tent where Ludie lies back, staring
at his blasted leg.  He looks at them bitterly --


84    INT. TENT - DAY


                         LUDIE

              What do you want?


85    INT. BRIDEY'S CABIN - DAY

C.E. is on his feet now --


                          C.E.

              I heard him myself.


                         BRIDEY

              No.  He wouldn't.

                          121

85    cont.

                    C.E.

          They's a whole crowd of fellas around
          him, I see him laughin and waving that
          letter an I come over to see what's so
          funny --


                    BRIDEY

          (despairing)  A lot of fellas?


C.E. puts a hand on Bridey's shoulder, in control
now --


                    C.E.

          You mind if I take a drink, honey?   It
          aint pretty what I got to say.


84    cont.  INT. TENT - DAY

Ludie won't look Joe in the eye --


                    JOE

          We gotta do somethin to bring the men
          together and we gotta do it fast --


                    LUDIE

          How bout we find the sonuvabitch that
          give us away to the Baldwins and nail im
          to a tree?  Your colored friend there
          can hold the hammer --


                    122

86    INT. BRIDEY'S CABIN - DAY

C.E. sits next to Bridey on the bed now, Bridey
drinking straight from the bottle --

                    C.E.

          "--trailin after me like a dog in heat,"
          he says, "sniffin round my legs like a
          brood bitch--"

                    BRIDEY

No!

                    C.E.

          "She don't wear no drawers,"  he says,
          "so's she can be ready for whatever
          stumbles down the pathway."

                    BRIDEY

Lyin bastard!

                    C.E.

He said you did it with one of the
colored.

                    BRIDEY

(crying)   Naw.  He didn't --

                    C.E.

          Now Bridey -- I think it's worse than
          that.  I think he might be a spy, in
          with the coal operators.  But he's got
          the fellas so turned around with all his

                    123

86     cont.

                    C.E. (cont.)

          talk -- well, I need you to help me,
          Bridey. And sometimes you got to tell a
          little bit of a lie to get the truth
          acrost --


87    INT. TENT - DAY

Some of the other miners have come in, listening to
Joe uneasily --


                    JOE

          I'm not gonna bullshit you fellas and
          tell you there won't ever come a time
          when the people that run this state send
          down the word to have us all murdered.
          But if we don't stand together now, as
          workers, we got no hope at all --


Ellix hurries in, gives a dark glance to Joe, and
whispers into Ludie's ear. Ludie stares coldly at
Joe --


                    LUDIE

          (to Ellix)  Help me up.


                    JOE

          You goin somewhere?


                    LUDIE

          Miners' business. An you aint no miner.
          (points to Few and Fausto)  You two come
          along.


                         124

87    cont.

Ludie grabs a crutch and hobbles out of the tent --


88    INT. BRIDEY'S CABIN - DAY

Ludie, Ellix, Stennis, Fausto, Few and other crowd
around C.E. and Bridey.  Bridey is pretty loaded,
looking only at C.E., who nods encouragingly as she
speaks --


                    BRIDEY

          So he comes in last night an he's all
          drunk -- and I says how I don't want
          nothin to do with him, that I'd call
          some of you fellas to help, but he says
          all of you is taken care of --


                    LUDIE

          Taken care of, huh?


                    BRIDEY

          So when I seen there wasn't no help he
          kind of -- forced me -- he forced me --


She hesitates.  Ellix looks at Few Clothes --


                    ELLIX

      C.E.?


                    C.E.

      Huh?

88    cont.

Ellix nods toward the black man in the room --

                    C.E.

          That's okay.  He'd better hear this
          firsthand.  Go ahead, honey.  What
          happened then?

                    BRIDEY

          Well -- hit were -- hit were unnatural.
          Afterwards he thrown money on the bed,
          like I was some kinda whoo-er --

There is a silence.  Bridey looks to C.E. for
reassurance --

                    C.E.

          You done just right, honey.  Now why
          don't you sit out front for a minute
          while we figure what we're gonna do
          about this?

Bridey steps out past the men, eyes downcast.  Few and
Fausto eye her suspiciously, then give each other a
look.  When she is gone, C.E. pulls something from his
pocket --

                    LUDIE

          So he don't have no sense with women --
          so what?  You know how Bridey builds
          things up --

126

88    cont.

                    C.E.

          Take a look at this that our friend left
          layin on the floor last night --


The men crowd closer to see --


     ENVELOPE

A torn, empty envelope.  On the front is typed Joe's
name.  The return address is the Baldwin-Felts
Detective Agency, Bluefield, W.Va. --


                    FEW (off)

          What's it say?


                    LUDIE (off)

          Hit's a death warrant is what -- for Mr.
          Joseph Kenehan.


89    INT. HICKEY'S ROOM - NIGHT

Danny walks down the corridor with a pile of linen in
his arms, mouthing the words of the sermon he's
preparing for tonight.  He knocks on the door to
Hickey's room.  No answer.  He fishes out a key, goes
in, plops the linen on the bed.  He sees a gun laid
out for cleaning and an army medal, both on the
dresser.  Fascinated, he moves to look at them --


90    INT. BRIDEY'S CABIN - NIGHT - CU C.E.'S HAND

Holding a fistful of broomstraws.  The men each pick
one out as C.E. talks to them --

90     cont.

                         C.E.

            Now the rest of us want a good alibi.  I
            figure in that prayer meetin tonight,
            right under the preacher's nose --


Few Clothes draws the short straw.  We PULL BACK to
see the others looking at him --


                         C.E.

            Welcome to the union, son.


91    INT. HICKEY'S ROOM - NIGHT

Danny has the gun in one hand and is hefting the
service medal in the other when he hears the MEN
COMING.  Panicking, he puts them back on the dresser
and hops in the closet, closing himself in --


      CU DANNY

Light striping his face from the door slats, he tries
to hold totally still as Hickey and Griggs come into
the room talking --


                    HICKEY (off)

            -- so it's gonna be goodbye Mr. Kenehan
            tonight.


                    GRIGGS (off)

            The miners?  How'd he manage that?

91     cont.

> HICKEY (off)

> That tramp that goes to meet the
> passenger trains?  Seems she got the eye
> for Kenehan, so he's put it in her head
> that Kenehan is badmouthin her around
> town.  He's got her crying to the miners
> right now, and then he's got these
> papers from Bluefield --

Hickey stops in mid-sentence.  A long pause --

> HICKEY (off)

> I didn't leave my Colt like this.

Another pause.  Danny is petrified.  Then WHOOSH!  The
closet door is flung open and Hickey yanks him out,
shaking him with one hand and waving his gun with the
other --

> HICKEY

> Little spyin bastard, whad you hear?
> Huh?  Whad you hear?

> DANNY

> Nothin.

> GRIGGS

> Horseshit.  Hit im, Bill.

Hickey sits Danny down on the bed, calming a bit.  He
scoops the army medal off the dresser and holds it in
front of Danny's face --

91    cont.

                         HICKEY

          Know how I won this, preacher boy?  Huh?
          I was sittin alone in a ditch in France
          and this Kraut jumps in next to me and I
          stick my bayonet in his face.  Another
          jumps in and I stick him too, and
          another and another.  They kept coming,
          one at a time, all night long.  After a
          bit I got worried they weren't all dead
          so I'd stick em all again a couple
          times.  In the morning they said I was a
          war hero.


He leans his face close to Danny's --


                         HICKEY

          I'monna stay close tonight, preacher
          boy.  You let a wrong word fly and I put
          one in your skull and do the same for
          your pretty mama.  You know I aint lyin,
          don't you?


92    EXT. TENT CAMP - NIGHT

Joe sits warming his hands by the fire.  Few appears
and squats by him, nervous --


                         JOE

          What's the story?


                         FEW

          Ludie got word the Baldwins be comin for
          you tonight.  I'm suposed to stick by
          you.

92    cont.

                    JOE

          (smiles)  Got the shit detail again,
          huh?


93    INT. ELMA'S DINING ROOM - NIGHT

All present tonight.  Danny hangs his head, pushing at
his food.  Hickey and Griggs have a bottle of liquor
at the table and are in high spirits --


                    ELMA

          You all right, Danny?


No response --


                 MRS. KNIGHTES

          You got your sermon memorized?


                   GRIGGS

          Bet he don't know any more scripture
          than I do.


                   HICKEY

          An that aint a whole hell of a lot, is
          it, Griggsy?


                   GRIGGS

          You know any?

                         HICKEY

            Dint get no further than "In the
            beginnin there was the Word."  Guess we
            both doomed to the hot place.


                         GRIGGS

            The Lord relies on little shits like
            this one to spread His word, I don't
            want no truck with Heaven.


                         HICKEY

            And as for hell, well, we **been** to West
            Virginia.


    Danny gets up and stalks away from the table, the
    Baldwin agents laughing at him.  They begin to sing --


                         HICKEY

            There is powr
            Powr
            Wonder-workin powr
            In the blood --


                         GRIGGS

            In the blood --


                         HICKEY

            Of the Lamb --


                         GRIGGS

            Of the Lamb --

94    INT. FREEWILL CHURCH - NIGHT - CONGREGATION

Up and singing where the Baldwins left off --


                        CONGREGATION

              Yes there's powr
              Powr
              Wonder-workin powr
              In the precious blood of the Lamb!


They sit, closing their hymnals, and we TRACK down the
center aisle from the front of the hall -- passing
Elma, Mrs. Knightes, Cabell and Jessie, and a row full
of all the inner-circle native miners, looking grim in
their starched shirts -- then CONTINUE all the way
back where Hickey and Griggs sit alone in a pew,
whispering and giggling.  C.E. stands by the back
door --


95    INT. HILL CABIN - NIGHT - CU SEPHUS

Sephus wakes in a sweat and sits up with a look of
horror -- he looks around.  He is in a bed, shirtless,
bandages wrapped around his shoulder and middle.  He
tries to lift himself out of bed, stands for a moment
(we see that his leg is splinted) -- then collapses
back onto the bed.  Missus comes hurrying in --


                        MISSUS

              What in God's name you doin, son?  I
              just got all your leaks stopped up an
              here you're tryin to bust em open again.


                        SEPHUS

              I got to get down there.  They got to
              know.

95    cont.

                         MISSUS

          You aint goin nowheres yet, less it's in
          a pine box.  Where's your sense?


                         SEPHUS

          I got to.  Hit's lives at stake --


96    EXT. TENT CAMP - NIGHT - CU FEW CLOTHES

His face tight with the pressure of his mission --


                          JOE

          Wish those fellas would get here.


Few is startled out of a private thought.  He looks to
Joe.  They sit next to each other by a fire.


                          FEW

Huh?


                          JOE

          If they're comin I wish they'd hurry up.
          I don't want any more shootin in the
          woods.


                          FEW

(nods)  Yeah.


                          134

                    Joe

            You ever use one of those?


                    FEW

            (nods)   Yeah.   Tenth Cavalry, in Cuba,
            back in ninety-eight.


                    JOE

            San Juan Hill.   Pretty rough down there?


                    FEW

            I did what I had to.


A silence.   Few tries to work up a little more hatred
of Joe --


                    FEW

            It true you a Red?


                    JOE

            Yeah, I spose it is.


                    FEW

            Then how com you don't carry a gun?


                    JOE

            (smiles)   We carry little round bombs.
            Don't you read the papers?

                    135

97    INT. FREEWILL CHURCH - NIGHT - DANNY

At the pulpit, thinking, troubled.  We hear Hickey and
Griggs in the rear, giggling over some whispered joke.
Danny makes up his mind --

                    DANNY

          I wanna tell you tonight -- bout the
          blackness in the heart of man.  Gon warn
          you -- bout the many an devious ways in
          which Satan will hide from you the truth
          -- of who your real friends are.  Gon do
          it with a story from the Patriarchs.


     ELMA

Wondering about this change of sermons --


                    DANNY (off)

          Now we all know about Joseph --


     INNER-CIRCLE MINERS

Listening, but their thoughts elsewhere --


                    DANNY (off)

          -- and how out of all Jacob's twelve
          children he was the smartest and the
          smoothest, and how his brothers got so
          jealous --


98    INT. SID'S OFFICE - NIGHT - SID

He sits at his desk cleaning his guns by the light of
an oil lamp.  He works the trigger mechanism of one --
his hands tremble.  He makes fists, takes a deep
breath.  He goes back to work, hands a bit steadier --


                      136

97    cont.   INT. FREEWILL CHURCH - NIGHT - HICKEY AND
               GRIGGS

Giggling in their rear pew, oblivious to Danny's
sermon --


                    DANNY (off)

          So when this fella Potiphar bought him
          for a slave, Joseph just smiled and
          vowed he was gonna be a <u>good</u> one.  Makin
          the best of a bad situation.


          PULPIT, DANNY


                    DANNY

          He put his heart to his work and was
          honest and friendly in his dealins an
          fore you knew it he was just about
          <u>run</u>nin Potiphar's household and fields
          and all his business for him.  The only
          trouble was Potiphar's wife.  Now she
          was what you might call a loose woman --


99    INT. BRIDEY'S CABIN - NIGHT - BRIDEY MAE

Sitting alone, drinking, tears slowly working down her
face --


97    cont.   INT. FREEWILL CHURCH - NIGHT


                    DANNY

          -- an Joseph said "I been good to
          Potiphar an he been good right back to
          me, how can I go slippin round with his
          wife?  Don't you tempt me, woman."


                         137

100   EXT. TENT CAMP - NIGHT - JOE AND FEW

Joe is deep in thought as he speaks --


                    JOE

          When I was in Leavenworth there was a
          bunch of Mennonites -- in cause they
          wouldn't fight in the war.  Gainst their
          religion.  It's also gainst their
          religion to shave their beards of wear
          buttons on their clothes, and they was
          bein forced to do both by the prison
          guards.  So they refused to work.  Went
          on a strike, right there in Hell's Half
          Acre.

          They were handcuffed to the bars of a
          cellhouse, eight hours a day for two
          full weeks.  They were put with their
          arms up like this, so's they had to
          stand on their toes or those cuffs would
          cut into their wrists.  Can't nobody
          stay on their toes eight hours.

          Pretty soon their fingers would start to
          swoll up, they'd turn blue and then
          they'd crack open and the blood would
          run down their arms -- eight hours a
          day, day after day, an still they
          wouldn't work, still they tore the
          buttons off their uniforms every time
          they were sewed back on.  Tore em with
          their teeth, cause their hands wouldn't
          close no more.

          Now I don't claim a thing for myself --
          but them fellas, never lifted a gun in
          their lives, you couldn't find any
          braver in my book.


They sit silent for a moment --


                    JOE

          Wish them guys would get here.


                    138

97    cont.    INT. FREEWILL CHURCH - NIGHT

                    DANNY

          Also in Potiphar's employ at this time
          was a couple of spies from one of his
          enemies --


     CONGREGATION

Confused, whispering to each other as Danny begins to
depart from Scripture --


                    DANNY (off)

          They seen the wanton lust of Mrs.
          Potiphar and seen it would be good for
          their purposes to get shed of young
          Joseph.


     SOFTSHELL PREACHERS

One leans to whisper to the top dog, REV. JUSTICE,
upset --


     C.E.

Puzzled and concerned --


     INNER-CIRCLE MINERS

Looking confused --


                    DANNY

          So they come to Potiphar's wife --

101   EXT. TENT CAMP - NIGHT - FEW CLOTHES

Watching something --


      JOE - FEW'S POV

Joe squats by a fire several yards away, talking with
a miner and his wife --


      CU FEW

Biting his lip --


      CU FEW'S HAND

Fingering the gun in his belt --


97    cont.   INT. FREEWILL CHURCH - NIGHT


                    DANNY

            "Your servant Joseph," she says to
            Potiphar, "he come in here and tried to
            make me lie with him.  Only when I
            called out he fled, leavin this here
            garment as evidence."


      CONGREGATION

Wondering over this version --


                    DANNY (off)

            "An not only that, he been spyin and
            plottin against you with your enemies.
            He means to take over here and have you
            kilt --"


                    140

97   cont.

We CHANGE FOCUS to see the inner-circle miners, who
turn and look at the rear as subtly as they can manage
-- we CHANGE FOCUS again to see Hickey and Griggs
talking to each other, paying no attention to the
sermon --


                    DANNY

          Potiphar had no reason to misbelieve his
          wife.  Joseph was a slave an a
          foreigner.  So he gathered up all his
          servants and household workers and they
          went and slew Joseph dead.


     ELMA

Beginning to realize what the metaphor is, worried --


                    DANNY (off)

          Cut him from gut to gizzard and left him
          bleedin in a stream.


     CONGREGATION

Totally lost, turning to one another --


     REV. JUSTICE, PREACHERS

Scandalized, conferring as they look at Danny --


     C.E.

Slipping out the door --


     PULPIT - DANNY



                         141

                          DANNY

          An lo they never learnt of Mrs.
          Potiphar's lies, and went to their Maker
          unrepentant, with innercent blood on
          their hands.


He stares at the congregation till they quiet, then
looks to Ludie --


          LUDIE

Nods, understanding --


                          DANNY

          Draw your own conclusions.


More buzzing as Danny turns and walks from the pulpit.
We hear Rev. Justice taking the pulpit and announcing
the next hymn as the word is passed down in whispers
from Ludie to Hillard.  The congregation begins to
SING.  Hillard picks a moment when Hickey and Griggs
aren't looking, then crawls down the aisle to the
exit --


102   EXT. TENT CAMP - NIGHT - JOE AND FEW

Seen from a distance.  They sit together by the fire,
the only ones still up in the camp --


          JOE AND FEW - CLOSER


                          JOE

          Gettin awful late --

102   cont.

                    FEW

         Shhh!  You hear somethin?


                    JOE

         No. You?


                    FEW

         Thought I did.  Like somebody moanin.


                    JOE

         Maybe it's the fellas.


                    FEW

         Maybe we best go out there an take a
         look --


103   EXT. BRIDEY'S CABIN - NIGHT

Hillard comes sprinting up the path, disappearing
around the bend just as Bridey stumbles out and flops
into her porch chair --


104   EXT. WOODS - NIGHT - JOE AND FEW

Moving through the trees, crouched low.  They move a
few steps, listen, then move again, Few in the lead --


     CU FEW'S HAND

Fingering the gun as he walks --

A104 WOODS - NIGHT

Hillard scrambles past us, winded, breathing heavily.
Just as he disappears, Sephus breaks out onto the path
from the side, hobbling in the opposite direction --


104   cont.   CU FEW CLOTHES

Sweat beading his forehead.  He stops walking, takes a
breath --


        WIDER

Few pulls his gun, cocks the trigger, turns and faces
Joe, looking scared.  Joe looks at him, puzzled.
There is a WHISTLE from behind --


                    HILLARD (off)

            Few Clothes?


Few exchanges a puzzled look with Joe, ducks into the
brush.  We HOLD on Joe.  Few comes back, a huge grin
on his face --


                    JOE

            Who's that?


                    FEW

            Hillard.  Meetin been called off.


He slaps Joe on the back, beams.  Joe is confused --


                    JOE

            We better get back to camp.

                    144

104    cont.

FEW

Just a minute --


Few turns, fumbles, pees into the bush --


JOE

Least we didn't waste our trip.


105    EXT. MAIN ST. - NIGHT - CU CABELL

Fire lighting his face as he watches something burn --
a FIRE BELL CLANGS down the street --


C.E.'S RESTAURANT

In flames --


106    INT. RESTAURANT - NIGHT - CU MENU

On the wall, burning --


PHOTOGRAPH

Of C.E. and Mother Jones, burning --


105    cont.    EXT. MAIN STREET - NIGHT - CABELL

He turns, agitated, and walks to Sid, who looks on
casually --


CABELL

You gonna do something?

105  cont.

                          SID

          Don't worry.  Hit won't spread.


                         CABELL

          You think C.E. is inside?


Sephus hobbles past, a knot of angry miners behind
him --


                        SEPHUS

          No such luck.


                         CABELL

          (confused)  I thought he was dead.


107  EXT. RIVER - NIGHT

C.E. wades out from behind camera into the Tug Fork,
pausing in the middle to look back at the commotion in
town --


     CU C.E.

Reflected firelight dancing on his glasses.  His face
shows more resolution than fear.  He turns and wades
off into the dark --


108  EXT. TRAIN STATION - DAY - BRIDEY MAE

Her face blank, a ticket clutched in her hand, she
waits for the outgoing train --


                          146

109   EXT. BOARDING HOUSE - DAY

Elma appears at a second-story window with a bundle of
supplies -- she looks back over her shoulder and then
lets it go -- we FOLLOW it down to Danny.  He signals
a thank you and runs off --


        WINDOW

Elma watching him go, then elbowed out of the way by
an angry Hickey.  PAPPY'S NARRATION begins on the
track --


                        PAPPY (VO)

                Hit were then that Joe Kenehan and me
                really begun to bring the men
                together --


110   EXT. CLEARING - DAY

By the tent camp.  The white miners play baseball
against the black miners while the Italians watch in
confusion.  We see armed miners watching the woods for
a possible attack.  Few Clothes swings and knocks one
out of sight --


                        PAPPY (VO)

                Once they seen how they'd almost done a
                innercent man, it was like Joe couldn't
                say no wrong.


111   EXT. CLEARING - DAY

Danny stands on a box, making a speech to a handful of
miners as Joe looks on --


                        DANNY

                -- I'm talking about is the sacred
                brotherhood of workers and how they are

                            147

111   cont.

                    DANNY (cont.)

          bein robbed out of the fruits of their
          labor --


                    PAPPY (VO)

          We moved out into Mingo County then,
          spreadin the word about the union --


A111   EXT. ROADSIDE - CU TREE - DAY

Someone nails a handbill to a tree, the headline
reading --

                    UNION RALLY

          Coal Miners your hour is NOW


                    PAPPY (VO, cont.)

          -- spreadin like wildfire --


B111   EXT. CLEARING - PLATFORM - JOE

Addressing another group --


                    JOE

          -- whose sweat was it that built those
          mansions?  Whose work, whose blood --


                    PAPPY (VO)

          -- over to Red Jacket, to Ragland and
          Delbarton, all up and down the Tug Fork
          River --


                         148

C111  EXT. CLEARING - PLATFORM - DANNY

Addressing yet another gathering --


                    DANNY

          -- that the Lord helps them that helps
          themselves.  Well, they been <u>helpin</u>
          themselves to our land and our labor for
          too damn long!


                    PAPPY (VO)

          -- bringing the union out to all the
          folks what needed help, puttin the
          spirit into em and trying to shut down
          the whole southwest field.  Joe Kenehan
          said how there was a new day acomin --


113  EXT. MAIN STREET - DAY

Union relief day -- Joe and his three-man committee
passing out money to a long line of miners as Hickey
and Griggs walk down one side of the line staring men
in the face and Sid walks on the other, not taking his
eyes off the two Baldwins --


                    PAPPY (VO, cont.)

          -- and sometimes I could just about see
          it.  But hit were dangerous livin for a
          union man, and you didnt' dare turn your
          back.


     CU JOE

Framed by the Baldwins on one side and Sid on the
other, he looks to each party, then goes back to
doling out relief payments --

114    EXT. MRS. ELKINS'S TENT - DAY

She sits in front of her tent, peeling a turnip.  One
of Rosaria's toddlers wanders close, staring at the
turnip hungrily --


                         PAPPY (VO, cont.)

              Hit was hard times and hit was hungry
              times, too.  The union relief was spread
              thin and the hope of a new day can feed
              your soul but leave your belly
              arumblin --


Mrs. Elkins eyes the little boy grumpily, then waves
her hand at him --


                         MRS. ELKINS

              Scoot!  Go on --


The little boy just smiles at her --


115    EXT. ROSARIA'S TENT - DAY

Rosaria and Gemma sit on the ground puttin greens into
a pot of boiling water, surrounded by their gang of
kids, all looking pretty hungry.  Rosaria is muttering
to Gemma in Italian --


                         ROSARIA

              We cross an ocean crowded together like
              cattle, travel all the way down here,
              have people shoot at us at night -- what
              for?  We could have starved back in
              Milano --


Her little boy comes up by the fire, eating a small
apple --

115   cont.

                    ROSARIA

          Where have you been?  Where did you get
          that?


Mrs. Elkins appears standing over them.  She has a
dead rabbit in one hand, a sack of dry beans and a
bunch of ramps in the other --


                    MRS. ELKINS

          Lady?


Rosaria looks up at her, surprised --


                    MRS. ELKINS

          Seein as there's just me an Hillard an
          you got all these little ones -- well --


She holds out the rabbit --


                    MRS. ELKINS

          You know what to do with this?  Hillard
          brung it in --


                    ROSARIA

          Coniglio?


                    MRS. ELKINS

          Hit's for you --


                         151

115 cont.

                    ROSARIA

          (Italian)  You're giving it to us?


                    MRS. ELKINS

          I aint gonna see no babies goin hungry.
          Go on, take it --


Rosaria accepts the rabbit --


                    MRS. ELKINS

          Here's some navy beans, and these is
          ramps -- you can cook with em and
          they'll put a taste in your stew --


Rosaria smells the ramps --


                    ROSARIA

          Aglio --


                    MRS. ELKINS

          Anyhow --


                    ROSARIA

          (Italian)  Anyhow -- would you like to
          sit down?  (indicates)


Mrs. Elkins understands and sits down.  The kids stare
at her as Gemma expertly begins to skin the rabbit --

                    MRS. ELKINS

          I figure -- you know -- we's all in this
          together.


The little boy with the apple sit on her lap --


                    MRS. ELKINS

          You sure got some pretty babies.


116   EXT. CLEARING - DUSK

Joe and Danny play pitch and catch behind the tents --


                    DANNY

          Some folks say the Sox just laid down
          but I don't believe it.  You just lookit
          the Series Joe Jackson had.  My faverits
          on the Reds is Ed Roush an Heinie Groh,
          even if they is Germans.


                    JOE

          Who's your favorite pitcher?


                    DANNY

          Hod Eller.  He's from Logan County.


                    JOE

          You get to play ball much?

                    DANNY

        Not when the mines is open.   (thinks)
        Joe?


                     JOE

        Yeah?


                    DANNY

        You ever kill anybody?


                     JOE

        What brought that up?


                    DANNY

        (shrugs)   Bet Sid has.   He were in the
        war.


                     JOE

        All I saw was just workers killin
        workers.   Wasn't any point in it.


                    DANNY

        And they thrown you in jail cause you
        wouldn't go?


                     JOE

        (smiles)   If them two years kept me from
        killin some poor stiff who got pushed
        out on a battlefield by rich folks and
        politicians, then they were worth it.

116    cont.

He puts the ball and glove under his arm --


                        JOE

          Gettin dark, Danny.  You'd better go get
          that coal.


117   EXT. HILLSIDE - DUSK

Danny and Hillard climb to the tipple in the waning
light.  They pause and look back toward the town --


                        DANNY

          See there, right there by the railroad
          trestle?  At's where Cap Hatfield an his
          boy Joe Glenn kilt three men.  Boy
          weren't but thirteen.


                        HILLARD

          (nods)  Used a Winchester.


                        DANNY

          Think it hurts much, a bullet?


                        HILLARD

          (shrugs)  Beats dyin in a damn coal
          mine.


                        DANNY

          (nods)  He weren't but thirteen year
          old, Joe Glenn.

118   EXT. MINE SHAFT - NIGHT

Deserted in the moonlight --


119   EXT. COAL YARD - NIGHT

A rail car sits on the tracks that lead out of the
mine opening, a canvas tarp thrown over the coal left
in it.   There is no one in sight --


120   EXT. HILLSIDE - NIGHT - DANNY AND HILLARD

Crouched in hiding, looking down at the shuttle.
Hillard indicates a watch shack to the other side of
it --


                    HILLARD

          He must be in there.


                    DANNY

          Coleman?   He allus sleeps with the
          lights on.   We just got to be quiet is
          all.


They pass out of the shot and we begin to SLOW ZOOM IN
on the lit window of the watch shack --


121   INT. WATCH SHACK - NIGHT

Dimly lit.   Turley sits behind a cluttered desk,
survey charts and tonnage schedules tacked up on the
wall behind him.   We HEAR but don't see C.E. Lively,
moving around the room as he talks --

                        C.E. (off)

The owners in Logan and Mingo County
have pooled up their money and come to
Mr. Felts --


                        TURLEY

We're still diggin coal in McDowell --


                        C.E. (off)

Mr. Turley, it's like a disease.  I seen
it before.  We're not talkin bout a
half-dozen holes shut down for a spell,
we're talking bout the whole way we <u>live</u>
in this country.  Your mountain people
get holt of these ideas and it makes
them sick, like a dog get holt of a
rabies-skunk.  There's only one way to
deal with that kind of infection once it
gets started --


                        TURLEY

I know these people --


                        C.E. (off)

Of course you do.  That's why I know
you'll understand what I've got to do
next.


C.E.'s body partly obscures the screen in the
foreground, Turley looking up at him --

121 cont.

                    C.E.

          This situation here's been left to
          simmer long enough -- I'm gonna have to
          bring it to a <u>boil</u>.


122   EXT. COAL YARD - NIGHT

Danny's hand appears, cutting the tarp loose with a
jackknife.  We PULL BACK to see him and Hillard
stealing coal -- Danny scoops lumps down as Hillard
holds the sack open.  They work quickly, till -- BLAM!
A SHOTGUN BLAST scatters coal just behind Danny.  He
hops down and starts to run with Hillard --


          DANNY

We FOLLOW him running, terrified, across the dark coal
yard.  We hear someone running behind him.  There's a
string of railroad cars ahead -- Danny dives under one
of them --


          DANNY

Pressing himself against the inside of a wheel -- he
watches under the car as Hillard sprints past,
followed by the mine guard, then we hear SHOUTS as
somebody else tackles Hillard out in the dark.  Danny
holds his breath as he sees Hillard's legs and the
legs of the guards as the boy is dragged back to the
side of the car Danny is under --


          COAL YARD, MEN

A pair of guards have Hillard pushed up against the
railroad car as Hickey and Griggs stroll over to
them --


               GRIGGS

          Well, well.  What we got here?


                    158

122   cont.

UNDER CAR - CU DANNY

Eyes wide with fear as he recognizes the voice --


COAL YARD - HILLARD, MEN

Smack!  Griggs slaps Hillard in the face --


                    GRIGGS

          Smarts a little, don't it, boy?  Hold
          his arms --


The two guards pin Hillard's arms behind him and ram
him against the coal car --


                    HICKEY

          Now how about you tell me who your
          ringleaders up in Logan are?  Gimme five
          names, boy, that's all, and we'll let
          you go.  At's fair enough, int it?


                    HILLARD

     Never.


Griggs smashes Hillard on the nose with the heel of
his hand, blood spurting out as Hillard SCREAMS.
Griggs grabs Hillard by the hair and pulls his head
back --


                    GRIGGS

     Talk to us, boy.

122  cont.

No response.  Griggs flicks Hillard on the nose with a
finger --

                         GRIGGS

          Talk to us!

                         HILLARD

          I'll rot in hell first.

                         HICKEY

          Okay.  Have it your way.  (calls)  Mr.
          Lively!


     UNDER CAR - CU DANNY

Listening hard as he sees a new pair of legs
approaching --


     COAL YARD - MEN

Hillard's eyes widen as C.E. steps out of the
darkness, comes up and stares at him close range.  The
guards step away.  Griggs pulls his gun and aims it at
Hillard's head --

                         GRIGGS

          Boy, I sentence you to death for the
          crime of stealin company property and
          bein a dirty Boleshevist union man.  You
          got ten seconds to talk.

122  cont.  HILLARD

His back to the coal car, trying to look brave.  We
look at him over the muzzle of Griggs's gun.  BAM!
Griggs shoots just to the left of Hillard's head, the
boy flinching to cover himself.  The men laugh.
Hillard starts to cry.  BAM!  Griggs shoots two feet
to the right.  BAM!  BAM!  BAM!  Three more shots,
only inches away from Hillard's head.  He sinks to his
knees, sobbing.  C.E. stands over him --


                    C.E.

        Talk?


Hillard manages to shake his head no.  Griggs points
the gun at his forehead --


        CU HILLARD, GUN

Hillard closes his eyes, trembling.  Griggs moves the
gun down next to Hillard's ear -- BAM!  Hillard jumps,
shakes even more but keeps his eyes shut --


                GRIGGS (off)

        Pheeew!  What a smell!


                HICKEY (off)

        Boy dirtied his diapers.


                C.E. (off)

        We want names, son.


                HILLARD

        I can't!  I sworn on a Bible!


                    161

122   cont.

                    C.E.

          Then we gonna have to get down to it,
          son.  ˉUse the razor --


     GRIGGS, HICKEY

Griggs takes a razor out, opens it, moves behind
Hillard and puts it to his throat.  He slices an inch,
blood trickling --


                    C.E.

          Get it off your chest, son.


Blood is bubbling from Hillard's mouth and nose --


                    HILLARD

          P-Plyant Mount, Bill Mahan, Asa Radnor,
          J.T. Keadle --


                    GRIGGS

          Five.  Give us five.


                    HILLARD

          An -- an Harley Shilton.


                    C.E.

          Kill im.


Griggs swipes hard with the razor, the men gasp.
Hickey is surprised --

122    cont.

                              HICKEY

                    Jesus, Griggs --


        UNDER CAR - CU DANNY

Horrified as Hillard hits the ground a few feet away
from him, choking and jerking spasmodically --


        MEN

Looking at Hillard twitching on the ground --


                              GRIGGS

                    So where do them fellas he named live?


                              C.E.

                    Clay Hill.


                              GRIGGS

                    Where's that?


                              C.E.

                    It's a cemetery.  Them are all fellas
                    was kilt in a gas fire, five, six year
                    ago.


C.E. squats to look Hillard in the eye --


                              163

122    cont.

                    C.E.

          Nothin like a young boy dyin to stir
          things up.


123   EXT. TENT CAMP - NIGHT

Joe sits poking at a fire in front of his tent.  There
is a distant WAILING -- people begin to come out and
peer into the darkness to see what it is.  Danny
appears first, in a state of shock, shaking.  Then
comes Sid Hatfield, lugging Hillard's body, wrapped in
a sheet, blood staining through.  Mrs. Elkins follows
him, wailing, hysterical with grief.  Sid gives Joe a
look as they pass --


                    SID

          Baldwins comin in the mornin, Kenehan.


124   EXT. TRAIN TRACKS - DAY

Rounding a corner, then heading straight at us,
closer, closer, then right over the camera --


125   EXT. TRAIN STATION - DAY

A group of BALDWIN-FELTS AGENTS in dark suits and
bowlers stand at the platform.  They look like an
undertakers' convention.  LEE and AL FELTS, the most
expensively dressed, lead the way into town.  We
FOLLOW along with their joking gun thugs, some
carrying rifles in cloth cases.  DOOLIN, the youngest,
is pumping the others for information --


                    DOOLIN

          Fellas have any idear what's waitin for
          us?


                    164

                        BASS

(winks)  You mean they didn't tell you?


                        DOOLIN

I just seen a line in the papers --


                        JAMES

"Opportunity for red-blooded American
men.  Immediate openings, high pay,
travel, chance for advancement.  Apply
Baldwin-Felts and write your own
ticket."  Whenever the natives get
restless someplace they put that out.
Hook some more cannon fodder.


                        BASS

Ever hear of the Hatfields and McCoys,
son?


                        DOOLIN

Course I have.


                        BASS

This Matewan is their stomping grounds.


                        JAMES

The'll put a bullet in your brain as
soon as look at you.

125   cont.

                    BASS

          (points)  See that fella?


     CU BUCHANAN

A grim-looking character bringing up the rear of the
group --


                    BASS (off)

          Buchanan.  Most decorated soldier outa
          this state in the Great War.


     MEN

Doolin is impressed --


                    BASS

          If they sent him along they must be
          expectin <u>bloodshed</u>.


126  EXT. MAIN STREET - DAY

Sid and Cabell stand facing the two Felts brothers.
Hickey and Griggs join them, smirking --


                    LEE

          Sid, we got authorization to put these
          miners off company property here in
          town --


                    SID

          Not from me you don't.


                        166

                    AL

        We've also got a warrant for your
        arrest.  If you give us any trouble --


Cabell takes the warrant from Al, glances at it --


                  CABELL

        This aint worth shit and you know it.


                   LEE

        (shrugs)  One way or another, we're
        gonna carry out these evictions tomorrow
        morning.  Gentlemen?


The men all pass around Sid and Cabell, checking them
out, and head for Elma's.  Sid turns to watch them --


                   SID

        They come to kill me.


127   EXT. HILLARD'S GRAVE - DAY - CU DANNY

Danny is saying a eulogy, having a hard time finding
the right words --


                  DANNY

        Hillard was my friend.  When I first
        come down to the mines it was Hillard
        shown me what to do.  He were a good
        coal miner and a good union man and he
        always took care of his mama.  I don't
        know how they could have done him like
        they did.

127   cont.   WIDER SHOT - GRAVEYARD

A little family plot on the hillside.  Miners are
gathered, Joe, Elma.  Rosaria supports Mrs. Elkins,
who sobs quietly.  Sid stands to the rear, a dark
presence --


                    DANNY

          All he wanted to do was live decent.
          That's all.  Sometimes people say how
          God willed it.  You know, how everything
          is His plan?


        CU DANNY


                    DANNY

          Well I don't think God planned on
          Hillard alayin amongst all these
          Elkinses here.  Not this young in his
          life.  I think all God plans is that we
          get born.  And then we got to take up
          from there.  So you rest in peace,
          Hillard.  You rest easy, cause we gonna
          take up where you left off.  Amen.


        GRAVEYARD

One of the mountain women steps forward and begins to
SING a mournful ballad --


        JOE

Sephus moves in next to him, keeping his eyes on the
grave as he speaks --


                    SEPHUS

          You gonna tell us to turn the other
          cheek, Joe?


                    168

127  cont.

                         JOE

              Shootin is what they want now.


                       SEPHUS

              Maybe it's what <u>we</u> want too.  You expect
              too much outa people, Joe.  You're still
              after that one big union and rest of us
              we can't see past this holler.


Joe looks over to see Ludie and Ellix whispering with
Sid --


                         JOE

              I need to talk to the men.


                       SEPHUS

              (nods to the grave)  Wouldn't be decent
              now.  I'll call a meeting for the
              morning, first thing.


Sephus moves away.  Joe catches Elma's eye across the
grave.  Tears roll down her face -- she turns away
from his gaze --


128  EXT. COAL TIPPLE - DUSK

We hear the woman finishing her SONG as the sun sets
behind the coal tipple --


127  cont.  EXT. HILLARD'S GRAVE - DAY

We PAN from the singer around the grave, looking at
the faces of the men and women gathered, ending with
Mrs. Elkins --

129   EXT. TENT CAMP - DUSK - FIDDLER

He plays the last notes of the song outside his tent.
Someone nearby lights a lantern as the night falls
quickly --


130   EXT. TENT CAMP - NIGHT

Few and Tom listen to the HARMONICA playing mournfully
as they build a small fire --


                         FEW

               Spread the word to stay out from town
               tomorrow.


                         TOM

          Somethin up?


                         FEW

               (shrugs)  I got a feelin.  You know how
               white fokes is when they gets all
               excited.


131   EXT. ROSARIA'S TENT - NIGHT

Next door Mrs. Elkins sits in front of her tent
staring into the distance.  Rosaria sits a few feet
away, being with her but not intruding.  Fausto comes
and kneels by her.  They speak in Italian --


                         FAUSTO

          How is she?


                         ROSARIA

          What do you think?

131 cont.

                    FAUSTO

          The company men came today.  Men with
          rifles.


                    ROSARIA

          (crossing herself)  God have mercy on us
          all.


132  INT. TENT - NIGHT - DANNY

Sighting down a rifle barrel, his expression grim.
Joe comes in, looking warily at the rifle.  Danny puts
it down but won't look Joe in the eye --


                    JOE

          Nothin's gonna bring Hillard back, you
          know.


Danny turns his face away --


                    JOE

          I came here to help --


                    DANNY

          (angry)  Sure you did.  First people
          come in here to help us with some money,
          and next we know we got no land.  Then
          they say they gonna help us with a job
          and a place to live.  So they put us in
          some damn coal camp and let us dig out
          their mines.  Now you come in and want
          to help us bring in the new day.  But
          Hillard aint gonna see no new day.  We
          had about as much help as we can stand.
          We got to take care of ourselves.


                      171

132   cont.

                    JOE

        We got to take care of each other --


Danny picks up the rifle and sights down the barrel --


133   EXT. BOARDING HOUSE - NIGHT

The lights are out --


134   INT. ELMA'S DINING ROOM - NIGHT

Elma walks through the dining room to the parlor of
the darkened house, tiptoeing past several of the
Baldwins who sleep on pallets on the floor.  Only
Doolin is awake, too nervous to sleep.  He darts a
look at Elma as she passes, then looks away.  Elma
goes to the window, looks out on the street --


135   EXT. MAIN STREET - NIGHT - SID

Eerie FIDDLE MUSIC is echoing down from the hillside.
Sid walks along the shuttered Main Street buildings.
There is a light from the apothecary window.  He looks
inside.  Jessie sits at the counter.  When she sees
him she comes to the window and they look at each
other for a long moment through the glass.  Finally
Sid breaks away and continues his lonely walk --


136   EXT. MAIN STREET - DAY

A nervous, head-hanging cur skulks down the empty
street --


137   EXT. MAIN STREET - DAY - CABELL

Hurrying along till he finds Sid sitting on a doorway
stoop across from Elma's.  He sits beside him to wait.
Sid hardly looks at him --

137   cont.

                              SID

          No need for you to be in on this.


                            CABELL

          Hit's my town, too.   They're my people.


138   INT. TENT CAMP - DAY - JOE

He starts awake as Fausto shakes his shoulder --


                            FAUSTO

               (whisper)  The men go to town.   They
               take rifle.


139   EXT. MAIN STREET - DAY

The Felts brothers step out first, followed by Hickey
and Griggs, then the rest of the Baldwins, their
rifles unwrapped and ready.   The Felts start straight
across the street, the others fanning out behind
them --


     STREET - SID AND CABELL

They start to walk out toward the agents --


     CU DANNY

Watching from behind a post --


A139   PARLOR WINDOW - ELMA

Watching the street, uneasy --


                             173

139 cont.   LONG SHOT, STREET

Sid and Cabell square off with the Felts brothers.  We
hear a TRAIN WHISTLE approaching in the distance.  The
other Baldwins spread out around their bosses --


     CU SID

Tense.  The TRAIN WHISTLES again, closer --


     FELTS BROTHERS

Dead-eyed.  The TRAIN WHISTLE SCREAMS warning -- we
can hear the WHEELS RUMBLING now --


140   EXT. MAIN STREET - DAY - JOE

Sprinting down the footpath into the edge of town.  He
stops, sees --


                         JOE

          No!


139   cont.   EXT. MAIN STREET - DAY

The TRAIN WHISTLES, very close and shrill, drowning
out Lee Felts's words and Sid's reply.  They go for
their guns at the same instant --


140   cont.   EXT. MAIN STREET - DAY - JOE

Running --

                         JOE

          No!!!


174

139  cont.  EXT. MAIN STREET - DAY

Al Felts gets a shot off into Cabell but Sid has his
guns up and shoots both brothers pointblank in the
face.  A half-second stunned pause, then the street
explodes with GUNFIRE, bullets zinging in from every
direction.  The Baldwins duck and scatter --


          SEPHUS

Firing from the side of a building --


          LUDIE

Firing from on top of a roof --


          MINER

Firing through an open window --


          MINER

Stepping out from a storefront, shooting --


          SID

Runs for a doorway, shooting as he goes, bullets
tearing up the dirt all around him --


          HICKEY

Shooting as he runs for cover --


          BALDWIN

Hit twice, three times, falling --

139   cont.   STENNIS

Stepping out to shoot and getting hit in the
shoulder --


        BASS

Frozen on the street, turning in every direction to
shoot, finally cut down --


141   INT. HOUSE - DAY - JAMES

Running into a house and kicking the door in -- we
FOLLOW him in as he pushes a woman and dives to hide
under the bed but is caught by the ankles and dragged
back outside by Ellix and Tolbert, who shoot him in
the head --


139   cont.   EXT. MAIN STREET - DAY - GRIGGS

Running, head low.  He smacks right into Sephus and
they both go down.  Griggs shoots Sephus in the leg as
he rolls and Sephus grabs Griggs's face and shoots him
in the throat --


        THREE BALDWINS

Charging a doorway, killing the miner standing in it,
but all three are cut down by a hail of bullets before
they get inside --


        SID

Popping out from cover to wing Hickey in the leg as he
runs past --


142   EXT. BOARDING HOUSE - DAY - HICKEY

Hopping and running, he reaches the fence at the side
of Elma's house and rolls over it --

142   cont.   HICKEY - CLOSER

Breathing hard, he crawls under a maze of hotel
bedsheets that hang above him.  He gets his breath,
gets to his feet.  He has a good shot at the street.
Ludie walks past, not seeing him, carrying a rifle.
Hickey takes aim.  He hears a metallic CLICK behind
him.  He turns -- Elma stands facing him, body
obscured from the chest down by the hanging laundry.
Hickey starts to swing his gun around -- BLAM!  A
shotgun blast sends him sprawling backward against the
sheets --


        CU ELMA

Face twisted with hatred as BLAM!  she lets loose the
other barrel --


        HICKEY

He falls tangled in sheets, blood spattered and
smeared on the pellet-torn ones that still hang behind
him --


143   EXT. RIVER - DAY - DOOLIN

Running, unarmed, away from town, closer and closer to
the river.  He SCREAMS and skids to a halt as Danny
steps out in front of him, rifle leveled.  They stare
at each other for a long moment, Doolin petrified,
Danny thrilled and sickened --


                    DOOLIN

            Aw Jesus.  Jesus, please don't shoot
            me --


        DANNY

His finger tenses on the trigger --

143  cont.  CU DOOLIN

Standing helpless, waiting for what comes next --


CU DANNY

His arms trembling, he sight down the rifle -- then
relaxes his finger on the trigger.  He jerks his head
and Doolin scrambles into the Tug and splashes toward
the Kentucky hills --


144  EXT. TRAIN - DAY - TRAIN WHISTLE

Blowing, signaling arrival --


145  INT. PASSENGER CAR - DAY

The conductor faces us, calling to the passengers --


CONDUCTOR

Matewan!  Watch your step!


146  EXT. TRAIN STATION - DAY - TRAIN DOOR

Thrown open -- there kneels a Baldwin, bloody and
dying.  He slumps forward toward the train --


CONDUCTOR

Horrified.  He looks down the street --


147  EXT. MAIN STREET - DAY

We TRACK down the street, across the dead Baldwin
bodies, past Cabell sitting on the ground, gutshot,
holding his stomach and crying, past Sid Hatfield,
guns up and ready, amazed to be alive, and finally to
Mrs. Elkins, who stands with a revolver, pumping shots
into a dead Baldwin --

148   EXT. MAIN STREET - DAY - ELMA AND DANNY

Looking down at something.  Elma drops her shotgun to
the ground --


          JOE

Joe is sprawled out on the street, shot several times,
dying.  He reaches his hand out.  Danny kneels to take
it.  They lock eyes and we TRACK IN very tight on
Joe's face.  The sound of GUNSHOTS FADES, replaced by
the DRIP of a damp mine shaft.  We SLOWLY FADE TO
BLACK --


149   INT. COAL MINE - DAY - BLACKNESS

There is a tiny dot of light in the distance --


               PAPPY (VO)

               There was a trial but there wasn't
               nobody gonna pass guilty on Sid Hatfield
               in Mingo County.


The tiny dot of light begins to move toward us.  It is
the beam from a headlamp --


               PAPPY (VO, cont.)

               Sid got married to Mayor Testerman's
               widda and then the Baldwins they caught
               him unarmed awalking up the steps of the
               McDowell County Courthouse down in
               Welch.  They shot fifteen bullets into
               him right in broad daylight, then C.E.
               Lively stepped in and put one right
               through his skull.  Wasn't even a trial
               on that one.

               That were the start of the great
               Coalfield War and us miners took the
               worst of it like Joe said we would.
               "Hit's just one big Union, the whole
               world over," Joe Kenehan used to say,

179

149   cont.

                              PAPPY (VO, cont.)

          and from the day of the Matewan Massacre
          that's what I preached.  That was my
          religion.


The beam is close enough now so we can tell it is a
single miner walking to us --


                              PAPPY (VO, cont.)

          We buried him with our own.  My mama she
          thought he wouldn't never stay, but now
          he's with us for always, alayin up here
          in these West Virginia hills.


The miner is Danny.  He walks into a CLOSE-UP, gives
us a direct look, then passes out of the frame.
Blackness.  CREDITS ROLL.